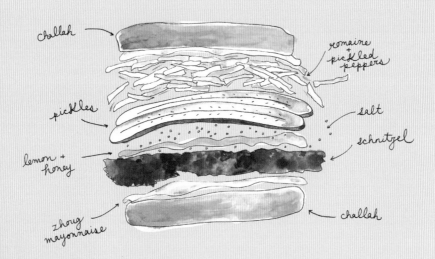

challah

romaine + pickled peppers

pickles

salt

schnitzel

lemon + honey

zhoug mayonnaise

challah

Like Arthurs itself, this cookbook is full of big restaurant energy and the passion and commitment to reinventing traditional Jewish dishes and creating fun and innovative new classics. As you read and cook through the recipes in this book you'll be laughing at the authors' hilarious and uncensored stories (and the odd disagreement!). And it's all encased in a joyful design with oodles of gorgeous photography and playful illustrations.

Arthurs is the perfect cookbook for everyone who loves to cook—and anyone who has ever craved a nosh.

ARTH

Home of the Nosh

BY RAEGAN STEINBERG, ALEXANDRE COHEN &
EVELYNE ENG · PHOTOGRAPHY BY KAROLINA JEZ

A Big Personality Cookbook
of Delicious Jewish Deli Favorites

appetite
by RANDOM HOUSE

Appetite by Random House® and colophon are registered trademarks
of Penguin Random House LLC.

Library and Archives Canada Cataloguing in Publication is available upon request.
ISBN: 978-0-525-61228-5
eBook ISBN: 978-0-525-61231-5
Photography by Karolina Jez
Illustrations by Vanessa Laberge; illustrations on pg. 326 by Melissa Wood
Book and cover design by Kelly Hill
Typeset by Sean Tai

Printed in China

Published in Canada by Appetite by Random House®,
a division of Penguin Random House Canada Limited.

www.penguinrandomhouse.ca

10 9 8 7 6 5 4 3 2 1

appetite
by RANDOM HOUSE

Penguin
Random House
Canada

To our beautiful children, Freya and Abel. To Marilyn, Liliane, and Solomon.
To Pumak, our late Alusky, and of course, to Arthur Steinberg, The Bear.
Hopefully you two are sitting side by side right now.

Contents

Long Live

The Bear

Preface

by Raegan Steinberg

The day my father passed, a huge snowstorm hit. It was one of those whiteouts where the snow is so heavy you can't see a few feet in front of you. I was on a mission. A few months prior, my dad had bought a brand-new black BMW 740. Pretty much the only place he had driven it to was the hospital. I would be the one to bring it back home. I got in the car and made my adjustments, pulling the seat forward and tilting the rearview mirror downward, rearranging everything to suit my 5-foot-2 body instead of the 6-foot-2 one it had held before. My only goal was not to crash.

In the beginning, the only sign my dad—Arthur—had that something wasn't right was a really long period of hiccups, which we dismissed as a weird reaction to blueberries. Who links hiccups to cancer? The symptoms worsened, until he walked through the front door one evening and announced the diagnosis to my mom, my little sister, my big brother, and me: non-Hodgkin lymphoma. Then he sat down at the head of the table and began to eat his dinner, as if it were any other night.

I was 21 then and didn't believe he was going to die. He kept saying, "No, everything is gonna be fine, we're gonna deal with it," but eventually the doctors kept saying, "It's really resisting the treatments." I had him slurping down shark fin soup and knocking back shots of wheatgrass. We called hospitals as distant as Israel, pursuing clinical trials with the slightest potential. All the while, we continued our ski weekends in Stowe and he even agreed to a boys' trip to Vegas. Arthur wanted to live.

For a year and a half, he never said anything about the fact that he was dying, not even when he ended up at a cancer center in Texas. The doctor said they had never seen someone take so much chemo. They could no longer treat him. Arthur was not going to live.

He was moved to the Jewish General, where he was told he had two weeks left. My family spent all day and night sitting with him, my mom always the last to leave, not returning home until 11 p.m. One of those nights, I was lying alone awake in their bed, in the house we had shared my whole life, telling myself over and over, "Prepare yourself. This is what it's going to be like."

2 a.m. and my mom still wasn't back. We got the call.

By the time we arrived at the hospital, my father was completely unconscious. I lay at the foot of the bed, holding his hand. We all drifted off to sleep, and that was when he left us. He was 58 years old.

I walked out of the hospital and drove that black BMW through the white city like a zombie. But I didn't crash. We sold the car and the house, and after many years, the painful memories gave way to joyful ones.

In his youth, Arthur Charles Steinberg had been a bear-fighting, rock 'n' roll–loving, LSD-dropping, Woodstock-crashing, Harley-riding, helicopter-skiing, bodybuilding, vodka-drinking, 250-pound investment BANKER. He was absolutely incomparable.

The only child of Otto Steinberg, a war vet, and Rita Pedvis, a prim lady, Arthur couldn't have conformed less to his parents' ideals. Despite his untamable nature, he eventually fell in love with a beautiful and innocent girl from Ottawa, my mama, Marilyn. After he stole her from right under his best friend's nose, they married grandly at the Ritz-Carlton in Montreal. Arthur changed from frat party king into husband, father, and provider, never losing his lust for adventure.

Anyone who knew Arthur loved Arthur, and he knew everybody. He was always running into familiar faces, to the point where I would be embarrassed at how often he'd stop to chat in public. His funeral was so jam-packed that people were spilling out from the synagogue doors onto the street.

As a father, Arthur was selfless,

supportive, and incredibly honest. He told me everything from his wild past and everything I could expect from a wild life of my own. When I screwed up, he's who I called, knowing he would always know what was best. He took me anywhere at any hour, from ski racing in Vermont at 7 a.m. to karate at 7 p.m. Because of him, I had everything I ever wanted, without realizing how hard he had to work for it.

My dad made sure that food was of utmost importance in our house. We sat down together for every home meal and booked vacations according to how well we could eat when we got there. At breakfast, we were planning lunch, and at lunch, we were planning dinner. He would set me on his motorcycle and we'd take off around the city for all kinds of treats, starting in Little Italy for cappuccinos and panettone and ending in our favorite greasy spoon for all-dressed steamies and fries. By the age of six, my little sister was munching on steak tartare and fries with mayo without raising an eyebrow (our six-year-old, Freya, now does the same). Food was our happy place, imprinted in our DNA through him.

My husband, Alex, and our children will never know Arthur, and it breaks my heart. He would have adored the fact that I married a chef. But I feel my heart warm when I see our children with Alex, knowing that they'll have the same kind of relationship with their dad that I had with mine.

Our restaurant is the best homage I could think of to pay my dad. Without his passing, it probably wouldn't exist at all. Arthurs Nosh Bar is an embodiment of his bright and generous spirit and, of course, his passion for a good nosh.

Introduction

Reagan: We know that Arthur's death is a sad story to open a cookbook, but we have done so because, well, it is the beginning. From that immense loss came this whirling adventure of a life that shows no signs of slowing.

While I've always been smart and capable, in my 20s I found myself lacking direction and majoring in poli sci—need I say more? It truly wasn't until my dad passed away that I began to make decisions about what I wanted for my life. Post-graduation, I was working for a catering company dominated by a total douchebag boys' club. I wanted to be taken more seriously in the field, and I couldn't stand being in Montreal in the aftermath of my family tragedy. I needed to escape for a while, and culinary school in Vancouver offered a way out. It wasn't long before I was fully committed to that world. It gave me a sense of purpose, like I had these new skills that were of some value.

Alex: Like Raegan, I didn't have any childhood dreams of becoming a chef. Through my mom's cooking, I had always appreciated eating well, but surely never envisioned myself pursuing it as a career. My thing was professional online gaming, and my side gig was dishwashing. One night I was asked to fill in for a missing cook, who of course never came back. I took his job, and from there grew my passion for cooking. I really still don't consider myself a chef; I don't think I've gone through the proper trials and training to win that title. I think the important part of what I and any other cook does is make food that tastes good, regardless of technique and tradition. That's the maximum any of us can do.

R: The food industry is also how we met, in a way (you can see our full story on pg. 86). It's also a big part of what we bonded over and how we could plausibly date, with both of us working late nights. I also convinced him to stop gaming, which I deeply regret; those guys make so much money now!

A: After a few years of us dating and working in various restaurants, we ventured into our own project, Back of House Catering. We ran it out of our first apartment using a 1950s electric oven and a Foreman grill to cater pitiful events like high school parties. After the fire alarms went off during a Portuguese chicken incident, we realized it was time for a new space. We found a shared kitchen at 4621 Rue Notre-Dame Ouest that was perfect, but after a few bar mitzvah and wedding jobs, we decided the spot was too good to waste on catering alone. One day we just said "fuck it" and took a risk. We named our new restaurant in honor of the late Arthur Steinberg. Arthurs Nosh Bar came to life.

R: Even though the evening before opening day was pretty much just me having a panic attack, creating the restaurant was a largely therapeutic endeavor. It helped me create a lasting legacy for my father and ensure he would never be forgotten. The walls are lined with photos of him and our family, and we all speak his name daily (even a replication of his exact signature is used to write "Arthurs" on all our products).

I don't know where I would be if my dad were still alive. There is almost nothing I wouldn't sacrifice for just one more day with him, but there is so much good that has been made possible because of his passing. I certainly wouldn't be running this restaurant with my incredible husband or telling our ridiculous tales to the public. Sometimes I can't help but think that our success has a little to do with my guardian angel watching over us.

Making a "Jewish" Restaurant

We knew that we wanted to cook what was familiar to us. Alex is a big believer in generational food memory, the idea that the food and flavors your ancestors loved are genetically passed down. For Alex, those ancestors are Moroccan-Spanish-Sephardic, and for Raegan, Romanian-Russian-Ashkenazi. Fred Morin once gave Raegan the advice "Cook what you know," and that's what we set out to do through Jewish food.

Plus it had been years since Montreal had seen a sit-down Jewish restaurant open, and the ones already in existence were cemented institutions, meaning that they were under pressure to not change a thing about their aesthetic, menu, or attitude. This is not a criticism—we adore these establishments. But we wanted the liberty to do something different in our city's Jewish food scene.

Opening a recognizably Jewish restaurant, at least in Montreal, means putting certain items on the menu: bagel and lox, latkes, matzo ball soup, etc. In other words, it means being Ashkenazi-forward. Otherwise, would most people really consider us as a "Jewish restaurant"?

So we have those obvious dishes on the menu (no, not just out of obligation, but that's part of it). At the same time, one of us is Sephardic, and we wanted a way to showcase aspects of that cuisine, which is essentially Middle Eastern and North African. If we serve too much of that kind of food, however, we'd no longer be called a "Jewish restaurant," but rather a "restaurant owned by Jewish people." Not to make it into some high-stakes thing, but it is a semi-fine line that we're walking. For the most part, we serve whatever we want, but the Ashkenazi element will always be prominent in our work.

It's a given that certain clients complain about the menu, claiming that we don't carry every Ashkenazi dish in existence. Hey, if you really want to know why we don't have gefilte, just flip to pg. 145. Happy reading.

The Beauty . . .

Cooking is like a human relationship. You go into it with a certain idea of what you want. But the factors inherent in each person (or ingredient, for the sake of this somewhat confusing analogy) combine to produce outcomes that are never exactly what you expected. The more you work on it, though—trying with different attitudes, levels of care, perspectives, timing, temperatures, and moods—the closer you might get to reaching what you want. It involves the whole self. And when you get it right, and the relationship is where it feels good, it can silence a room. It can bring joy to a sad moment and tears to a happy one. It can make you remember tastes you didn't even know were in your memory. It is different, every single day, and never perfectly replicable. But you can also just screw around for the fun of it, without risking too much. Unless you have a deadly allergy you don't know about. Then you're fucked.

Running a restaurant is invigorating. We love walking through the dining room and hearing the commotion of the customers' conversations, the loudness of the open kitchen, all that clinking and clamoring filling the atmosphere. We like to think of the nosh bar as a little spot where you go for a bite with people you actually like spending time with. Our restaurant is born from that idea: tiny and intimate, yet loud with conversation and laughter. Whether you're seated at the actual bar, in a booth, or at a two-top, you're likely to end up elbow to elbow with the person next to you, overhearing a telephone game of local rumors and ravings. Arthurs is definitely not what we'd call a tranquil place, and we don't want it to be.

Yet the more the restaurant ages (and the more we age), the more we feel the time we have left to enjoy it slipping away. We disperse our time a bit differently now; when we first opened, we lived right around the corner. Once Raegan got pregnant, we changed homes and lifestyles. Working on a recipe until 3 a.m. is not something we typically do anymore, and that's okay if it means getting to be there for the little moments with our kids, Freya and Abel. Losing a parent young teaches you that life is fragile. This could all be gone tomorrow.

We speak as if we've mastered the work-life balance, but that's far from true. We struggle with being present for ourselves, our children, and our business. To this day, Alex worries, "This is the day they all look up from their plates and see that I'm a fraud." But the walls are still up and the line is still miraculously out the door, so something's working. In utopia, we would build our restaurant and family and be there for every little thing, but in the precious world that we do have, with all its constraints, we just do our best.

. . . and the Bullshit

We were terrible bosses in the beginning. We had trouble delegating tasks, taking responsibility for our mistakes, keeping our marital spats out of the kitchen, planning finances, filtering out other people's opinions, and recording recipes (which caught up with us in the writing of this book). Our stress came through in our unprofessionalism.

We needed to right these wrongs very quickly. The most important part of the restaurant is the staff, and what each person gives to their position is irreplaceable. It was essential that we learned to become leaders that they could respect, give them the room and ability to grow professionally, be a bit of a psychologist and friend to each of them, and create a positive kitchen environment—in short, to make sure they love their jobs (and that we do too!).

When we first opened, we said we wouldn't be like the kind of bosses we had as line cooks, who offered wretched hours, an unsupportive atmosphere, and overbearing expectations. By the time we had sort of figured out how to effectively avoid that and fix all our initial errors, we were hit by the pandemic. With dining rooms closed, we switched to takeout and made cuts to the menu. We pulled through surprisingly well, with a mix of luck and extremely loyal staff. Everyone worked together to adjust to the new rhythm.

What we struggled with during the pandemic was the idea of paring things down, simplifying, and focusing more on the business side of things. Somewhere in there, we slightly lost our way. We're still trying to find a middle ground between being a business and a passion project. What degree of perfectionism can we strive for without driving ourselves and our staff insane? How can we create a well-oiled machine without disregarding the mental state of the individual? In this industry, what level of stress is productive and what level is destructive? Where is the line between being a boss and a friend? How can we remain relevant without letting outside voices sway our intuition? We will never find these answers.

But what are we saying here? We're not curing cancer. We're just trying to make stuff that tastes good without wrecking anyone in the process. And without losing our minds over rude Google reviews and Instagram comments. (You'd think that after eight years, we'd have turned off notifications.) The most we can do is listen to our gut and trust that both of us will get our shit done.

It goes without saying—even though we just ranted about it for a whole page—that the restaurant industry is a tough one, and we're part of the fortunate few who have it relatively easy. Amidst all our bitching, we hope you detect our immense gratitude and love for all of it, bullshit included. Every day, we get to work alongside eager, talented, complex people who care about food as much as we do. It is one of life's greatest gifts.

Why Write a Cookbook?

We didn't quite grasp the scope of what we've accomplished at Arthurs until we were trying to stuff it all into one book. It has proved impossible to fit every recipe, story, and tip into these pages, but that is part of what makes this cookbook such a fitting image of Arthurs. Without really planning to, we went from a little catering company to a so-called (*not* self-proclaimed) Montreal institution. This book is intended as a snapshot of our 47-seater, bursting with all the tastes and sounds and labor that have filled it over the last nine years.

It is also crucial to us that we share snippets of the cutting reality of restaurateuring, a domain that, for all its passion and gratification, tends to quickly wear down its workers. We do not wish to censor those aspects—staff turnover, financial barriers, COVID-19 repercussions, failed recipes—because without them, the restaurant would not be what it is today. We also do not wish to censor ourselves; as we bicker and rant in real life, we bicker and rant in writing. It is an inevitable part of running a business with a spouse, two kids, and an Alusky, and it's not something we'd ever give up. In fact, we already have so much going on that Alex didn't want to do this book at all. He also feels we're not well known enough for anyone to read it, but we've put so much effort (and money) into Arthurs that it seems wrong to not share it all with you, regardless of how daunting the task felt.

One joy of writing recipes for a home cook is that we can finally make them as we have always wanted to, such as frying latkes and schnitzel in a pan rather than a deep fryer,

or charring vegetables in a cast-iron skillet rather than under an oven broiler. Some recipes were made in-house before we gained a following and had to outsource them to meet the demand, such as Basement Babka. Some of these recipes never even made it onto the menu due to constraints on staff, budget, or time, while others were short-lived because customers preferred to order our bigger sellers, like the Syrniki and McArthur. Others are flat-out absurd, like the Caputo and Best Fudging Chocolate Pie.

We believe that all this is best conveyed in the hard-copy cookbook. *Arthurs: Home of the Nosh* is a physical piece of our history that we are proud to pass from our home to yours, especially to those who aren't within reach of Montreal. This book will look alright on your coffee table, but we would be much more satisfied if you stain it with flecks of fudge, schmears of schmear, tipsy mimosa marks, and schmaltzy fingerprints.

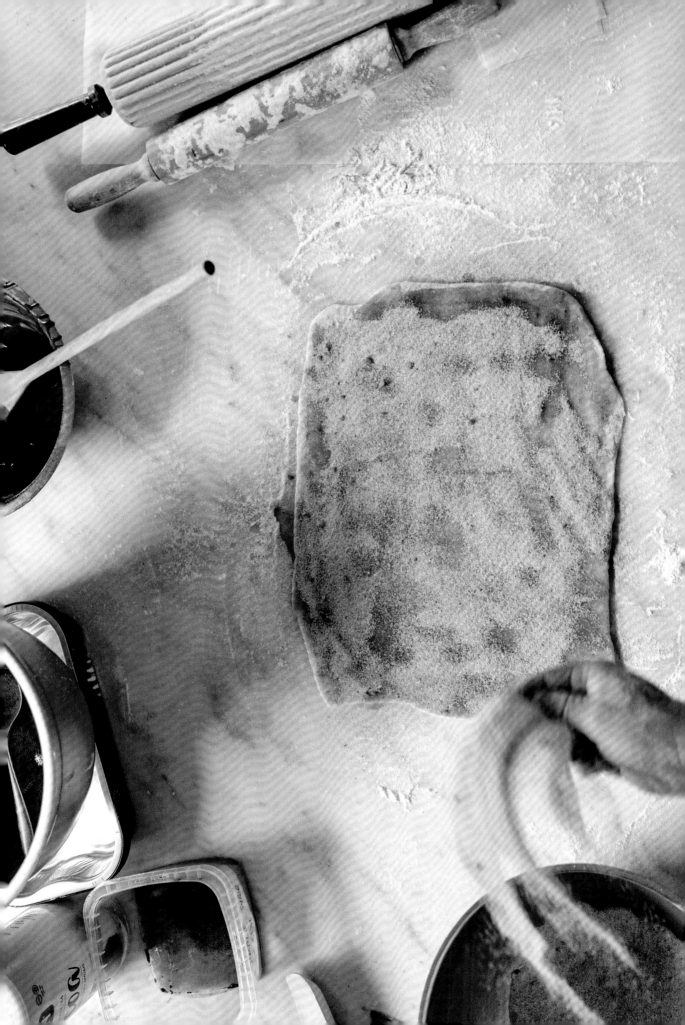

Notes on the Recipes

(DO NOT SKIP THIS PART OR A CURSE WILL BE BESTOWED UPON YOU AND YOUR BRETHREN)

We want you to love cooking the recipes in this book. Whatever you make from these pages, the goal is that it always be delicious.

If you cook something and it is anything short of that, we want you to understand why. Some of these recipes go deep into explaining exactly why we use certain methods or ingredients. If you have the will to listen to (not just read) the recipes, including their footnotes, they will help you become a more conscientious, generous home cook with a basic understanding of why some things work and others less so. Here are some things that will help you as you cook through this book.

Ingredients

Salt: Every time salt is listed as an ingredient, assume it means Diamond Crystal kosher salt unless otherwise stated. Different brands of kosher salt vary in saltiness and coarseness. One teaspoon of Morton, for example, is equal to about ½ teaspoon of Diamond Crystal. So taste as you go, using our quantities as the baseline, and stay away from iodized or table salt. For finishing, we always use Maldon because it melts in your mouth and crushes easily if you want a finer grind. If you prefer fleur de sel or any other flaky salt, it's perfectly fine to use that instead. Our belief is that salt is the most important ingredient; if you're going to cut corners on costs, don't do it on salt.

Spices: We toast and grind a lot of spices from whole because it makes a difference in freshness and flavor. This is especially important for cumin; whenever you see "ground cumin" in a recipe, we are referring to whole cumin seeds that have been freshly toasted then ground at home. If you use pre-ground spices, start with half the given quantity, then taste and adjust from there.

Sugar: Granulated sugar refers to your basic white sugar. For brown sugar, we've specified for each recipe whether dark or light is best, but use whichever one you already have.

Flour: Anytime you see "flour" in this book, it's all-purpose unless otherwise specified. You probably won't notice the discrepancies between higher- and lower-quality flours, unless you're really into this stuff. Use whatever brand you usually do.

Eggs: The eggs we use are large. If you can, buy pasture-raised ones. They taste better, look better, and are better for the chicks. Cage-free, free-range, and organic eggs are only slightly better than regular eggs in terms of these three factors. So if you're gonna spend the extra money, do yourself and the chickens a favor and spend it on pasture-raised.

Butter: Butter is so expensive that we won't tell you to buy the nicer kind, unless you actually have the money for it and believe you'll taste the difference. If possible, choose grass-fed or cultured, and look into the European end of the market for things like buttering toast. Otherwise, just use what you can afford. If making clarified butter (see below), definitely use the least expensive option. And when we say "butter" in the recipes, it means unsalted.

Clarified Butter: We like to use clarified butter, aka ghee, for almost anything we fry in a pan or on the flattop griddle (save for toast). It has a high smoke point and is healthier and better-tasting than most neutral seed oils. You can buy it or make your own. Melt butter in a saucepan or in the microwave until the milk solids separate. Skim out the milk solids, and what remains is clarified butter. If you're careful about not burning them, you can reserve those milk solids for seasoning a variety of things with a toasted milky flavor, like crumbles and ice cream. Ghee is pricey, so if it's better for your wallet to do a 50/50 ghee-oil mix, do that. A little ghee is better than none at all.

Seasoning

Seasoning (by which we mean salting) is the most important thing in cooking. Imagine you're sitting down to a gorgeous plate of food at a restaurant. You cut off your first bite, put it in your mouth, and the first thing you think is, "Dang, this could use some salt." An otherwise perfect dish, ruined. To prevent this, you can use whatever salt you want; just be mindful of how different ones season to differing degrees (see "Salt," pg. 13, for more). The crucial matter is that you season every single step or layer of a recipe as you go (except for most soups and other liquids with a long cook time, in which the flavors evolve toward the end). In a sandwich, for example, don't heavily salt the chicken but put no salt on the lettuce, thinking they'll balance each other out. They just won't. Sometimes we even instruct you to season certain ingredients before you cook them, whether it be to remove excess moisture, improve texture, or some other reason. Do not skip this step! Even a chocolate milkshake benefits from a small pinch of salt. Point being, when in doubt, add salt—without overdoing it, of course. (If you do oversalt something like soup, a pro tip is to add a potato and simmer until it's soft, then remove; that potato will suck up all the salt it can. A matzo ball works too!)

As for black pepper, it's not always necessary. Think of it as a way of balancing out salt. If you don't like it, though, don't use it.

A catchphrase to remember to season is this: Every time someone eats an unintentionally under-seasoned dish, a kitten loses its home. That should help you.

Icons

The Devil indicates something in the text that Alex finds annoying, like Avo Toast (pg. 42), or a recipe he's created that's complicated as hell. Do not be dissuaded by the devil, but do expect some mayhem.

The little green Clock indicates a recipe that is going to take a long time to complete. These recipes are worth the wait but you need to be prepared in advance.

Scale

At the restaurant, we typically measure our ingredients by weight. There are a few reasons for this:

1. Grams are exponentially more precise than cups and teaspoons. The latter can differ for some ingredients from brand to brand, and the way they are measured can differ from person to person. Using a scale ensures that your final result matches ours as closely as possible (so if you use a scale and the recipe still turns out like shit, you can blame us).

2. Scales have a bad rap for being only for the fancy-pants cook, but they're actually for the lazy. You have less cleanup and fewer scooping and scraping motions to do. If you do use imperial, don't scoop directly with the cup. Spoon the product into the cup gently; otherwise, it'll be too packed.

For most recipes in this book, we've converted our weights to volume measures and included both measurements for you. Overall, it was an inaccurate and annoying-as-hell process. For most savory recipes, it's perfectly fine to use cups and so on because you can go with feeling and adjust along the way. Some recipes require precision work, however, and it's often better to be safe than sorry, especially when it comes to desserts. So for the Dessert chapter, you'll see that the weight measures come first. A scale can cost as little as $15. Plus, you can use it for weighing various household objects and microdosing shrooms. Go buy one, *please*!

Go Cook!

All that being said, this is anything but a rulebook. It is a basic reference to send you in the right direction. If you cook something from this book and your reaction is "that's fine" or "that's okay" (the worst two phrases to describe food), it doesn't necessarily mean that you failed to follow instructions properly. It is more likely a sign that you didn't give your whole self to it, by which we mean that you didn't taste at every step, use quality ingredients, adjust to your preferences, and so on. Or, you know, maybe we screwed up during testing. In a few years, we're likely to have changed our perspectives on the way we cook anyway—as should you.

Use these recipes as guidelines to make the food yours. Cooking has as much to do with intuition and emotion as it does with capability or know-how. Your food should grow with you, and for this to happen, you need to invest some love into it. It should stir something within you.[1]

---

1 Raegan thought this last paragraph was embarrassingly cheesy and needed to be removed completely, but Alex refused.

BREAK

FAST

break · fast:

the breaking of the fast, the first meal
of the day, whenever that may be

Fuck the dinner dates. I want
to get breakfast with you.
You and me at a diner—
sweatpants, bedhead, and still
groggy from the night before.

Anybody can dress up
to spend the night together.
But the ones who are willing
to spend the morning with
you? Those are the ones
who mean something.

—UNKNOWN

It's 7:30 a.m. at Arthurs. One at

a time, the cooks throw open the front door (seeing as the back one is locked with a spoon) and plod past the walk-in fridge, then down to the basement to change into their stained kitchen clothes. Clomp-clomp back up the stairs to light the gas and click-click on the burners. Cutting boards, knives, and mixing tools get snatched up from the dish pit, and it's time to get started on the prep list. At 8:00, the opening servers start sauntering in, tying on their aprons and tying up their hair as they murmur about last night's happenings. It's 8:45 when the coffee pots get to brewing and the glass domes showcasing the sprinkle cookies are clinking back into place.

Before anyone knows it, it's 9:00, and the first customers are filing through the sage-green door of 4621 Rue Notre-Dame Ouest. The restaurant rapidly swells with the sounds of servers chatting with customers, music flowing from the AUX, latkes bubbling, and cooks calling out bills. The printer continually tch-tch-tches with new orders: Smorgasbord, Sandwich Déjeuner, Eggs & Salami, Avo Toast, Almond Oats, Syrniki. Some mornings it feels as if the whole of St-Henri has come for their daily dose of eggs and toast. Even by 11:00, when they have the whole lunch menu to order from, many diners continue to opt for oeufs brouillés. By the time the last customers are seated, around 3:00, the line cooks are whistling along with Popeye, their arms bulging from a long day of whisking.

Arthur always said that breakfast is the most important meal of the day. It would be convenient to say that we've run Arthurs on this principle. What's closer to the truth, however, is that we've remained a breakfast (and lunch) restaurant because, in the beginning, we were overwhelmed by the long hours, small staff, and big menu. One of us wanted to create an entirely new repertoire for the dinner service, and the other absolutely did not. There was our staff's well-being to consider too, and the amount of pressure they'd have to undergo. All things considered, we probably could've found a way, but then COVID came around. So we've stuck to eggs, and there's not too much bad we can say about that. Breakfast is, after all, still the most important meal.

Syrniki

R: If these pancakes were on a talk show, the host would introduce them with "our guest today needs no introduction." They have taken on a life of their own, generating three-hour wait times for those seeking a taste of what has become our most iconic dish.

The inspiration for these thick, moist, fluffy pancakes hearkens back to my 20s, when I was working at a 20-seater wine bar making everything from scratch. One of our Saturday brunch specialties was a creamy ricotta pancake, and I wanted to produce something similar for Arthurs' brunch menu without using ricotta (this was at the height of the ricotta-everything trend). Alex did his standard intensive research and stumbled upon something called a syrniki, an Eastern European cottage cheese pancake. Merging a syrniki with a buttermilk pancake, he unwittingly created what would become our bestseller. Alex didn't want to serve them all week; he wanted to reserve them for the weekend to make them more "special." But I pushed to have them on the regular menu, and I think people would be pretty pissed if we ever changed that.

Drench them in syrup; sprinkle them with semisweet chocolate; speckle them with wild blueberries; or fry until crispy and top with scrambled eggs, maple syrup, and hot sauce (clearly, an invention of my strange husband). No matter what you add to them, we can proudly say that these are likely the best pancakes you will ever eat!

1⅓ cups (320 ml) buttermilk, at room temperature

1⅓ cups + 1 tablespoon (320 g) 14% sour cream, at room temperature

1¼ cups (280 g) full-fat cottage cheese, at room temperature

4 eggs, yolks + whites separated, at room temperature

1 teaspoon pure vanilla extract

Generous 1 tablespoon butter, melted and cooled slightly

3 cups (420 g) flour, sifted

1½ tablespoons granulated sugar

2 teaspoons baking powder

2 teaspoons salt

Clarified butter or neutral oil, for cooking

Maldon salt, for serving

Pure maple syrup, for serving

In a large bowl, use a hard spatula to thoroughly mix together the buttermilk, sour cream, cottage cheese, egg yolks, and vanilla. Drizzle in the melted butter and mix until combined.

In a separate large bowl, combine the flour, sugar, baking powder, and salt. Make a well in the center. Gently stir in the wet mixture, being careful not to overmix. Small curds of cottage cheese should still be visible.

In a stand mixer, whip the egg whites to soft peaks, about 4 to 5 minutes.

With a spatula, gently fold the egg whites into the batter until just combined.

Let the batter rest for 10 minutes in the fridge (chilled batter will achieve pancakes with greater height and structure).

Heat a large nonstick skillet or seasoned cast-iron skillet over medium heat and grease it with clarified butter or oil (butter will burn). Scoop the batter onto the skillet in a mound to form one pancake, or as many as you can fit in your skillet without crowding (we use about ⅓ cup of batter per pancake, but make whatever size you want, reducing cook time if making smaller ones). Resist the urge to spread the batter around—the goal is tall, voluminous pancakes.

Fry the first side of the pancake over medium heat for 5 to 6 minutes. This batter won't bubble to tell you it's ready to be flipped. Rather, when the edges become matte, use a thin spatula to gently lift the pancake to check the bottom. When it's golden, flip over. Cook for another 5 minutes. If the sides appear uncooked, stand the pancake on its side and roll it to seal the edges (or finish it in a 300°F oven for 5 minutes). Repeat with remaining batter. The internal texture should be very moist, but not raw, with the cottage cheese curds still wholly visible. There will be some dark brown and black spots where the cottage cheese has caramelized.

Serve with a generous pinch of Maldon and lots of maple syrup. The pancakes are best served right away but can be kept warm in the oven on its lowest setting.

Jack Johnson

MAKES 12 TO 14 PANCAKES (SERVES 6 TO 8)

Syrniki batter, ready to be fried (pg. 21)

2 to 3 bananas

Granulated sugar, for caramelizing

Maldon salt, for serving

Maple syrup, for serving

Complete the Syrniki recipe up until the batter has chilled and is ready to fry. Continue the recipe as outlined, delicately adding about 6 banana slices to the top of each mound of batter after it is placed in the pan, and sprinkling on a bit of sugar to help the bananas caramelize. Serve topped with Maldon, maple syrup, and fresh banana slices if you'd like.

Strawberry

MAKES 12 TO 14 PANCAKES (SERVES 6 TO 8)

Syrniki (pg. 21)

3 cups (about 400 g) halved good strawberries

Granulated sugar, for macerating

Lemon, for macerating

Maldon salt, for serving

Maple syrup, for serving

While the Syrniki are frying, place the strawberries in a bowl, and mix in some sugar and a bit of lemon juice, adjusting both to taste depending on how sweet your strawberries already are. Let the strawberries macerate for about 15 minutes, until the sugar has dissolved. When your Syrniki are plated, top with Maldon, maple syrup, and the macerated strawberries (about ½ cup per 2 pancakes).

Blueberry

MAKES 12 TO 14 PANCAKES (SERVES 6 TO 8)

Syrniki batter, ready to be fried (pg. 21)

3 to 3½ cups (about 500 g) blueberries, preferably wild

Maldon salt, for serving

Maple syrup, for serving

Complete the Syrniki recipe up until the batter has chilled and is ready to fry. Carefully fold about 1 cup (150 g) of the blueberries into the batter, doing your best not to squish them. Finish the recipe as outlined, and serve topped with Maldon, maple syrup, and a pile of fresh blueberries (about ⅓ cup per 2 pancakes). Toss the blueberries with a tiny drizzle of maple syrup before plating to help them stick together.

Chocolate

MAKES 12 TO 14 PANCAKES (SERVES 6 TO 8)

Syrniki batter, ready to be fried (pg. 21)

1 cup (about 170 g) dark chocolate pastilles

Maldon salt, for serving

Maple syrup, for serving

Complete the Syrniki recipe up until the batter has chilled and is ready to fry. Finish the recipe as outlined, delicately adding the pastilles in one layer to the top of each mound of batter after it is placed in the pan, and adjusting the heat as needed to avoid burning. Serve topped with Maldon and maple syrup.

PERFECT SCRAMBLED EGGS

R: It was a Friday night in high school and my friend and I were just a tad high. We sat, stooped over a little bench table in my family's compact kitchen, chomping on our late-night cereal. My dad came home from his own night of fun with the boys, walked over to the stove, and started making scrambled eggs and fried potatoes. I was saying to myself, "DON'T LET HIM KNOW," and the funny thing was, he was surely thinking the same thing toward me. He sat down directly across from us, and we ate our munchies together in silence. We all placed our dishes in the sink, went our separate ways to bed, and never spoke of it again.

My dad was able to cook three things: pancakes, steak, and scrambled eggs. Early in the morning, I'd come downstairs to find him with his tie thrown over his shoulder, patiently scrambling eggs for us before he drove us to school blasting OutKast. Sometimes he'd throw in leftover mashed potatoes or onions and turn it into an omelet of sorts. It wasn't fine dining, but it certainly hit the spot.

Everyone is entitled to eat their eggies however they like, but our parents' way, and now the Arthurs way, is the best way of all—creamy, custardy, and ooey gooey.

SERVES 2

6 eggs

½ teaspoon salt

1½ tablespoons butter or fat of choice, preferably at room temperature

Crack the eggs into a bowl. Whisk them extremely well, preferably with an immersion blender (to incorporate minimal air), until zero streaks remain.

Whisk in the salt. Let the eggs sit for 5 to 10 minutes, which will ensure that the egg proteins don't bind too tightly during cooking, resulting in a creamier scramble (thanks, J. Kenji López-Alt). Without pre-salting, it's as one of our chefs said: "C'est comme si tu mets pas de lubrifiant quand tu baises!"

Add the butter and salted eggs to a medium nonstick pan on low heat—like most good things in life, making creamy scrambled eggs requires patience. Slowly whisk (preferably with a silicone whisk to not scratch your pan) until the butter is melted. As you whisk, small curds will begin to form, then the mixture will thicken slightly as larger ones form. Grab a heatproof spatula and use it to slice through the big curds and scrape along the sides and bottom of the pan. Slide the pan on and off the heat as needed to ensure even cooking. If the eggs are cooking too quickly, remove the pan completely from the heat, tilt it, scrape the eggs to one side, and keep mixing. Low and slow is key!

Just before you reach perfect doneness, remove the pan from the heat. The eggs should look a tad runny, but when you run a spatula through them, there should be no liquid at the bottom of the pan. It is important that they're a bit underdone, as they will continue to cook on your plate.

Plate the eggs and crack some black pepper on top.

Egg Basics

A: The first thing your dad teaches you about cooking is how to toast bread and fry eggs. Your mom teaches you how to butter your toast and perfect your eggs. If your mom didn't do that for you, here is your guide to making eggs. Some methods are a bit tedious, but they get you a perfect egg every time. You can use whatever fat you want, but we always recommend clarified butter (see pg. 14 for why).

Sunny-Side Up

This will teach you how to fry the perfect sunny egg, including how to get rid of the nasty raw egg membrane on top. It takes a delicate hand but becomes simple with practice.

Slick a nonstick skillet with clarified butter and set over medium heat.

Crack an egg into the pan. Once the egg white has set slightly, take a spoon and delicately slide the membrane off the yolk (the membrane is that transparent, mucus-like part of the egg). Spread the membrane over the white, circling it slowly around the yolk, so that it disperses and cooks. This ensures that your egg is snot-free. Immediately season with salt and black pepper.

Over-Easy

Over-easy eggs are perfect for sandwiches. They have a bit more thickness to them than a sunny egg and are quicker and easier to cook. Plus you're sure to avoid eating any of that raw egg membrane.

Slick a nonstick skillet with clarified butter and set over medium heat.

Crack an egg with whatever method you want. If you have very little fat in the pan, you can drop the whole egg, in its shell, into the pan (then remove the shell). Unconventional, but 9 times out of 10 it will break the egg perfectly.

Cook the bottom of the egg until the white has cooked and the yolk membrane is still raw. The bottom should have little to no color. Generously season with salt and black pepper.

Use a fish or plastic spatula to flip the egg. There isn't any special trick to doing this well, other than confidence and practice. It helps to flip in the direction in which the yolk is leaning and to keep it close to the pan. If you fuck up with enough faith, it'll look like you did it on purpose.

Cook the second side for less than half the time you cooked the first.

Slide the egg onto a plate, with the first side you cooked facing up. This will allow any residual heat from that side to release, preventing the yolk from congealing as quickly (over the top, we know, but this is for a truly perfect fried egg).

Hard-Fried

The hard-fried, or wok-fried, egg is an amazing vehicle for anything with stronger flavors, such as salsas and pickled salads. Browning the bottom of the egg brings out the—there's no other way to say this—egginess of the egg. This, in addition to the air pockets and crispiness created by high heat, makes the egg sturdy enough to hold its own beside more pungent ingredients.

Grab a well-seasoned carbon-steel wok, or a stainless-steel or cast-iron skillet (nonstick is bad with high heat). Add 2 to 3 tablespoons of clarified butter, animal fat, or neutral oil, and get the pan ripping hot.

For the crispiest egg, crack an egg into a fine-mesh strainer to strain out the water. Carefully slide the strained egg into the pan to avoid splattering.

Once the egg starts to bubble, spoon the fat from the pan over the egg in a basting motion. This will cook the egg whites without needing to flip the egg. Watch the egg carefully, as it can overcook in seconds. Season with salt.

Poached

Yeah, you can probably find a faster and better description of how to do this online (Nigella Lawson and Helen Rennie have good videos on YouTube). I'm not gonna give you some secret recipe, unless you want to learn how to make 300 eggs.

Hard-Boiled

Nobody likes a gray egg. Whomever you feed it to will hate you and call you smelly egg guy forever. So don't make one of those. How do you know if you've overcooked it? Your whole kitchen will smell like farts.

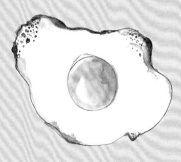

SMORGASBORD

R: In its loosest sense, a smorgasbord is simply an array of foods. What we're interested in is the "Ashkenazi" smorgasbord, a light brunch spread of toast, schmear, smoked salmon, eggs, and caviar. The Arthurs smorg draws inspiration from this concept and scales it down to a single plate. It is our most diverse breakfast dish, a colorful gathering of challah, latkes, scrambled eggs, gravlax (an original feature of the Swedish smörgåsbord), and cucumber salad.

This last aspect came about from my love of tomatoes and cucumbers as a breakfast side (like how many people eat a side of fruit). We initially tried serving them on spears and it looked awful, so I got Alex to put together a cucumber salad instead. Nearly every Middle Eastern cuisine has a rendition of it—salad-e Shirazi, salata falahiyeh, Israeli salad, etc.—so you may recognize it under another name (and don't worry too much about getting the proportions exactly right).

A: I'd like to meet the jackass who said, "Let's put shitty fruit next to eggs." Imagine you ordered a steak at dinner and they gave you a brochette of underripe pineapple, banana, and melon. Get that out of my sight. The only time fruit belongs with eggs is in Thai pineapple fried rice. Now that's delicious.

People have come in and complained that we don't even serve our breakfast with a side of fruit. Yes we do—it's called a fruit salad, and you can order it in the summer as a *side dish*. What, you think the other places are gifting you that out-of-season fruit? Nothing in life is free. Trust me, you're paying for those mushy berries and single lettuce frond. Might as well pay for the good stuff.

SERVES 2

2 challah rolls or breakfast bread of choice

Butter, for cooking and toasting

4 eggs

4 slices (about 3½ oz/100 g total) Gravlax (pg. 163)

½ cup Arthurs Cucumber Salad

2 Latkes (pg. 178)

Caviar, for topping

14% sour cream, for topping

Roasted Applesauce (pg. 216), for topping

Chives, finely chopped, for topping

Slather the challah rolls on all sides with butter and season with salt. Place in a skillet and toast on each side, pressing the rolls with a heavy object, until deeply golden brown. Set aside and cover with a kitchen towel to create steam and keep the rolls tender inside and crispy outside.

In a small nonstick skillet, scramble the eggs, following the instructions for Perfect Scrambled Eggs on pg. 27.

Cut each challah roll in half. Plate the Gravlax and Arthurs Cucumber Salad first on one side of the plate, then the Latke, eggs, and challah on the other side of the plate to avoid mixing hot and cold. Top the Gravlax with a small amount of caviar, and the Latke with sour cream, Roasted Applesauce, and chives. Season the eggs with black pepper.

Arthurs Cucumber Salad

MAKES 2½ CUPS

5 Persian or Lebanese cucumbers, finely diced[1]

2 Roma tomatoes, finely diced[2]

½ Vidalia onion, finely diced

1½ teaspoons minced fresh dill or parsley, mint, or whatever is fresh in your region

1 tablespoon Red Wine Vinaigrette (pg. 217)

1½ tablespoons extra-virgin olive oil

1 clove garlic, crushed (optional)

Juice of ¼ lemon

Place the diced cucumbers and tomatoes in a colander set over a bowl, and season with salt to drain excess water. Transfer to a large bowl and add the onion and dill.

In a small bowl, whisk together the vinaigrette and olive oil. Pour it over the veg mixture and add the garlic. Toss until evenly distributed. Season with salt and lots of black pepper to taste, and adjust dill and vinaigrette levels as desired. Right before serving, stir in the lemon juice.

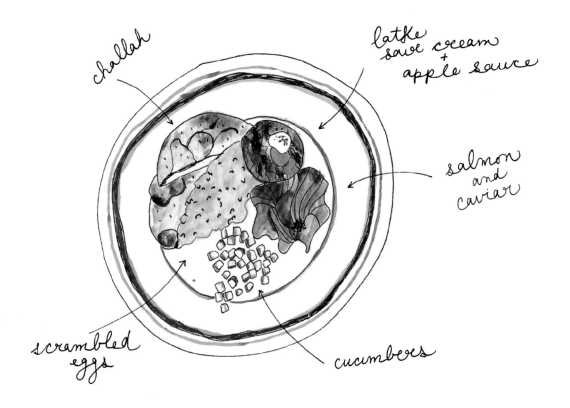

challah

latke
sour cream
+
apple sauce

salmon
and
caviar

scrambled
eggs

cucumbers

---

1 We like Lebanese cucumbers because they have less water and more flavor than English cucumbers. If using English ones, we recommend you scoop out the middle part with all the seeds to remove excess water.

2 If tomatoes are in season, feel free to use whichever kind are best at the market. Just be wary of water content.

MARINATED BREAKFAST SALAMI

R: All-beef kosher salami is a staple in the diet of a Jewish household. I like mine super crispy, practically charred. My family likes it cold, sandwiched between challah with yellow deli mustard. At Arthurs, we like it bathed in this delicious marinade of maple syrup and hot sauce that my hubby dreamt up after tasting his friend's grilled, brown-sugar-rubbed salami ;) If you come by Arthurs any time our kids are there, you'll catch our daughter snacking on salami the way she likes it—marinated, cold, and swiped from the flattop station in fistfuls when her mommy's not looking.

MAKES 1 TUBE'S WORTH OF SALAMI

1 tube (about 1.1 lb/500 g) all-beef salami

3 tablespoons dark brown sugar

⅓ cup (80 ml) water

1½ teaspoons Tabasco

¼ cup (80 g) pure maple syrup + more to taste

Remove the salami casing and slice the salami into ½-inch-thick rounds.

In a large pot, combine the brown sugar and water. Bring to a boil, then remove from the heat. Stir in the Tabasco and maple syrup and set aside to cool.

Place the salami in a plastic bag, pour in the marinade to cover it, and seal. Marinate for at least 10 minutes at room temperature and up to 24 hours in the fridge, flipping halfway through. You could leave it for up to 10 days, but it will become almost candied when you fry it.

Drain any excess marinade from the salami.[1]

On a BBQ or in a skillet set over medium heat, fry the salami for 2 minutes on each side, or longer if you like it a bit burnt on the edges.[2]

Drizzle with extra maple syrup if you want it sweeter.

---

[1] Extra marinade can be reused for your next batch of salami. It will keep in the fridge for up to 2 weeks.

[2] If you want to make the cleanup process easier, place parchment paper in the skillet and cook the salami on top of it.

EGGS & SALAMI

A: Every Jewish or Greek diner that serves Jewish people in Montreal has something akin to mishmash, a mélange of eggs, processed meat, and a veg or two, usually fried on a flattop. Raegan grew up eating hers at Beautys, but I had never heard of that place until I was in my 20s. My idea of a mishmash was my mom's kosher salami or leftover Shabbat lamb enveloped in scrambled eggs.

In a perfect world, I'd put mishmash on the menu. In the real world, there's no damn space for it in our kitchen, and this is the best we could do. Maple-syrup-marinated all-beef salami seared and served with scrambled eggs, buttery challah, and a deep-brown latke.

SERVES 2

8 slices Marinated Breakfast Salami (pg. 34)

2 challah rolls or breakfast bread of choice

Butter, for toasting

4 eggs

1 small handful shredded aged cheddar (optional)

2 Latkes (pg. 178)

14% sour cream, for topping

Roasted Applesauce (pg. 216), for topping

Chives, finely chopped, for garnish

Pure maple syrup, for finishing

In a skillet over medium-high heat, fry the salami slices for 2 to 3 minutes on each side, until darkened and beginning to char at the edges.

While your salami's sizzling away, swipe the challah rolls with butter, season with salt, and toss on the grill. Take the hockey puck you have lying around and use it to press the challah for maximum toasty surface space.

In a small nonstick skillet, scramble the eggs, following the instructions for Perfect Scrambled Eggs on pg. 27. Grate in a bit of cheese.

You can throw all this on two plates and move on with your day, but if you're feeling extra, here's how to plate it the Arthurs way:

Grab two hot plates. Each plate is now a clock. At 5:00, place a Latke. Top with a dollop each of the sour cream and applesauce. Sprinkle with chives.

At about 3:00, place your eggs. Season with coarsely ground black pepper. Slice the challah in half, and place one half at 9:00 and one at 12:00, cut side facing the eggs so that the bread is eating them like Pac-Man.

From 6:00 to 7:00, fan out the salami slices. Drizzle them with a wee bit of maple syrup. Top the eggs with coarsely ground black pepper and more cheddar.

challah

scrambled eggs

salami

latke
apple sauce
+
sour cream

THE SCRAMBLE

R: I am a creature of habit, and nowhere else in life is this more apparent than in my choice of omelet: spinach, onion, and tomato.

A: You can take the woman out of the omelet but you can't take the omelet out of the woman.

R: . . .

A: You can't put raw spinach and tomato into an omelet. It's WAY too much water. I don't know why you still do it.

R: I mean, it's not supposed to be some high culinary thing. I like it because it makes me feel energized and healthy, and the acidity of the tomatoes is nice. What's wrong with that?

A: Literally everything . . . Look, if you want to put watery vegetables into eggs, you've gotta cook them and squeeze all the liquid out first. And if you're going through the trouble of that, don't make an American diner omelet or, worst of all, a frittata. Browned scrambled egg is one of the most off-putting flavors in existence, unless you're doing a dish that specifically benefits from it (like bánh xèo). But this dish is not that.

In response to the disgustingness of an American omelet, I threw together The Scramble, which is essentially just sautéed kale and onions with soft-scrambled eggs and a few toppings. Be warned: if you get lazy and don't remove the juices from the kale and onion, your finished dish will look like vomited-up eggs.

SERVES 2

Extra-virgin olive oil, for cooking

¼ cup (40 g) finely diced Vidalia onion

2 cups (120 g) finely chopped curly kale leaves

6 eggs

2 tablespoons shredded aged cheddar

Butter, for toasting

2 thin slices black Russian bread or bread of choice

14% sour cream, for topping

Salsa (pg. 211), for topping

Avo Spread (see Avo Toast, pg. 42), for topping

Heat a medium skillet over medium-low, and add a generous splash of olive oil. Add the onion and cook until translucent. Adjust the heat if necessary to avoid browning.

Add the kale and cook until wilted but still a vibrant green. Season with salt. Remove from the pan and set aside to cool. Once cooled, squeeze out any residual liquid.

In the same pan, start scrambling the eggs (see Perfect Scrambled Eggs, pg. 27). Just before they're done, throw in your desired amount of kale-onion mixture (use any leftovers for a stupid frittata) and the cheese. Time it well because if you add these ingredients too early, the eggs will become snotty!

Meanwhile, butter, salt, and toast the bread in a pan.

Divide the eggs between two plates. Dollop the sour cream, Salsa, and Avo Spread on top. Crack some black pepper over everything. Serve with the toast.

BREAKFAST SANDWICH

R: Alex and I had grand delusions for this breakfast sandwich. We thought people passing by in the morning on their way to work would pop in and grab it for a nosh on the run. But as they say, the best-laid plans of restaurateurs often go awry. This sandwich doesn't lend well to travel at all. The eggs are soft-scrambled and lightly sealed, cradled in leaves of crisp iceberg lettuce and slices of sweet salami blanketed in melted American cheese. All this gets sandwiched between a tender, freshly toasted challah roll schmeared with spiced mayo. This is the kind of sandwich you sit your ass down to eat, with a fork and knife, a stack of napkins, and a strong black coffee.

MAKES 1 SANDWICH

1 challah roll

Butter, for cooking

2 eggs

2 slices Marinated Breakfast Salami (pg. 34)[1]

1 slice American cheese

Zhug Mayo (pg. 219)

2 leaves iceberg lettuce (the soft, exterior leaves only)[2]

Slather the challah roll all over with butter and season with salt. Toast it on both sides in a pan, pressing it with something heavy. Set aside and cover with a kitchen towel.

In a small nonstick pan, make scrambled eggs (see Perfect Scrambled Eggs, pg. 27). When they are done, shape them into a round. Cook on low for 1½ minutes, then flip and cook for just long enough to seal the eggs. Keep the heat minimal to avoid any browning whatsoever. At Arthurs, color is the enemy of scrambled eggs!! If you want them well done, simply cook for longer (although if a customer asks for this during a rush, you bet we're gonna brown the hell out of it over high heat, unless you're a baby or pregnant with one, or really old).

While the eggs are cooking, heat another small pan over medium-high heat. Fry the salami slices. Lay the cheese on top. Fry until the cheese is melty, and the salami is darkened and the edges have caramelized.

Cut the challah roll in half. Schmear a thin layer of Zhug Mayo on the inside of both halves. On the bottom half, place the lettuce so that it curves upward and makes a nice pocket for the remaining layers. Lay the eggs down, then the salami and cheese. Season with black pepper, then top it off with the remaining challah half.

Stab the sandwich with a toothpick so it doesn't go slipping and sliding. Good luck if you plan on cutting it in half.

---

1 For a vegetarian version, replace the salami with half of a seasoned avocado.

2 According to sandwich science, using the ribs (the hard parts) of lettuce in a soft-scrambled egg sandwich will place too much pressure on the eggs, causing them to fall out upon first bite.

AVO TOAST

R: Avo toast . . . one of Alex's many demons. As much as you might want to hate it, it's kind of the perfect healthy breakfast plate: bright, savory, and satiating. Daina Antikacioglu, our sous chef from the early days, had just come back from LA and put this recipe together as a special. It was such a hit that we kept it on the menu and never changed a thing. I'm sure if my husband had his way we wouldn't serve this anymore because he's convinced "Instagram has taken it and destroyed it." But what can I say? Happy wife, happy life.

SERVES 2

2 to 4 thin slices tomato[1]

Red Wine Vinaigrette (pg. 217), for seasoning and drizzling

Butter, for toasting

2 (½-inch-thick) slices black Russian bread or rye bread

Clarified butter, for cooking

2 eggs

¼ cup to ⅓ cup Avo Spread (recipe below)

Zhug Sauce (pg. 209), mixed with a splash of extra-virgin olive oil, for topping (or hot sauce of choice)

2 small handfuls sprouts (like cilantro or pea)

Place the tomato slices on a paper towel–lined plate and season with salt, pepper, and Red Wine Vinaigrette. Let sit for a few minutes to release excess water.

Butter and salt the bread and toast it in a skillet.

Meanwhile, set a second skillet over medium-high heat and slick it with clarified butter. Fry the egg however you like, preferably over high heat for the crispy egg whites (see pg. 29).

While the egg is frying, start building your toasts. Schmear the Avo Spread all over each piece of toast. Make a dip in the center for the remaining toppings. Lay down the tomato slices and a fried egg. Season with salt, pepper, and a bit of Zhug Sauce. Grab a small handful of sprouts and place in a mound on top of each egg.[2]

Season the sprouts and splash with Red Wine Vinaigrette. Make it shine. Don't you dare take a picture of it.

Avo Spread

MAKES ABOUT 2 CUPS

½ clove garlic (optional)

4 ripe Hass avocados

½ Marinated Long Hot (pg. 152), finely chopped

2 tablespoons freshly squeezed lime juice

1 tablespoon extra-virgin olive oil

2 teaspoons finely chopped fresh cilantro

2 teaspoons salt

Crush and then mince the garlic. Let sit for 5 minutes to let some of the flavor release and lessen in intensity before using.

Combine the garlic and all other ingredients, plus some black pepper to taste, in a medium bowl or mortar and pestle. Mash everything together with your hands, a fork, or the pestle, until you have a range of textures, from smooth to large chunks. To store, place the spread in a container, tap it on the counter to remove air pockets, plastic wrap the surface, and cover. It will keep for 4 days in the fridge, or longer if you scrape off the browned bits as they come up.

---

1 If you can't find good tomatoes in season, thinly sliced Lebanese cucumbers are a good substitute.

2 Fancy people can also add Smoked Salmon or Gravlax from pg. 163.

MATZO BREI

R: Neither one of us grew up on this quintessentially Ashkenazi dish. Alex's family is Sephardic, which is not a matzo brei–eating culture, and my family only loosely kept Passover. But Alex happens to really like it, so of course we worked on a recipe for the holiday menu. Passover 2023 it finally happened, and it sold out instantly. Our recipe is both sweet and salty, hence the added onions, but you can remove them for a purely sweet version. We do hope you'll sear the matzah before adding it to the eggs for extra toastiness and caramelization, but it is definitely optional if you're feeling lazy. All in all, this is one of the easiest things for a non-chef to recreate: eggs scrambled with cinnamon-soaked matzah, a side of seared hash and beef bacon, and a finishing touch of maple syrup and powdered sugar. Crispy crunchy ooey gooey salty sugary cozy goodness!

MAKES 2 MATZO BREI

1 full sheet (35 g) Streit's egg matzah

1 teaspoon + 1 pinch granulated sugar

⅓ teaspoon cinnamon

½ cup + 2 tablespoons (150 ml) whole milk

4 eggs

2 tablespoons butter

¼ sweet onion, sliced

½ tablespoon clarified butter

Pure maple syrup, for topping

Powdered sugar, for topping

Maldon salt, for topping

Latke batter (pg. 178), for serving (optional)

Viens Beef Bacon (pg. 167), fried, for serving (optional)

Using your hands, break the matzah into quarter-sized pieces, and place in a large bowl. Stir in the 1 teaspoon sugar, the cinnamon, and the milk. Let sit while you prepare the eggs and onion.

Crack the eggs into a bowl, and season with a couple pinches of salt. Whisk with a whisk or hand blender until they become one homogeneous color.

In a nonstick skillet, melt 1 tablespoon of the butter over medium heat. Add the onion and remaining pinch of sugar, and cook until golden brown. Transfer the contents of the pan into the bowl with the eggs. Let the pan cool slightly off the heat.

Place the soaked matzah in a fine-mesh strainer set over a bowl. Do not press or squeeze the matzah—you want the pieces to remain as intact as possible. Meanwhile, heat the clarified butter in a small skillet set over medium heat. Add the matzah, and sear on both sides until golden. Set aside.

Place the pan used for the onions back over low heat, then add the remaining 1 tablespoon butter and the onion-egg mixture. Stir occasionally with a spatula, roughly following the technique for Perfect Scrambled Eggs on pg. 27.

Once the eggs are three-quarters of the way cooked, fold in the matzah. Raise the heat slightly to dry out the matzah a bit, then remove the pan from the heat when the eggs are still a tad underdone, allowing the residual heat to finish them.

To serve, top with a bit of black pepper, maple syrup, powdered sugar, and Maldon. If desired, sear some Latke batter as you would hashbrowns to use as a side, along with some crispy Viens Beef Bacon.

THE CLASSIC

R: The Classic is a rite of passage in Ashkenazi culture and got its name for good reason. It is the perfect ratio of bagel, lox, and cream cheese, conveniently packaged in sandwich form. We prefer lightly smoked salmon and the airiness of whipped cream cheese, which can be prepared by hand or with a mixer, but of course regular works just as well. Use whatever bagel you like; Alex prefers poppy seed, but imagine the photoshopping that the influencers would have to do to remove all those black dots in their teeth. Sesame is the decidedly more photogenic choice.

MAKES 1 SANDWICH

Butter, for toasting

1 bagel of choice, halved

A little or a lot of cream cheese (preferably Philadelphia)

3 slices (2.6 oz/75 g total) Smoked Salmon (pg. 163)

1 large pinch Pickled Vidalia Onions (see pg. 154)

1½ teaspoons capers

1 pinch finely chopped fresh dill

1 thin slice tomato (preferably in season)

Red Wine Vinaigrette (pg. 217)

1 lemon wedge, for garnish

Butter the inside of the bagel and toast in a pan until lightly golden. Place one half, inside facing down, on a plate, then stack the other on top, inside facing up. This will lightly steam the outside, creating the effect of a very fresh, yet toasted, bagel. Let cool slightly so the cream cheese doesn't melt when you schmear it on.

With a spatula or hand mixer, whip up the cream cheese. Schmear a thin layer of it onto the inside of both bagel halves.

On the bottom half, begin layering with the salmon. Season with salt and black pepper. Continue stacking with the pickled onions, capers, dill, and tomato. Season again with salt and black pepper, and lightly dress everything with the vinaigrette.

Close it up with the remaining bagel half, and top with a lemon wedge.

HONEY BUTTER TOAST

R: I am a bread-and-butter annihilator. Challah, in particular, has a special hold on my heart. Whenever my mom bought a fresh loaf, I'd reserve two extra-thick slices for toasting. I was very particular about the buttering: I'd butter each piece end to end, and there had to be enough to reach all the way through to the core of the toast. The real test of the butter-to-bread ratio was the first bite. My lips needed to be heavily glossed over, and my teeth marks needed to contain evidence of a butter-soaked interior. It's an evolutionary mutation—when my mom was a kid, she would crouch behind the kitchen counter and munch on a stick of butter as if it were a chocolate bar.

The honey portion of this recipe came to me when I was 13, still a chubby pre-teen. My godfather, my dad's BFF from summer camp, had invited us to stay at his terracotta-tiled, sunlit, super SoCal home in Bel Air. As I was mulling over the toast toppings he had laid out for breakfast, he gently suggested that I forgo my usual jam and opt for honey. I squeezed that serene little bear and the rest is history.

Our poor children have since inherited my butter-devouring gene. If you leave a stick of butter out overnight, it's guaranteed to be gone the next day. It's our little Christmas morning.

A: Not everyone had some futuristic Bel Air toaster with slots big enough to toast challah, RAEGAN. In my house, we had to work together to stuff challah slices into our skinny toaster, which was really only useful for POM bread and pita. Then we had to pry the bread out with our hands and some non-child-friendly utensil because it was too big to pop out properly. Every Friday and Saturday, the whole house smelled like dafina and burnt toast. Pan-frying, you ask? We'd never heard of it.

SERVES 1

1 very thick (2-inch) slice challah

An excessive amount of butter, at room temperature

Creamy honey, for spreading

Maldon salt, for serving

Slather both sides of the challah in butter (for reference, we use a paintbrush or dough scraper to do this at Arthurs).

Toast the challah in a skillet over medium heat. Flip after 2 to 3 minutes, or when the first side is deeply golden, and toast the other side until it looks the same. For a crosshatch effect, use a panini press or grill pan.

While the challah is still hot, generously drizzle creamy honey onto one side. Spread the honey with a knife so that it coats the entire surface and is just about to drip down the sides.

Finish with a flourish of Maldon. Devour while it's warm and gooey, or at room temperature a few hours later, which Alex claims is better.

ALL-DRESSED ALMOND OATS

R: Creamy oats are not at all what I grew up eating. The oats of my youth came from the Quaker Oats instant packets that you find at a ski hill and buy out of desperation. So for most of my life, I've been turned off by oatmeal, porridge, grits, and all their mushy cousins. It wasn't until I started dating my hubby that I began to understand what legit oats should be like. Alex loves bowls of anything creamy in the winter, and I still don't—I'm more of a crunchy-crispy girl myself—but now I can at least appreciate them. We added oats to the menu when the almond milk craze was going strong—

A: Okay, first of all, not everyone eats instant oats "out of desperation." Some of us kids ate it regularly. Also, almond milk had nothing to do with this recipe at first. As mentioned, I love oats, so I wanted to make some for Arthurs, using normal-person milk. You, however, thought almond milk was healthier and would accommodate vegans, so we used that instead. Everyone thought dairy was the devil. But you know that quote, "The greatest trick the Devil ever pulled was convincing the world he didn't exist"? Baudelaire was talking about store-bought almond milk, aka Big Nut.

R: There you have it. Almond oats.

SERVES 4 TO 6

4 cups (960 ml) water

2 cups (400 g) granulated sugar

Juice of ¼ lemon

3 medium Bosc pears

1 tablespoon pure maple syrup

2 teaspoons dark brown sugar

Heaping 2 cups (300 g) steel-cut oats

2 cups + 1 tablespoon (495 ml) almond milk + more as needed

1 large pinch cinnamon

Fresh fruit (like pomegranate seeds, finely diced Granny Smith apples and pears, and sliced banana), for topping

Almond butter, for topping

Cinnamon sugar, for topping

Hemp seeds, for topping

In a large pot, bring the water and sugar to a boil, stirring to dissolve the sugar. Remove from the heat and stir in the lemon juice.

Peel the pears and add them to the pot with the cooled sugar water. Bring to a simmer over medium heat, and cook until a knife inserts easily into the pears with little resistance; they should be soft, but still firm enough to be diced.

Remove the pears and transfer to a bowl. Pour over enough of the poaching liquid to completely cover them. Once cooled, dice 2 of the pears into ½-inch cubes. Set aside, and keep the third pear submersed in the syrup for up to 1 week in the fridge; we recommend eating it with chocolate sauce for dessert.

In a large pot, combine the maple syrup, brown sugar, oats, almond milk, and cinnamon. Simmer over medium-low heat until cooked to your desired consistency—anywhere from al dente to overdone—adding more milk as necessary. Be patient! This can take over 1 hour to accomplish. Stir frequently to ensure that nothing sticks to the bottom and burns. When the oats are done, stir in the pears. Season with a small pinch of salt.

To serve, top with anything you'd like. The Arthurs way is pomegranate seeds, finely diced Granny Smiths and pears, sliced banana, a scoop of almond butter, some cinnamon sugar, and hemp seeds. (The Alex way is peanut butter, scrambled eggs, and maple syrup.)

GRANOLA

R: Everybody loves granola. It follows that my husband needed to make it into literally the world's most complicated recipe. He tried so many ways to simplify and shorten it, but he failed. So here we have it, a three-part granola. No, you cannot just combine all ingredients together at the beginning; it doesn't turn out well. You can, however (if you're a sane person), choose just one of the parts and make a basic granola.

This makes a large quantity, almost six liters worth, but why would you make any less if you're gonna go through all the work? Store it in your pantry for whenever a granola hankering comes along, and if ever it goes stale, pop it back in the oven and it'll be like new again. Our daughter loves it and insists on eating it with her yogurt at least four times a week.

MAKES 24 CUPS

Part 1

¼ cup (50 g) light brown sugar

3⅓ cups (300 g) rolled oats

Heaping ½ cup (65 g) wheat germ

2 cups (250 g) roughly chopped almonds[1]

⅔ cup (85 g) pumpkin seeds, preferably toasted

½ cup (85 g) dried mulberries

1 tablespoon salt

1½ teaspoons cinnamon

½ teaspoon ground ginger

½ cup (120 ml) Roasted Applesauce (pg. 216)

Heaping 3 tablespoons pure maple syrup

Heaping 2 tablespoons honey

⅓ cup + 1 tablespoon (65 g) browned butter, cooled slightly

2 tablespoons neutral oil

Part 2

Packed ⅓ cup + 1 tablespoon (85 g) dark brown sugar

3⅓ cups (300 g) rolled oats

1¾ cups (200 g) cashews

Heaping ½ cup (80 g) sunflower seeds

2 teaspoons salt

1½ teaspoons cinnamon

½ cup (120 ml) Roasted Applesauce (pg. 216)

¼ cup (80 g) pure maple syrup

3 tablespoons honey

1 tablespoon neutral oil

Part 3

Packed ⅓ cup + 1 tablespoon (85 g) dark brown sugar

4 cups (355 g) rolled oats

1¼ cups (140 g) wheat germ

Heaping 1¾ cups (200 g) oat bran

Heaping 1 cup (140 g) roughly chopped pecans

1 cup (140 g) sunflower seeds

Heaping ¾ cup (100 g) roughly chopped walnuts

1 tablespoon salt

2 teaspoons cinnamon

1½ teaspoons pure vanilla extract

½ cup + 1 tablespoon (190 g) honey

½ cup + 1 tablespoon (135 ml) neutral oil

---

1 Don't overchop any of the nuts in this recipe because they give texture.

Preheat the oven to 300°F. Line three sheet trays with parchment paper.

Each recipe uses the following method, but must be cooked on separate sheet trays:

For each individual part, combine the brown sugar and all dry ingredients, minus the spices, in a large bowl.

In a pot, bring the spices, liquid sugars, and fats to a boil, stirring to combine. Once boiling, turn off the heat.

Pour the hot liquids into the dry ingredients and stir together. Spread in an even layer on the sheet tray.

Bake all three sheet trays at the same time for 30 minutes, until golden brown. Every 10 minutes, stir with a wooden spoon and rotate the position of the trays.

While the granolas are still hot, transfer them all into a large bowl and stir to combine. Spread the granola blend onto the trays and let cool to room temperature.

Store in airtight containers for at least 1 month. If it becomes stale, just place it back in the oven at 350°F for 5 minutes, then let cool.

YOGURT & FRUIT

R: If you couldn't tell by now, Alex is the creative mind of the pair (although he doesn't like to admit it). So when I asked him to come up with a yogurt dish, he delivered. In the summer, we use market berries, blueberry compote, and cottage cheese. In the winter, we coat juicy citrus supremes in fresh mint and peach jam, which slice through the fruits' acidity with herbal sweetness. Then Alex's tahini date spread goes on, darkening up the dish with a rich nuttiness, before everything gets covered in spiced, chunky granola. Tangy, sweet, creamy, and crunchy, this is a breakfast of contrasts.

Summer Yogurt & Fruit

SERVES 2

Blueberry Jam

½ cup + 2½ tablespoons (130 g) granulated sugar

3 tablespoons potato starch

2 teaspoons ground coriander seeds, toasted

½ cup (120 ml) water

⅓ cup (80 ml) freshly squeezed grapefruit juice

2 tablespoons freshly squeezed lemon juice

Heaping 4½ tablespoons (100 g) honey

1 heaping tablespoon salt

2 cinnamon sticks

4.4 lbs (2 kg) frozen blueberries

Assembly

¾ cup (180 g) full-fat Mediterranean yogurt, pressed if desired

2 tablespoons Blueberry Jam

¼ cup (55 g) full-fat cottage cheese

Turbinado sugar, for topping

½ cup seasonal fruit of choice (we like mangoes, blueberries or strawberries)

¼ cup Granola (pg. 52)

Creamy honey, for drizzling

Extra-virgin olive oil, for drizzling

MAKE THE BLUEBERRY JAM

In a small bowl, whisk together the sugar, potato starch, and coriander seeds. In a separate bowl, whisk together the water, citrus juices, honey, and salt. Add both mixtures to a large pot, along with the cinnamon sticks and blueberries.

Bring to a boil over medium-low heat, stirring occasionally to prevent burning, until it reaches 285 to 300°F. Remove from the heat and let cool. If it's too stiff, you can add a bit of water to loosen it up. The jam will keep in an airtight container in the fridge for a few months.

ASSEMBLE

Make a swoosh with the yogurt in each of two serving bowls, and swirl in the Blueberry Jam. Plop in the cottage cheese and top with a bit of turbinado sugar. Add the fruit and scatter the Granola all around. Drizzle with some creamy honey and the slightest bit of olive oil.

Winter Yogurt & Fruit

SERVES 2

Sweet Tahini Date Sauce

Scant ⅓ cup (45 g) pitted and chopped Medjool dates (nice and plump ones)

3½ tablespoons honey

Heaping 3 tablespoons tahini[1]

2½ tablespoons almond milk

1½ tablespoons pure maple syrup

2 teaspoons cacao powder

2 teaspoons coconut oil

1¼ teaspoons lucuma powder (optional)

1 teaspoon maca powder (optional)

1 teaspoon pure vanilla extract

1 teaspoon freshly squeezed lemon juice

¼ teaspoon cinnamon

Assembly

1 blood orange, supremed

1 Cara Cara orange, supremed

1 grapefruit, supremed

2½ tablespoons peach jam + more for serving

2 sprigs fresh mint, leaves only, ribboned

⅔ cup (150 g) full-fat Mediterranean yogurt, pressed if desired

3 tablespoons 14% sour cream

2 tablespoons Sweet Tahini Date Sauce

¼ cup Granola (pg. 52)

1 tbsp pomegranate seeds

A bit of creamy honey, for drizzling

MAKE THE SWEET TAHINI DATE SAUCE

Combine all ingredients, plus a pinch of salt, in a saucepan set over low heat. Bring to a simmer and cook until the dates have softened. Transfer to a food processor and blend until smooth; if you want extra smoothness, pass it through a sieve. Store any leftovers in an airtight container in the fridge for up to 3 weeks.

ASSEMBLE

In a small bowl, fold the citrus with the peach jam and mint. In another bowl, mix together the yogurt and sour cream.

Make a swoosh with the yogurt mixture in each of two serving bowls. Plop some more jam and a big spoonful of the Sweet Tahini Date Sauce on top. Add the citrus, Granola and pomegranate seeds. Top it off with a generous zigzag of creamy honey.

---

[1] Anytime you use raw tahini in a recipe, don't skimp on quality. If your tahini is bitter, it's because it's shitty, and if it's shitty, you'll taste that in the final dish.

BRUNCH

It's 8:45 a.m. on Saturday

morning and the line is already streaming out to the street corner, a string of sleepy, restless people. The servers glance out through the glass and put an end to their only chance at socialization—they're about to get slammed. The kitchen knows it too; before the first order is in, they've already plopped a preemptive row of pancakes on the flattop. Music is blasting as the bills rush in. The cooks call their tables with an urgency triple that of a weekday morning: "5 minutes on 42, 10, 60, 55, 26!" "I'm dropping the chicken for the Grand Slam!" "Can I get a re-call?!" "Plating all Moroccan Toasts!" "Can I talk to the server who punched this ASAP Waffle?!" "Guys, I need 3 more minutes on 26, I have no space for the Shakshukas!" The first-time customers trickle in at 11:00 and are greeted by the hostess: "We're looking at a 2½-hour wait. Would you like to put your name down?" (She once unknowingly said this to Rainn Wilson and Oscar Nuñez, and they left.)

You really can't talk about the food scene in Montreal without talking about brunch. It is a serious aspect of our food scene and can be experienced in nearly every form imaginable: Hole-in-the-wall diners with American-style omelets and frozen breakfast sausage (the best, in Raegan's opinion). White-tablecloth French establishments with champagne service, pain perdu, and house-smoked duck bacon. Distinctive Filipino brunch with coconut waffles and crispy pork belly. Delicious dim sum with steamed dumplings and buns plucked from rolling carts. Québécois locales, ever-reliant with their oeufs tournés, fèves au lard, cretons, and rolled-up crêpes, all splashed with sirop d'érable d'ici. Then there's us.

Arthurs does brunch in teeming towers of smoked salmon, colossal fried chicken gleaming with hot sauce, challah toasts assembled like sculptures, and decadent cottage cheese pancakes bathing in maple syrup. We may not have set out to be a part of Montreal's wild weekend dining scene, but we're grateful to have found our little pocket in it.

THE KAROLINA WAFFLE

A: Despite its lesser fame, our waffle is, in my opinion, better than our Syrniki (pg. 21). The syrniki is like a warm hug, and that's a nice feeling, but you can only enjoy a hug for so long. The waffle, on the other hand, is not something you get sick of. It's just so delicate and chewy and Eggo-y. You could eat 10 and feel like you had 2. I'm surely biased; in pursuit of the perfect waffle, I developed a frightening obsession. It was the first time I had really applied chemistry to cooking (hence the diastatic malt powder). I spent all my time on Reddit forums, YouTube tutorials, and the deep waffle web. The only reason I stopped was because Raegan was growing concerned for my health. We named the final plate after Karolina Victoria Jez, Raegan's dear friend, who had been begging for a waffle for some time. She also just so happens to be the brilliant photographer of the images in this book!

MAKES 10 TO 12 WAFFLES

Honey Butter

1½ tablespoons creamy honey

1 cup (226 g) high-quality salted butter, at room temperature[1]

Waffles

5½ cups + 2 tablespoons (595 g) pastry flour[3]

1⅓ tablespoons active dry yeast

1 tablespoon diastatic malt powder

1⅓ tablespoons granulated sugar

1 tablespoon salt

½ teaspoon baking soda

3 eggs, yolks + whites separated, at room temperature

4 cups + 2 tablespoons (990 ml) whole milk

¾ cup (170 g) butter

2 tablespoons artificial vanilla extract

Honey Butter, for serving

Powdered sugar, for serving

Pure maple syrup, for serving

Rainbow sprinkles, for serving

MAKE THE HONEY BUTTER

Using a spatula, whip together the honey and butter.[2] Any leftovers can be stored in an airtight container in the fridge for up to 4 days or in the freezer for up to 3 months.

MAKE THE WAFFLES

Into a large bowl, sift the flour, yeast, malt powder, sugar, salt, and baking soda.

In a separate bowl, whip the egg whites to soft peaks.

In a saucepan, slowly heat the milk, butter, and vanilla until warm (when you dip your finger in, it should be hot but not uncomfortable). Transfer to a medium bowl. Gradually whisk in the egg yolks until combined.

Add the wet mix to the dry mix and whisk together until no lumps, bumps, or humps remain. Gently fold in the egg whites. Cover and let rest for 20 to 30 minutes in a warm area.

Rewhisk the batter before using. Cook the waffles according to your machine instructions, adding enough batter so that it overflows slightly when you close the machine. Serve right away with a knob of Honey Butter, a dusting of powdered sugar, a side of maple syrup, and a pepper mill filled with sprinkles (full credit to Maison Publique for the cracked sprinkles concept). If absolutely necessary, you can keep the waffles warm on a wire rack in a warm oven, but they quickly dry out. Leftover waffles can be frozen and toasted like Eggos. Extra batter can be stored in the fridge for a few days.

---

1 If you forgot to pre-soften your butter, you can grate cold butter into a bowl to soften it instantaneously.

2 If making the Honey Butter in a larger quantity, use a firm whisk.

3 If you only have all-purpose flour, that's fine, but it will give you a softer waffle that loses its crispiness faster.

Challah French Toast

A: French toast is the middle child of our brunch menu, the overlooked and oft-forgotten delicacy whose glory has been stolen by the overachieving sibling, Syrniki (pg. 21). To make up for it, we've made this little walk-through of how we do our french toast, which may seem like overkill if you view brunch as a joke. I for sure used to view it as this stupid ordeal, but after treating it with as much care as lunch and dinner, I see that it should be taken just as seriously as any other meal that you pay for at a restaurant. If anything, it can be more challenging to succeed in brunch because diners expect something truly amazing after waiting in line for hours.

. . . But back to french toast. It is one of the first things I ever cooked, a dish synonymous with my childhood brunches—it was either this or Pearl Milling (previously Aunt Jemima's) pancakes. We can appreciate it through its three main components: bread, technique, and toppings. Below is a *rough* rundown on how we like to approach each of them.

Bread: Almost any bread can become french toast, but a truly versatile loaf is hard to come by. Sourdough gets a lot of fanfare, but its flavor is too distinct for my liking. White bread, by contrast, does not have a distinct enough flavor and is too soft, unless you can get your hands on a Texas white or Japanese milk. Brioche is lovely but too rich. Challah is our bread winner. It has good stretch and bounce, a subtle sweetness, a dense interior, and a tender crust that holds its own after extensive soaking and that stays moist if not soaked for long enough.

Technique: You could simply slice, dunk, and pan-fry your challah, which would give you a quick and satisfactory result. But why restrain yourself?

Pan-fried french toast is wonderful: thinly cut, simple, and minimally creamy with a subtle bite. But so is pain perdu, the soufflé style in which the bread is dried days in advance, soaked overnight in a batter of sorts, then baked until expanded.

At Arthurs, we begin with the pan technique but finish with the soufflé way. We dry our bread, soak it in a pseudo crème anglaise for a minimum of 30 minutes, then sear it on the flattop to caramelize the challah with control, an idea roughly pulled from crème brûlée. Right before serving, we finish it in the oven to puff it up, allowing us to prepare the dish well in advance (making it ideal for a brunch party).

Toppings: There's nothing wrong with drawing inspiration from other desserts to come up with a french toast flavor, but I am staunchly anti-copy-paste. For example, you can't just replace the cake with bread and red food dye, cover it with cream cheese frosting, and call it "red velvet french toast"—though if that's what you're into, power to you.

Now for what we love.

On our first day at Arthurs, we carefully dredged each 5-inch-thick slice of bread in cornflakes and seared it to order, a seemingly simple step. With little staff, large volume, and zero experience in the brunch industry, we quickly realized it was anything but.

Accordingly, we adapted with the seasons, using fresh fruit in the summer and junkier flavors (think fluffernutter) in the winter. In our later, more extravagant moments, we have made a whipped ricotta toast with poppy seed, meringue, and lemon filling; a cereal milk toast with honey butter cornflakes, crème anglaise, and a cereal milk yogurt sauce; and an apple pie toast with aged cheddar, black pepper, and pie crust crumble, just to name a few.

I know I may sound like a pompous ass, but the possibilities for this dish are limitless if you can figure out what your perfect base recipe is. In the end, the best french toast is just butter, maple syrup, and salt.

CHALLAH FRENCH TOAST

MAKES 8 SLICES (SERVES 4)

8 (2-inch-thick) slices challah

3 egg yolks

½ cup (100 g) granulated sugar

¾ cup + 2 tablespoons (210 ml) heavy cream

½ cup + ⅓ cup (200 ml) whole milk

1 tablespoon honey

½ teaspoon pure vanilla extract

½ cinnamon stick or ¼ teaspoon ground cinnamon

Clarified butter, for cooking

Place the challah slices in one layer on a sheet tray and leave in the fridge overnight, uncovered, to stale. Alternatively, you can dry them in the oven at low heat for 30 minutes.

When you're ready to make the french toast, preheat the oven to 325°F.

In a bowl, whisk together the egg yolks and sugar until you reach the ribbon stage (when you lift up the whisk, the batter that falls from it should form a thick trail that rests on the surface of the batter for a few seconds before disappearing).

In a saucepan, combine the heavy cream, milk, honey, vanilla, and cinnamon stick (if using ground cinnamon, add it after the liquids have been reduced in the next step).

Bring the mixture to a boil. Once it scalds, whisk down the bubbles and lower the heat. Reduce the mixture by 20%, whisking often so it doesn't burn. (If it does burn, do not scratch at the bottom. Instead, transfer the mixture to a separate pot and continue.) Remove the cinnamon stick (or, if using ground cinnamon, stir it in now).

Very, very slowly, stream the hot liquid into the egg and sugar mixture, whisking constantly so the eggs don't scramble. Allow to sit for 15 minutes so the air bubbles pop, then transfer to a large, shallow dish. Let cool slightly.

Submerge the challah in the mixture. Let soak for about 3 minutes, flipping a few times.[1] You know it's done when some liquid comes out of the bread when you squeeze it.

Slick a skillet, preferably cast iron, with clarified butter, and bring it to medium heat. Fry the challah on each side until golden brown.

Finish the challah in the oven for 3 minutes. You'll know it's done when it looks fluffy and bounces back when you poke it.

---

[1] The fresher the bread, the longer you soak it. The staler the bread, the shorter you soak it. If your bread is basically breadcrumbs, or if you've dried it in the oven, simply dunk it and take it out, otherwise it'll fall apart.

Strawberry Lime Tart[1]

MAKES 8 SLICES (SERVES 4)

Lime Tart

16 graham crackers
(9.1 oz/260 g)

Packed 2 tablespoons light
brown sugar

¼ cup + 2½ tablespoons (90 g)
butter, at room
temperature

½ teaspoon salt

6 egg yolks

1 (10 oz/300 ml) can condensed
milk

½ cup (120 ml) freshly
squeezed lemon juice

½ cup (120 ml) freshly
squeezed lime juice

Ritz Crumble

1 (6.3 oz/180 g) box Ritz
crackers

½ cup + 1½ tablespoons
(136 g) salted butter, at
room temperature

2 tablespoons granulated sugar

1 tablespoon dark brown sugar

1 teaspoon cinnamon

MAKE THE LIME TART

Preheat the oven to 350°F.

Place the graham crackers, brown sugar, butter, salt, and one of the egg yolks[2] into a food processor. Pulse until it reaches the texture of very wet sand. Press it evenly into the bottom of a 9-inch pie tin.

Bake for 8 to 13 minutes, until slightly darkened and puffed. As soon as it's out of the oven, press it down lightly with a metal measuring cup.

While the base is cooling, make the custard. In a bowl, whisk together the condensed milk, citrus juices, remaining five egg yolks, and a pinch of salt. Let sit for a few minutes to stiffen up, then rewhisk it before pouring it onto the crust. Tap the tin on the counter to remove air bubbles (you can also use the heat of a flame to do this).

Bake for 20 to 24 minutes, until just the center jiggles. If it cracks, you know it's overbaked. Leave the oven on for the Ritz Crumble. Let cool to room temperature, then freeze for at least 4 hours or overnight. When ready to assemble the french toast, cut into small cubes.

MAKE THE RITZ CRUMBLE

Crumble the Ritz crackers by hand into a large bowl. Add the remaining ingredients and mix together until it reaches the texture of crumbly wet sand.

Spread it evenly in the bottom of a 9-inch square baking dish or any dish large enough to obtain a ¼ inch-thick layer. Bake for 8 to 13 minutes, until darkened.

Let cool and break up into small pieces.

continued …

---

1 While Lime Tart is technically a dessert, we haven't put it in the Desserts chapter because it's not intended as a stand-alone recipe. We specifically designed its texture to work as a topping on the french toast. If you eat it on its own, you probably won't find it all that great.

2 You typically wouldn't put egg yolk in this kind of base, but because we're cutting it from frozen, we want a crust that won't crumble. The egg yolk gives it more of a chewy cookie texture, but if you want it slightly more crumbly, reduce the butter by 2 teaspoons.

Almond Cream

1 cup (100 g) almond flour

3 eggs, at room temperature

¾ cup (150 g) granulated sugar

¾ cup + 2 tablespoons (200 g) butter, at room temperature

1 cup (240 ml) whole milk

3½ tablespoons cornstarch

1 teaspoon pure vanilla extract

Mascarpone Whipped Cream

1 cup + 2 tablespoons (250 g) mascarpone

1 cup (240 ml) heavy cream

Scant ½ cup (50 g) powdered sugar

Assembly

Strawberries, halved if large, for topping

Granulated sugar, for macerating

8 slices Challah French Toast (pg. 63)

Almond Cream, for topping

Pure maple syrup, for drizzling

Mascarpone Whipped Cream, for topping

Ritz Crumble, for topping

Lime Tart, for topping

Powdered sugar, for topping

Lime zest, for finishing

Maldon salt, for finishing

MAKE THE ALMOND CREAM

Preheat the oven to 375°F.

Sift the almond flour and spread it out on a small sheet tray. Toast in the oven for 10 to 15 minutes, until lightly golden.

Set up a bain-marie: fill a saucepan with about an inch of water and set a large heatproof bowl on top; adjust the heat as needed to ensure that none of the simmering water splashes into the bowl during the cooking process. Place the eggs and sugar into the bowl and, whisking constantly, cook until thickened slightly (imagine the consistency of hollandaise sauce). Little by little, whisk in the butter until fully incorporated. Set the bowl aside.

In a medium pot over medium-low heat, heat the milk, cornstarch, and vanilla until it begins to bubble, stirring constantly. Whisking the egg and sugar mixture constantly, slowly stream in the milk mixture until fully combined. Whisk in the toasted almond flour. Press a sheet of plastic wrap on the surface of the cream and place in the fridge to cool completely.

MAKE THE MASCARPONE WHIPPED CREAM

In a stand mixer fitted with the whisk attachment, whip the mascarpone and cream until combined. Gradually add the powdered sugar and whip until just shy of stiff peaks.

ASSEMBLE

In a bowl, toss the strawberries with a bit of sugar and let macerate for 5 to 10 minutes.

For each serving, place two slices of Challah French Toast on a plate. Spread the Almond Cream on the first slice, then place the second slice on top. Top with a handful of strawberries, a bit of black pepper, and a squeeze of maple syrup. Add a good amount of Mascarpone Whipped Cream, a scattering of Ritz Crumble, and a few Lime Tart cubes. Dust with powdered sugar and finish with a bit of lime zest and Maldon.

Poached Peach Ricotta

SERVES 4

Poached Peaches

6 peaches (preferably free-stone, for easier pitting)

4 cups (960 ml) simple syrup, cooled[1]

2 cloves

1 cinnamon stick

½ vanilla bean

Whipped Ricotta

Heaping ⅓ cup (84 g) full-fat cottage cheese, at room temperature[2]

Heaping ⅓ cup (84 g) mascarpone, at room temperature

Scant 1 tablespoon cream cheese, at room temperature

¼ vanilla bean

½ teaspoon artificial vanilla extract

Heaping 1½ teaspoons honey

Heaping 1 cup (238 g) ricotta, at room temperature

Scant ½ cup (50 g) powdered sugar

¼ cup (60 ml) heavy cream, very cold

Assembly

Whipped Ricotta, for topping

8 slices Challah French Toast (pg. 63)

4 to 8 Poached Peach halves

Vanilla Crunchies (see Cinco de Mayo Pie, pg. 266), for topping

Shaved medium-aged cheddar, for topping

MAKE THE POACHED PEACHES

Bring a large pot of water to a boil.

With a paring knife, make a little X on the bottom of each peach. Boil them for 30 seconds, then transfer to an ice bath. Remove their skin, then halve and pit them.

Transfer to the simple syrup, along with the cloves, cinnamon stick, and vanilla bean. Let them sit for at least 8 hours before using. These last forever stored in the fridge.

MAKE THE WHIPPED RICOTTA

Blend the cottage cheese in a blender. Transfer to a large bowl and add the mascarpone, cream cheese, vanillas, and honey. Whip with a whisk, then fold in the ricotta with a spatula.

Sift in the powdered sugar and mix thoroughly. Cover and let sit in the fridge for a few hours or up to overnight.

Right before you're ready to use, whip the heavy cream to stiff peaks. Fold it into the chilled mixture. (If you want a sweeter Whipped Ricotta, add a bit of sugar to the heavy cream when whipping it.)

ASSEMBLE

To make each serving, dollop some Whipped Ricotta onto two pieces of stacked Challah French Toast. Top with one to two poached peach halves, a handful of Vanilla Crunchies, a bit of shaved cheddar, and a crack of black pepper.

---

[1] The powers that be have asked us to include a note on how to make this, so here we go: Boil equal parts sugar and water. Kill the heat and let cool, then store forever in the fridge. If you want more on that, google it.

[2] If desired, you can replace the cottage cheese and mascarpone with all ricotta.

LATKE SPECIAL

R: Here's a likable little brunch plate that takes only a few minutes of prep if you have leftover latkes and buy the salmon. It's a lazier version of the eggs Benedict concept, demonstrating one of the many ways you can use latkes as a base for a well-rounded dish. If you're doing a brunch gathering, simply lay out the ingredients and have everyone put it together however they like.

SERVES 1

1 egg

1 Latke (pg. 178)

2 to 3 tablespoons Avo Spread (see Avo Toast, pg. 42)

2 slices (1.8 oz/50 g total) Smoked Salmon (pg. 163)

14% sour cream, for topping

Caviar, for topping

Pickled Mustard Seeds (pg. 154), for topping

1 handful thinly sliced mixed lettuce (we like radicchio, endive, and whole arugula)

Red Wine Vinaigrette (pg. 217), for finishing

Poach the egg (see pg. 29 for our recommendation).

Spread the Latke with Avo Spread, then drape the Smoked Salmon on top. Make a small divot in the salmon, then place the poached egg there so it's stable. Season with salt and black pepper. Top it with a small dollop of sour cream, then equal bits of caviar and Pickled Mustard Seeds.

Splash the lettuce with the Red Wine Vinaigrette and serve on the side.

GRAND SLAM

R: Nearly every breakfast joint has a Grand Slam, the most excessive plate you can order. Ours came from an exchange with Setiz Taheri, our friend and neighbor from the clothing brand Quartier. We had decided on a collab. His business would create a sick T-shirt for us, and Alex would create something delicious for them. Enter the Grand Slam: two mini syrniki, two sunny-side up eggs, two strips of beef bacon, and—the pièce de résistance—Southern-style hot chicken.

SERVES 1

2 small Syrniki[1] (pg. 21)

2 eggs, fried (see pg. 28)

2 slices Viens Beef Bacon (pg. 167)

1 piece Noshville Chicken (pg. 200)

Nosh Sauce (pg. 213)

Maldon salt, for finishing

Pure maple syrup, for serving

Prepare your Syrniki, eggs, bacon, and chicken, timing it so everything is ready at about the same time and stays nice and hot. Lacquer the chicken with the Nosh Sauce so it shines, sprinkle the Syrniki with Maldon salt, and serve with a side of maple syrup.

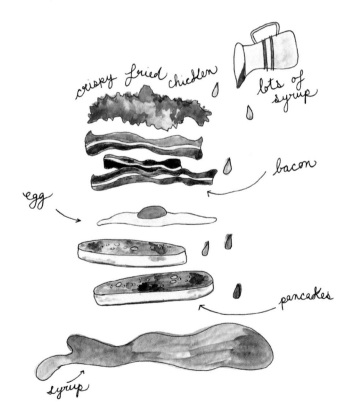

---

1 For Noshville Chicken and waffles, replace the Syrniki with The Karolina Waffle (pg. 61).

CHICKEN BUTTER BISCUIT SANDWICH

A: A lot of brunch menus have a fried chicken biscuit sandwich of sorts, but it's hard to find one that you can take more than two bites from before you're stuffed. To help with this, we make our biscuits with White Lily flour, which somehow produces a much more delicate result (unfortunately, they did not pay us to say that). You can use sifted all-purpose to similar effect.

In terms of topping, we went sweet. You can omit the Maple Glaze for a more savory biscuit, but we do hope that you make the Caramelized Honey, which somehow tastes almost exactly like its McDonald's counterpart. We're not saying that our sandwich is "light" in any sense of the word, but it is easier to eat your way through without feeling like a sack of bricks at the end.

MAKES 6 SANDWICHES

Maple Glaze

¼ cup + ½ tablespoon (63 g) butter

Packed ½ cup + 2 tablespoons (130 g) dark brown sugar

1½ tablespoons whole milk

1 tablespoon pancake syrup[1]

1 teaspoon maple extract[2]

1 cup (125 g) powdered sugar

Caramelized Honey

1½ cups + 2 tablespoons (550 g) honey

2 tablespoons white vinegar

½ teaspoon salt

Pinch cayenne or a few slices jalapeño (optional)

Buttermilk Biscuits

1¼ cups (300 ml) buttermilk

1 cup (113 g) self-rising flour, or 1 cup + 2 tablespoons (135 g) White Lily pre-sifted flour + 1½ teaspoons baking powder + ¼ teaspoon salt

MAKE THE MAPLE GLAZE

In a small saucepan over low heat, melt the butter and brown sugar together until the sugar is dissolved. Add the milk, pancake syrup, maple extract (for that '90s taste), and half the powdered sugar. Stir until smooth, then mix in the remaining powdered sugar.

Keep the glaze warm until ready to glaze, as it will harden as it cools.

MAKE THE CARAMELIZED HONEY

Place ¾ cup + 2 tablespoons (300 g) of the honey in a small saucepan. Bring to a boil, then lower to a simmer. There will be small, intense bubbles at first. When the honey calms down and large, slow bubbles form, turn off the heat. Stir in the remaining honey, the vinegar, and the salt. If you'd like a little spice, add a pinch of cayenne or a few slices of jalapeño. Let cool before using. This will keep on the counter for a long, long time. Use it with chicken nuggets, fries, and so forth.

MAKE THE BISCUITS

Preheat the oven to 475°F.

Place the buttermilk in the freezer for 15 minutes, until extremely cold.

continued …

---

1 You could use pure maple syrup, but it will cause the glaze to be softer, rather than dry out and crackle like a classic donut.

2 Maple extract is what adds that childhood maple-glazed donut flavor.

2 teaspoons granulated sugar

⅓ cup (75 g) cold salted butter, grated and frozen overnight or until fully frozen

Scant ¼ cup (50 g) shredded medium-aged cheddar (optional)

Butter, for baking and rubbing

1 egg, for brushing

1 tablespoon 14% sour cream, for brushing (optional)

Maldon salt, for finishing

Maple Glaze

Assembly

6 Buttermilk Biscuits

18 thin slices Otto's Dill Pickles (pg. 155) or bread-and-butter pickles

6 pieces Noshville Chicken (pg. 200), fried

Softened butter, for rubbing

Caramelized Honey, for drizzling

Sift the flour and sugar into a large bowl. Using a fork, toss and smash the frozen butter into the flour until you reach a very rough cornmeal texture. Stir in the chilled buttermilk in three additions, stopping once the dough comes together in a crumbly ball (you may not use all the buttermilk).

Turn the dough out onto a lightly floured surface. Shape it into a 1-inch-thick rectangle. Fold the dough in half, then rotate it 90 degrees. Roll it back into a 1-inch rectangle and repeat the folding and turning another five to eight times. Every 5 minutes during this folding process, place the dough in the fridge for 5 minutes so that it remains cold. If using cheese, add it in the third and fifth folds so that it melts in pockets when baked.

Using a ring mold, cut about six rounds from the dough (alternatively, use a knife to cut squares). Take care to twist the mold as little as possible. Place the dough on a sheet tray and let chill in the fridge for a final 5 minutes.

While the dough is chilling, add a knob of butter to a cast-iron skillet and throw it in the oven. We use a 9-inch skillet, but you should choose the pan size according to what kind of biscuits you want. For softer ones, use a pan small enough to fit the biscuits snugly. For crispier ones, use a pan large enough to spread out the biscuits, and reduce the bake time by 3 minutes.

Once the pan is hot (but not so hot that the fat is sizzling), remove it from the oven and add the dough rounds. In a bowl, whisk together the egg and sour cream, and brush on top of the dough. Bake for 15 to 20 minutes, until the biscuits are puffed and golden. Remove from the oven and immediately rub butter on the biscuits and sprinkle with Maldon. Let rest for 1 minute.

Dunk the top of each biscuit into the warm Maple Glaze and transfer to a wire rack set over a sheet tray. The glaze should harden almost immediately as it drips down the sides. If it's too runny, let the glaze cool a bit.

ASSEMBLE

Once the Maple Glaze has fully hardened on the biscuits, use a fork to open them up. Lay down three slices of pickles on one side of each biscuit, then a piece of Noshville Chicken. Rub a bit of soft butter on the hot chicken, then drizzle with the Caramelized Honey. Finish with a bit of salt and close it up.

MOROCCAN TOAST

A: Eggplant is a staple vegetable in Moroccan households. My family consumes it cold at Shabbat, pureed into baba ghanoush, or pan-fried with spices and tossed into a cold salad. Aptly, we gave our most popular eggplant dish at Arthurs the simple moniker "Moroccan Toast." When I first made it, it was just a thin piece of bread with eggplant, eggs, and sprouts. Everyone said it was "fine"—not to be dramatic, but I'd rather that they'd spit it out, smacked me in the face, and walked out than have used that word. I started over from scratch.

After much trial and error, we came out with the improved version: a thick slab of toasted challah schmeared with harissa mayo; blackened, creamy eggplant; lightly poached eggs (the most annoying task in a brunch restaurant); and an abundant scattering of vibrant herbs, seeds, sauces, and crunchy bits. (This recipe is obviously on the longer side, so be sure to read through the whole thing before beginning!) Bringing the Moroccan eggplant alone to a gathering is the equivalent of bringing a bottle of tequila; it just makes everything more fun.

MAKES 4 TOASTS

Moroccan-Style Eggplant

2 large eggplants sliced in ¾-inch rounds[1]

¼ cup (60 ml) neutral oil

¼ cup (60 ml) extra-virgin olive oil

¼ small Spanish onion, finely diced

½ red bell pepper, finely diced

3 large cloves garlic, minced

Packed 1½ tablespoons dark brown sugar

1½ teaspoons Moroccan or sweet paprika

1½ teaspoons ground cumin

1 teaspoon ground turmeric

Juice of ½ lemon

MAKE THE MOROCCAN-STYLE EGGPLANT

Place the sliced eggplants on two parchment-lined sheet trays. Lightly sprinkle both sides with salt. Let sit for 10 to 20 minutes, until some of the moisture is drawn out. Thoroughly pat dry with a paper towel. Do not be tempted to skip this step, or the eggplant will turn out bitter and wet.

In a large heavy-bottomed skillet, heat the neutral oil over medium-high heat. Turn on your hood fan to capture the smoke (alternatively, let your fire alarm go off so the good-looking firemen come over).

Working in batches, fry the eggplant until the exterior is just shy of burnt, about 5 to 7 minutes on the first side and 3 to 5 minutes on the second. Don't move them around too much. They will look very dark, but the interior should be white and creamy and feel soft when poked. Transfer to a paper towel–lined plate and set aside. Add more oil between batches as needed.

continued…

---

1 Select a glazed donut–face eggplant: its skin should be shiny, smooth, and firm.

Crispy Chickpeas

1 (14 oz/398 g) can chickpeas

¼ cup (60 ml) canola oil

1½ teaspoons za'atar

Assembly

8 eggs

Butter, for toasting

4 thick slices challah

1 cup Harissa Mayo (pg. 219),
    for spreading

2 cups Moroccan-Style
    Eggplant

1 cup Arthurs Cucumber Salad
    (see Smorgasbord, pg. 32)

½ cup Savory Tahini Sauce
    (pg. 216)

Toppings

Juice of 1 lemon

Paprika Oil (see Salade Cuite,
    pg. 222)

Crispy Chickpeas

Pomegranate seeds

Fresh cilantro, finely chopped

Fresh parsley, finely chopped

Za'atar

Sumac

Aleppo pepper

Black pepper

Lower the heat to medium-low and add the olive oil to the skillet. Sauté the onion and pepper until lightly browned and soft, about 2 minutes, then add the garlic and cook for another minute. Next, stir in the brown sugar, paprika, cumin, and turmeric and cook for another minute, until fragrant.

Return the cooked eggplants to the pan. Mash the mixture until it reaches a spreadable consistency and is beginning to stick to the bottom. The final color should be lightly golden. If it's dark, you've likely burnt and overcooked your eggplant, and you've fucked up.

Stir in the lemon juice and adjust salt and spices to taste (depending on the season, your eggplants may require more brown sugar).

MAKE THE CRISPY CHICKPEAS

Strain the chickpeas and pat them dry.

In a large skillet, heat the oil over medium-high heat. Add the chickpeas and fry until golden brown and slightly shrunken in size, about 5 to 7 minutes. Transfer to a paper towel–lined plate to absorb oil. Place in a bowl and toss with the za'atar and a generous pinch of salt. (You can also do this in an air fryer.)

Let cool. Store in an uncovered container until ready to use. These will keep for a few days but are best eaten the same day.

ASSEMBLE

Cook the eggs to your liking (we prefer poached, which can be done up to 24 hours in advance).

Lay out all your prepared components, like a real chef would.

Butter the challah and toast in a pan. For each serving, place one slice in the center of a large plate. Spread a couple table-spoons of Harissa Mayo all over the surface of the bread. Place about ½ cup Moroccan-Style Eggplant on top of each slice. Use a spoon to shape a mini crater in the center and add the eggs. Season them with salt and black pepper. Delicately spoon at least ¼ cup of the Arthurs Cucumber Salad over the eggs in a little mound. Drizzle 1 to 2 tablespoons Savory Tahini Sauce all over the Arthurs Cucumber Salad.

For topping, squeeze a bit of lemon over top and splatter around some Paprika Oil. Finally, scatter over the remaining topping ingredients to suit your taste. The finished plate should be kind of a hot mess—teetering, over-accessorized, and delicious.

SHAKSHUKA

A: No one quite agrees on the birthplace of shakshuka. Is it Israel, Yemen, the Ottoman Empire, or some ancient, unheard-of place? I'm sure as hell not the one qualified to tell you. When it comes to food, we're not big believers in singular origin stories. History is too muddy, with too many trade routes and conquests and migrations, to label any dish as "authentically" belonging to any one culture or region, with very few exceptions. Shakshuka is not one of them, and that's what makes it so enjoyable; there are a thousand ways to play with it.

The Arthurs Shakshuka never stops changing. Doing our best with Quebec's ingredients, we alter it according to what's in season to reflect various regions, hopping from India to Tunisia to the Middle East and beyond. This particular recipe is mostly influenced by South American flavors (chilies and roasted poblanos) and Israeli custom (chopped romaine and tomatoes).

Spicy and sweet, hot and cool, sour and comforting—these are just a few of the paradoxes that you'll find in this dish, along with a plethora of serving possibilities. You can eat it for breakfast and dinner. You can bake a fish in it and cook merguez in it. You can freeze it in bulk or eat the leftovers cold with hummus. You get the point.

SERVES 8

Shakshuka

7 red bell peppers

3 poblano peppers

2 jalapeños

6 vine tomatoes or 10 Roma tomatoes

4 small Spanish onions, 2 unpeeled + 2 peeled and thinly sliced

20 cloves garlic, 10 unpeeled + 10 peeled and minced

Neutral oil, for broiling

2 morita chilies

1 ancho chili

1 mije chili

3 New Mexico or guajillo chilies

2 chipotle peppers in adobo sauce

1 tablespoon apple cider vinegar

½ teaspoon granulated sugar

1 tablespoon unsalted chicken or vegetable bouillon powder

MAKE THE SHAKSHUKA

Preheat the oven to broil.

Spread the bell peppers, poblanos, jalapeños, tomatoes, and unpeeled onions and garlic on a sheet tray. Drizzle on a bit of oil and salt. Broil until they begin to burn, checking frequently, as each ingredient may be ready at different times. Let the bell peppers and poblanos cool slightly, then peel and slice into ½-inch strips. Set aside. Peel the tomatoes, onions, and garlic. Roughly peel, deseed, and devein the jalapeños.

In a small pan, lightly toast all the dried chilies. Remove only the New Mexico chili and set aside. Add a splash of water to the pan and boil for 1 minute. Transfer the contents of the pan to a blender and blend to a paste. Add the chipotles in adobo and the broiled jalapeños, onion, tomatoes, and garlic, and blend. Blend in the apple cider vinegar, granulated sugar, and chicken broth powder (if unsalted, add 1 teaspoon salt). Set aside.

In a small pan over medium-high heat, toast the cumin, caraway, and coriander seeds until you can smell them. Grind in a mortar and pestle or spice grinder.

Heat the Paprika Oil in a large Dutch oven, or other ovenproof pot with a lid, over medium heat. Add the toasted spices. Once they

continued...

1 tablespoon cumin seeds

2 teaspoons caraway seeds

1 teaspoon coriander seeds

½ cup (120 ml) Paprika Oil (see Salade Cuite, pg. 222)

3 tablespoons tomato paste

1 tablespoon light brown sugar

1 (28 oz/796 ml) can high-quality crushed tomatoes

⅓ small confit lemon (1 oz/30 g)

Assembly

8 to 16 eggs (1 to 2 per person, or as many as you want)

Side Garnishes (see suggestions below)

begin to stick to the pot, add the remaining 10 cloves minced garlic and the peeled, sliced onion and cook until softened and lightly golden. Stir in the tomato paste and cook until darkened to a brick red, about 5 to 10 minutes. Add the sliced roasted bell peppers and poblanos and the brown sugar. Once they begin to soften, cover the pot and let cook for 20 to 30 minutes.

Add the canned tomatoes and bring to a simmer. Add the toasted New Mexico chili and the chili-vinegar paste from earlier and bring back to a simmer. Add the confit lemon. Let simmer until thickened, about 20 to 40 minutes (it should be slightly thicker than tomato sauce). Taste and adjust the seasoning with salt and brown sugar.

PREPARE THE SIDE GARNISHES

You can really do whatever you want for garnish. Think of it as the plate served with pho, with all the herbs and sauces on it. Use our suggestions below as a reference point.

ASSEMBLE

Remove the shakshuka base from the heat. Create one little well for each egg and crack them in. If desired, crack them into a fine-mesh strainer first to remove excess water. Season with salt and black pepper. Gently shake the pan to spread out the egg a bit.

Place the pan back on the heat and cover. Bring to a simmer and cook for 5 minutes or longer, depending on how runny you like your eggs (we prefer a runny yolk). Crack the yolks to let them run a bit. Serve with the side garnishes.

SIDE GARNISHES SUGGESTIONS ——————————————————————————

Try your Shakshuka with any or all of these groupings of garnishes. Mix the components together beforehand, or plate them individually, and serve them on the side of the skakshuka or on top.

Option 1:

Pickled Vidalia Onions (pg. 154)

Extra-virgin olive oil

Mexican oregano

Habanero chili, deseeded and sliced

Freshly squeezed orange juice

Freshly squeezed lime juice

And/or option 2:

Whole leaves fresh mint

Whole sprigs fresh parsley

Whole leaves fresh cilantro

Pita or bread of choice

And/or option 3:

Marinated Long Hots (pg. 152), sliced

Garlic, minced

Extra-virgin olive oil

Black pepper

Maldon salt

And/or option 4:

Amba (pg. 210)

Savory Tahini Sauce (pg. 216)

And/or option 5:

Tomatoes, diced

Romaine, sliced

Sweet onions, sliced

Cascabella peppers or pepperoncini, sliced

Bulgarian feta, crumbled

Red Wine Vinaigrette (pg. 217)

Extra-virgin olive oil

FRENCH FRY CHILAQUILES

A: This dish is exactly what it sounds like: an imitation of chilaquiles in which the tortillas are replaced by fries because, well, why not. We've thrown in some fried eggs, à la huevos rotos, since my dad has always loved dipping his fries in eggs. It's a great hangover cure if you have a sober person willing to cook it for you.

MAKES 2 SERVINGS (MAY THE BEST ONE WIN THE 5TH EGG)

Salsa

4 guajillo or Hatch chilies (once you go Hatch, you never go back)[1]

3 puya chilies

7 chiles de árbol

1 morita chili

8 tomatillos[2]

3 cloves garlic, skin on

½ cup (120 ml) water

1½ teaspoons white vinegar

1 teaspoon chicken or vegetable broth powder

Granulated sugar, to taste

2 tablespoons neutral oil or fat of choice

Assembly

½ recipe Malt Vinegar Fries (pg. 183), fried

5 eggs

Salsa

Bread-and-butter pickles, chopped

Cotija or good feta

Sweet onion, sliced

Jalapeño, diced

Radish, diced

Fresh cilantro, chopped

Crema

Avocado, sliced

Freshly squeezed lime juice

Malt vinegar

MAKE THE SALSA

Halve and deseed all the dried chilies. Toast them lightly in a skillet, being very careful not to burn them. Set aside.

Broil, grill, or sear the tomatillos and garlic. Peel the seared garlic and place it in a blender along with the toasted chilies and a few of the tomatillos. Blend until smooth, then add the remaining tomatillos. Gradually add the water until smooth. Add the vinegar and broth powder. Season with sugar and salt to taste.

Heat the oil in a medium pot over medium-high heat. Pour in the Salsa; it should sizzle and "sear" a bit. Bring to a boil for 3 to 5 minutes. Remove from the heat and adjust the seasoning as needed. Let sit for at least 30 minutes before using to allow the flavors to come together.

The Salsa will keep for a few weeks in the fridge. The tomatillos will make it gelatinous, so simply use an immersion blender to smooth it back out.

ASSEMBLE

Place the hot fries on a rimmed plate.

Hard-fry your eggs according to the method on pg. 29, frying them as if they were one single egg. Season with salt and black pepper.

Drape your eggs over the fries and cover with some Salsa. Top it off with any or all remaining ingredients to your liking, ending with the lime juice and malt vinegar.

---

1 You can swap out different dried chilies for any of these. Just be sure you're substituting based on spice level (for example, don't replace the guajillo or puya with more árbol because it'll be too spicy, at least for our taste).

2 If you can't find fresh tomatillos, don't get canned ones. Instead, substitute with an equal weight of Roma tomatoes.

The
Meet-Cute

R: Way back in the early 2000s, I popped into Greasy Spoon for a meal. Through the open kitchen, I caught a glimpse of a cook wearing some stupid straw hat. I don't know, I thought he was cute. I asked somebody who he was and found out he was dating some supper club waitress. That was the end of that.

. . .

Until, two years later, after finding out my boyfriend of five years was cheating on me, I went for dinner with my mom at Lucille's in NDG.

A: I was working in the kitchen and noticed her sitting at the bar. I timed my smoke break for when they were finishing up their meal. Like a nervous little boy, I lingered outside an extra five minutes so I could open the door for them. Of course, I didn't say a word to her.

R: I vaguely recognized him from Greasy Spoon, but I mainly thought it was weird that he held the door—back of house isn't supposed to use the front door at all.

A: I went back inside and asked my manager about the girl with the bangs. He told me to forget her because she was taken. Instead, he gave me her sister's name, which I accepted because I knew it was the only way I could reach Hot Bangs Girl. I was obsessed from day one.

R: Soon after that night, my sister told me some creep had messaged her on Facebook and was trying to get my number.

A: For some reason, she consented to give it to me. I grew a bit overzealous with my texting to Raegan . . .

R: I eventually asked him to stop writing me. It was all too much, and I was trying to work things out with my ex. Obviously, that didn't happen.

A: She texted me two weeks later, newly single, asking if I wanted to go for a drink. I picked her up in a cab and we headed to La Distillerie on Ontario, that place with the mason jar cocktails that get you fucked up fast.

R: He was dressed horribly, wearing a super-deep V-neck and baggy jeans that were so long, they had a hole in the heel from being dragged on the ground and getting caught on his shoe.

A: Raegan was *so* hot (even hotter now, though). She dressed very badass, rock 'n' roll, motorcycle chick back then, with tight jeans, ripped tights, and chunky boots.

R: Rock 'n' roll? I think I've worn ripped stockings once on a date and was mortified.

A: She's lying. We got really, really drunk. It got to 2 a.m. and we still didn't want the night to end. We went to Bílý Kůň on Mont Royal, where we were literally the only two people. I remembered her telling me that her favorite song was that one that goes, "sitting on the dock of the bay . . ." The next time I got up for a beer, I asked the bartender to put it on. I pushed aside some tables and we slow-danced in the middle of the bar. That's when I knew I wanted to marry her.

R: On the ride back, I puked out of the side of the cab. It was the best date ever.

A: The next time I saw her, she made me blueberry pancakes at her place. I was living half out of my car and half out of my parents' house. I ended up overstaying my welcome and just never left. We did a lot of cooking and a lot of partying, until we got bored of the party and grew up.

R: We had many late-night, romantic rendez-vous after our kitchen shifts, and we'd stay up all night poring over cookbooks. Sometime after my culinary-school hiatus in Vancouver, I decided I needed a second, more grandiose escape. I made an eight-month plan to back-pack Asia, with or without Alex. He inevitably tagged along.

A: Two nights before we left, I proposed on a street corner in the day's last ray of sun. Here we are, nearly 15 years later, still together. I wouldn't be anywhere near where I am today without her . . . nagging.

R: He loves me too much—it's annoying. He's the kindest, most thoughtful, most solid man ever, and he makes everything fun. He is an *amazing* dad. Like, he literally cries every day because of how much he loves our kids, and I have to tell him to stop. We make each other better. There is no one else I'd rather do this life with.

A: And I'm the cheesy one??

THE SANDWICH

CHAPTER

"STRAWBERRY JAM SANDWICHES"

when i was young
ammi packed me lunch
one strawberry jam sandwich
cut neatly into squares
. . .
and finally
for some unknown reason
there were no strawberry jam sandwiches
but ammi still packed me lunch

it was tuna or chicken
maybe tomato and cheese
sometimes a pastry
i wasn't hard to please

and it never occurred to me
that my strawberry sandwiches
were gone

till one completely random day
i'm sitting with my friends
taking the first bite of my sandwich
a burst of strawberry fills my mouth
. . .
my strawberry jam sandwich came back
and i was bombarded by my childhood
playing on the swings sandwich in hand
red coated crumbs dotting my shirt
running out of class as soon as the bell rings
to munch munch munch
on my strawberry sandwiches

—NISH

A: How do we treat the sandwiches

we love? As my wife exquisitely puts it, "You just shove it into your face." Each chomp contains so much of everything you want that you just keep going and going, hardly stopping to swallow. You transform into some starved animal, as you do when you shovel fries in your mouth from the warm paper drive-thru bag or inhale a super-spicy dish, always chasing that first, perfect mouthful of salt or heat.

The bread hits first, crackly-crunchy and buttery or tender and pillowy, then gives way to the inner layers of flavor. Every mouthful is a symphony of salt, acid, sourness, sweetness, and fat (or at least a few among those). Maybe, before each bite, you dip the sandwich into a sauce or jus. Maybe it's late August, and you've inserted a slice of the last good tomato of the season, its juices running down your chin. Maybe it's less about the sandwich and more about where you are, at the beach on a hot day with a tuna sandwich or hunched over your counter with one made from Thanksgiving leftovers. It might even be a sandwich made of memories, a white bread with ham in your lunchbox.

From the bánh mì to the BLT, we all have "our" sandwich. You can say you're avoiding gluten or cutting carbs, but can you honestly say you don't like sandwiches? A great one can range from the childishly simple (Salami Sandwich, pg. 96) to the obnoxiously complex (Caputo, pg. 111). The sandwiches I was raised on were usually made from leftovers or just a few ingredients. One of my most beloved was the tomato and cheese sandwich from the cafeteria, with the squishy bread and salt and pepper packets.

My palate may have matured since my school cafeteria years, but I hold to the basic belief that a sandwich should always be made for ease and enjoyment, not just appealing to the eye. You should be comfortable eating it, not struggling to fit it into your tired jaw as it falls apart onto your plate, unless you're in the sacred privacy of your own kitchen. Nothing should be extraneous; if an ingredient serves no purpose other than adding "more," it shouldn't be there. Even if it's a particularly labor-intensive sandwich, you shouldn't be able to tell how much work went into each component; it should all come together seamlessly, like a good dessert. (Don't be fooled by the apparent simplicity of a meat and bread sandwich; that meat may have aged for years, and that sourdough starter may have been born before you.) Every single element, bread included, must be seasoned, with very few exceptions. And, above all—in Arthur's words—the bread makes or breaks the sandwich.

Anatomy of a Sandwich

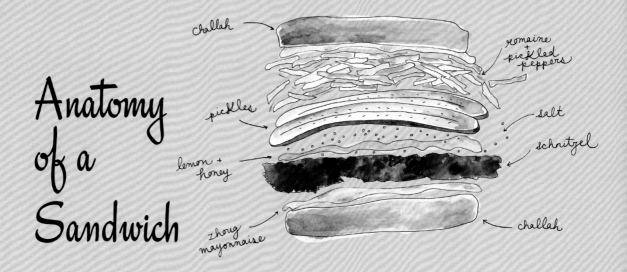

challah

romaine + pickled peppers

pickles

salt

schnitzel

lemon + honey

zhoug mayonnaise

challah

A: You've just made yourself a turkey, cheese, heirloom tomato sandwich, like the good little mainstream food media follower you are. You've got a little crispy iceberg in there, a little Duke's mayo. You've toasted the bread in a seasoned cast-iron skillet with a pat of European butter. You're doing well for yourself. And now you're sitting down on your couch to watch whatever series will be popular by the time this book is released.

You bite into your sandwich and the FUCKING TOMATO SLICES SLIP OUT ONTO THE FLOOR, their red juices splattering all over your shag carpet. Try removing tomato seeds from all those threads, not to mention what a waste of an heirloom tomato. That's like at least $1 a slice. Now you're left with a turkey cheese sandwich and a stain on a carpet you knew you never should've bought.

How could this have been avoided?

Well, there's no hard answer to how to "properly" layer a sandwich; it's mainly by feel. Generally, you want to layer from bottom to top, hardest to softest. In the case of the tomato, it should be layered near the top, with the lettuce, because that's where you have the firmest grip. If you put it toward the bottom, it's gonna slide right out.

At the end of the day though, you're gonna make your sandwich however you damn want. With that being said, we still have a few general suggestions to help you out.

Bread

Bread Types: I can tell you which bread I think is best for each sandwich, and in the recipes that follow I do, but in the end it's up to you. Here are "rules" to loosely abide by:

- Use the freshest bread you can get your hands on.
- Choose a baguette that won't rip the palate of your mouth when you bite into the sandwich.
- A New York bagel is better suited to sandwiches than a Montreal one. Crucify me.
- If you consider a tortilla a type of bread, please always toast it before using.
- Gluten-free friends, I'm afraid you're on your own; I am of the chosen few who can still digest gluten.
- For the love of God, don't replace bread with bell pepper.

Fat Options (for Toasting and/or Post-toasting): Butter, margarine, mayo, olive oil, or rendered fat. Remember: Bread needs seasoning too, especially if using unsalted fat!

Toasting Methods:

- Toaster: Ideal for light toasting and cold sandwiches (tuna, egg salad, turkey, etc.).
- Skillet: Ideal for deep, even toasting. Heat butter or clarified butter in a cast-iron skillet or slather it directly on the bread. Toast over medium heat.

Where to Toast?

- Both sides: The standard method, good for any classic sandwich.
- One side only: To recreate nostalgic, squishy bread. To steam the inside, like hoagies. To mold the bread around the sandwich so as to not squish out the insides, ideal for heavily layered sandwiches.
- No toasting: Reserved for the freshest sourdough, in my opinion.

Toast Tent: Once your bread is toasted, stand it up like a little tent, with the two slices leaning into each other, while you prepare the other sandwich ingredients. This will help the bread stay crispy, rather than steaming on one side, as it would if you laid it down flat.

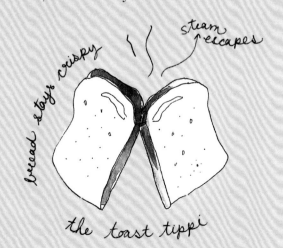

steam escapes

bread stays crispy

the toast tippi

Greens

The only "rule" we have for greens is that we hate mesclun mix. It's where salad goes to die. Besides that one exception, use whatever you want. A splash of Red Wine Vinaigrette (pg. 217) never hurts. If using a creamier sauce, place the greens in the sandwich, then lightly drizzle the sauce on top, rather than tossing the greens with it beforehand. Like this, it's more of a spread than a dressing, and you're less likely to overwhelm the whole flavor profile of the sandwich.

Another tip is to prepare everything for your sandwich on the same cutting board, so that by the end you have a nice little pile of seasoned juices, meat crispies, breadcrumbs, and so forth. Swipe all this into the same bowl as your lettuce, and mix it together before using in your sandwich. (Turkey and the Wolf, a Louisiana joint that really expanded the possibilities of restaurant sandwich making, calls this "Cutting Board Salad" in their book.)

Cheese

The most crucial thing to consider with cheese is temperature. Some cheeses are wonderful when heated but horrendous when cold, like American cheese. The reverse is true for cheeses like cheddar, which split when heated and quickly re-congeal into a rubbery, oily mess (although this doesn't stop a lot of people from using it in grilled cheese). Bottom line, it'll take some trial and error to learn your preferences, so try out everything that sounds promising.

And don't forget to SEASON EACH INGREDIENT!

MCARTHUR

A: Despite its fame, this sandwich doesn't have much of a story. A derivative of the Schnitzel Plate (pg. 197), the McArthur came to me in the middle of service during our soft opening. Then, the very morning of our hard opening, I completely changed it into what it is now: a deceptively simple schnitzel sandwich of challah (the sweeter Sephardic kind), iceberg slaw, pickles, and spicy mayo, somehow deemed by La Presse as "un nouveau classique montréalais."

MAKES 1 SANDWICH

Iceberg Slaw

½ French shallot, sliced in thin half-moons

1 tablespoon neutral oil

1 tablespoon extra-virgin olive oil

2 teaspoons red wine vinegar

4 cups (160 g) thinly shredded iceberg lettuce, core only[1]

1 tablespoon minced pickled peppers

Assembly

Fat of choice, for frying (see pg. 93 for suggestions)

½ piece Schnitzel (see footnote, pg. 193), ready to be fried

Creamy honey, for drizzling

1 lemon wedge, for finishing

Salted butter, for toasting

2 (1-inch-thick) slices challah

Zhug Mayo (pg. 219), for spreading

Otto's Dill Pickles (pg. 155), very thinly sliced

Iceberg Slaw

French Dressing (see Cobb Salad, pg. 120), for drizzling

MAKE THE ICEBERG SLAW

In a small bowl, mix together the shallots, oils, and vinegar. Let sit for 10 minutes and up to overnight. Right before assembling the sandwich, grab a spoonful of the shallots and transfer to a fresh bowl. Mix in the iceberg and peppers.

ASSEMBLE

Fill a large cast-iron skillet with enough fat to submerge the chicken halfway. Over medium-high heat, bring the oil to 350°F or until quick bubbles form around the end of a wooden spoon. Fry the Schnitzel (follow the instructions on pg. 194). Pull the chicken out of the fat and place it on a wire rack to drain. Immediately season both sides with salt. Wait 1 minute, then drizzle with honey from edge to edge. Let rest for 2 to 5 minutes. Right before you put it in the sandwich, squeeze a small wedge of lemon over it.

Meanwhile, generously butter the bread and toast the bread in a skillet over medium heat (if using unsalted butter, season with salt before toasting). Tent the toast slices together (see pg. 93) so that they retain their crispiness as you prepare the other components.

Evenly schmear a thin layer of Zhug Mayo on one side of each challah slice. Place the chicken on the bottom slice. Lay down enough pickle slices on top of the chicken so that its entire surface is more or less covered. Distribute a handful of the slaw over the pickles, and season lightly with salt. Lightly drizzle with French Dressing. Close up the sandwich. Slice it in half right before serving, otherwise the juices will seep out and quickly turn the bread into a soggy mess.

1 A note on iceberg: The entire core, comprising over half the head, should be shredded and used for sandwiches with harder fillings (like this one). Only the very soft, outermost leaves should be kept whole and used for sandwiches with softer fillings (like the Breakfast Sandwich, pg. 41). But, you know, use the whole head if you're gonna throw it out otherwise.

SALAMI SANDWICH

A: This sandwich doesn't sell well at all, but it's one of those classic Jewish things that'll always be around. Salami sandwiches were a major food group in both of our childhoods, and it's not something we ever want to put a bunch of shit on and change beyond recognition. There's not much to it; it's just good.

MAKES 1 SANDWICH

6 to 8 slices Marinated
   Breakfast Salami (pg. 34)

1 onion roll

Butter, for toasting

Yellow mustard, for spreading

1 small handful drained Vinegar
   Coleslaw (pg. 151)

Grill or sear the salami in a pan. Set aside while you toast the onion roll—hot sandwiches taste better once they've cooled a bit so don't worry about the salami cooling while you're toasting. Plus, the grill marks on the salami will have time to crackle and candy a bit (not to mention you'd burn the hell out of your mouth, so don't try to be a tough guy about it).

Halve the onion roll and butter it end to end. Toast the inside faces in a pan. Flip them over, then place the top bun, domed side down, on top of the bottom one for a moment. This will help the exterior of the top bun steam and get extra soft.

Schmear a layer of yellow mustard on both buns. Lay down the salami, then the coleslaw. Close the lid. Put the whole sandwich back into the pan and squish it with a spatula for a few seconds. Flip and repeat.

TUNA MELT

A: Most tuna melts make me feel all sluggish and sleepy when I eat them for lunch. In my mind, midday tuna sandwiches are made for hot weather and should be cold and fresh (not that there's anything fresh about canned tuna, but you get the point). When figuring out our tuna melt, therefore, we decided to make the only hot elements the cheese and the bun. Everything else works together to keep things light; eggplant puree serves as a barrier between the hot bread and the cold tuna, while a very thin layer of Caper Mayo (pg. 218) cuts any heavy, fatty feeling with brininess. The Monterey Jack is fried to a delicate crisp for toasty cheese flavor, while sprouts add a hint of crunch and grassiness. No tuna melt lethargy here.

MAKES 1 SANDWICH

1 onion roll

Butter, for toasting

Caper Mayo (pg. 218), for spreading

Clarified butter, for frying

2 to 3 slices Monterey Jack

1 tablespoon Rita's Eggplant (pg. 149)

⅓ cup Tuna Salad (pg. 147)

1 small handful sprouts

Hot peppers (preferably pickled or brined, such as Pickled Red Chilies (pg. 152)) (optional)

Halve the onion roll and butter it end to end. Toast the inside faces in a pan. Flip them over, then place the top bun, domed side down, on top of the bottom one for a moment. This will help the exterior of the top bun steam and get extra soft.

Thinly spread the Caper Mayo on the inside faces of both buns. Lay the cheese on the face of the top one. Add a touch of clarified butter to the pan and fry it, cheese side down, so that the cheese gets lightly browned and crispy on the edges.

Beginning with the non-cheesy bottom bun, place some Rita's Eggplant, then Tuna Salad, then sprouts and hot peppers.[1] Close the lid.

---

[1] The photo shows the cheese in the middle of the sandwich but it tastes better attached to the top bun.

EGG SALAD PARTY SANDWICHES WITH CAVIAR

R: Party sandwiches, a mainstay at family gatherings from birthdays to shivas, are an age-old part of most Jewish delis. Usually they're filled with egg or tuna salad. Sometimes they're layered with mixed deli meats and yellow mustard, or formed into pinwheels with smoked salmon and a little gherkin (apparently the least favored of all, according to recent polls). In Montreal, Snowdon Deli is king of the party sandwich. If you're in the know, you can even specially request a box of their peanut butter and jelly ones. We've come up with a somewhat trendier party sandwich, the egg and caviar. Alex literally hates it because he thinks caviar is overused, but that's to be expected considering he's not the fun one in the relationship (his words, not mine). We recommend you purchase decent caviar; anything super cheap will ruin the whole point of doing something fancy like this. As my husband says, "If you have some money to burn, by all means, go for it."

MAKES 4 FULL-SIZE SANDWICHES OR 16 PARTY SANDWICHES

8 slices white grocery-store bread (the squishy one you know wasn't made by hand)

Butter, semi-cold, for spreading

2 cups Fluffy Egg Salad (pg. 148)

Good caviar (I like sturgeon), for topping

Slice the crusts off the bread. Spread a thin layer of butter on one side of each slice of bread. The butter should be cold enough that it remains solid in the sandwich, as its goal is to protect the bread from getting soggy.

Using the buttered sides of the bread to make the inside of the sandwiches, evenly spread a generous layer of Fluffy Egg Salad onto four of the slices. Ideally each layer should be the same thickness as two slices of bread.[1]

Close up the sandwiches and cut each of them into four equal squares or triangles. Plop a small spoonful of caviar onto each portion.

---

[1] If you'd like, you can fill the layers with less egg salad and make triple decker sandwiches instead (as pictured here).

GRAVLAX SANDWICH

R: This is a cult sandwich at Arthurs. While The Classic (pg. 46) will always be a classic, the Gravlax Sandwich is simply *more*: more acid from more lemon juice and red wine vin, more tangy sweetness from more varieties of onion, more juiciness from more tomato, and more herbiness from more fresh dill and sprouts. More is more!

MAKES 1 SANDWICH

Caramelized Onion Cream Cheese

2 to 4 tablespoons thinly sliced onion

Butter, for cooking

Granulated sugar, for seasoning

1 (8 oz/226 g) block cream cheese (preferably Philadelphia)

Roasted garlic and peppers seasoning, to taste

Assembly

1 to 2 slices tomato

Butter, for spreading

2 very thin slices black Russian bread or bread of choice

Caramelized Onion Cream Cheese, for spreading

3 slices (about 2.6 oz/75 g total) Gravlax (pg. 163)

1 small handful Pickled Vidalia Onions (pg. 154)

1 teaspoon capers

½ teaspoon finely chopped fresh dill

Lemon wedge, for finishing

1 generous handful sprouts

Red Wine Vinaigrette (pg. 217), for drizzling

MAKE THE CARAMELIZED ONION CREAM CHEESE

In a pan over medium-high heat, sweat the onions with a bit of butter. When they start to steam, pour a bit of water in, lower the heat to medium-low, cover, and cook for 10 minutes. Uncover, season with a little sugar and salt, and raise the heat back up to medium. Keep cooking until the onions are the color of dark brown sugar. Stir in the cream cheese until fully combined and smooth. Season with roasted garlic and peppers seasoning as desired. Store in an airtight container in the fridge for as long as your opened cream cheese lasts.

ASSEMBLE

Place the tomato slice(s) on a paper towel–lined plate and season with salt and black pepper to release excess liquid.

Butter and toast the bread on one side (you can do this in a pan or a toaster on the bagel setting). Because this bread is sliced so thinly, toasting only the inner face will ensure that that side soaks up any juices, making the bread more malleable so that it doesn't break apart.

Schmear some Caramelized Onion Cream Cheese onto the toasted side of both slices. On the bottom slice, begin with layering the Gravlax and season with salt and black pepper. Continue layering with the pickled onions, capers, dill, and tomato. Season with salt and black pepper and a light squeeze of lemon.

Finish with the sprouts and drizzle with Red Wine Vinaigrette, then sprinkle with salt. Close the lid and cut in two.

LOBSTER SANDWICH

A: I thought that I knew lobster rolls until I had them in Maine, where the proper seafood shacks stuff hot dog rolls with an entire lobster, nothing covering the crustacean but the perfect amount of butter. In true Maine fashion, we wanted our lobster sandwich to be as pure as possible. Each sandwich holds the meat of one full, steamed-in-house lobster dunked in hot garlic butter. Besides those two ingredients, there's not much else.

This sandwich is also very annoying to prep in restaurant quantities, and we made almost zero profit from it, despite selling about 80 of them a day at over $40 each. Our hands were covered in cuts at the end of each day, and we went through an absurd number of rags. We once evacuated the entire dining room because a line cook steamed the lobster with too much Tabasco and burnt everyone's eyes off. I felt too guilty about the whole thing—lobster death count included—and took it off the menu for many years (until my wife forced me to put it back on).

All things considered, this sandwich is still worth it. We have you steam the lobster, unless you plan on driving to the coast and using seawater, because boiling dilutes the flavor. If you're gonna invest money and labor into lobster, you might as well get the most out of it.

MAKES 1 SANDWICH

Garlic Butter

1 lb (454 g) cold butter, cubed

1 stalk celery, peeled and diced

¼ French shallot, diced

3 cloves garlic, minced

½ teaspoon granulated sugar

¼ teaspoon salt

Lobster

1 (1¼ to 1½ lb) lobster[1]

Juice of ½ lemon

A few shakes Tabasco

Assembly

Butter, for spreading

1 challah or egg roll, halved[2]

Garlic Butter, for dunking

Lemon wedge, for squeezing

MAKE THE GARLIC BUTTER

Add ½ lb (227 g) butter and 2 tablespoons water to a small pot set over low heat. Once the butter has melted, stir in the celery, shallots, garlic, sugar, and salt. Cover the pot partially with a lid; this will help prevent the milk solids from splitting before the flavors have had time to infuse. Cook until the butter and water are emulsified and the aromatics are fully cooked.

Turn off the heat and let the mixture sit on the burner for 5 to 10 minutes to infuse. Strain out the solids, then return the butter to the pot. Slowly incorporate the remaining cold butter so that by the end it has a spreadable consistency and every bit of butter is infused with flavor. Leftover butter can be stored in the fridge for up to 3 weeks or in the freezer for up to 3 months.

COOK THE LOBSTER

Fill a large pot with about 2 inches of water and bring to a boil (the pot should be large enough to fit 2 lobsters; don't use too

continued . . .

---

1 When selecting a lobster, opt for a smaller one, preferably female. These tend to be sweeter ;)

2 You can use a brioche or potato bun, but we find that these can be too buttery or dense. You

could also reach for the classic hot dog bun, which is just as good as the challah roll, if not better.

small a pot, or your cooking time will have to increase, making it easier to overcook the lobster). Season the water with the lemon juice, Tabasco, and a generous amount of salt. (You can season the water with whatever you want—insane people would buy seaweed from the fishmonger and use it in place of a steam basket.) Add the lobster to a steam basket placed inside the pot, lower to a simmer, then cover the pot with the lid. Steam the lobster for 10 to 12 minutes, depending on the size of your lobster.[3]

Transfer the lobster to a tray and place in the fridge to cool for up to 2 days. Do NOT use an ice bath, unless you've really overcooked it, or it will suck out all the flavor.

Break down the lobster and extract the meat. We recommend you google this, but here is the basic method: Remove the legs, claws, and knuckles first. Flip the lobster on its head and twist out the tail, then cut it in half. Keep the roe if desired (we encourage you not to throw this away; the internet is full of ideas for how to use them if you're averse to simply eating them). DON'T throw out the legs—they have some of the sweetest meat. Extract the meat from the legs by rolling over the legs with a rolling pin. Do what you'd like with the head and shells; ideally, reserve them for stock. Keep the meat in the fridge until ready to use.

ASSEMBLE

Butter and salt both sides of the bread and toast it in a skillet. Remove from the pan and keep under a towel to lightly steam it.

Meanwhile, melt the Garlic Butter until hot. This is important! If the butter is only warm, it will congeal in the sandwich, and that's disgusting.

Take the lobster meat straight from the fridge and dunk it directly into the hot Garlic Butter for 10 seconds. This is just long enough to warm and tenderize the outside but still preserve a chilled, bouncy interior. Transfer the lobster to a paper towel–lined plate to absorb excess butter. Taste, and season both sides of the lobster lightly with salt and black pepper.

Lay the lobster onto the bottom bun, placing the two claws on opposing sides on the outer perimeter of the bread so that they form a "wall" to encompass the rest of the meat. Squeeze a bit of lemon juice over top, close the sandwich, and serve.

---

3 Because we don't transfer the lobster to an ice bath to retain as much flavor as possible, it is better to undercook than overcook the lobster, as it will continue to cook after being removed.

VERMONT THANKSGIVING TURKEY

A: A lot of Thanksgiving sandwiches look sloppy and overstuffed—perfect for eating at home—but we needed something less messy for the restaurant. We therefore eliminated mashed potatoes and gravy, instead incorporating their flavors into a "stuffing" loaf. Since the point is to use Thanksgiving leftovers, substitute or add anything you have on hand and adjust accordingly. You can buy canned cran jelly, mix mayo and Dijon into non-creamy coleslaw, cut up roasted turkey, form patties out of any kind of stuffing, use gravy like dip, or even schmear mashed potato onto each bite.

MAKES 1 SANDWICH

Stuffing

½ loaf (6.7 oz/190 g) challah

Schmaltz (pg. 169) or turkey schmaltz, for cooking[1]

10 (1 oz/30 g total) saltine crackers

½ cup + 1 tablespoon (126 g) butter

3 tablespoons water

½ large Spanish onion, finely diced

2 stalks celery, peeled + finely diced

2 cloves garlic, minced

Packed ½ tablespoon minced fresh sage leaves, stems reserved

½ teaspoon minced fresh thyme leaves

½ teaspoon minced fresh rosemary leaves, stems reserved

2 large lightly flavored sausages, cases removed[2]

---

1 To make turkey schmaltz, simply replace the chicken fat with turkey fat in Schmaltz (pg. 169).

2 We use a mix of chicken and turkey, but feel free to use anything not spicy, as long as it's not beef.

MAKE THE STUFFING

Preheat the oven to 425°F.

Slice the crust off the challah and cut the bread into 1-inch cubes. Toss with a bit of melted Schmaltz and season with salt and black pepper. Spread the challah on a sheet tray. Toast in the oven until the outside is golden and dry but the very middle of it is still chewy, about 5 minutes. Stir halfway through to ensure even browning. Set aside to cool.

Transfer the croutons to a bowl, along with the saltine crackers. Using your hands, break the crackers into dime-sized pieces. Set aside.

In a large pot, slowly melt 6 tablespoons (84 g) of the butter with the 3 tablespoons water. Add the onion, celery, garlic, and herb leaves, and cook on low heat until translucent but not browned. Stir continuously, making sure the butter does not separate from the water. Transfer to a large bowl.

Set the same pot back over medium-high and throw in a knob of Schmaltz. Brown the sausage meat, breaking it down slightly with a wooden spoon. Remove the sausage and transfer to the same bowl with the cooked vegetables and butter mixture.

Add the Chicken Soup Stock to the same pot. Bring to a boil, then lower to a simmer for 15 minutes. Stir in the reserved herb stems. Continue simmering on low until reduced by about half (you want to end up with 1⅓ cups/320 ml). Scratch at the bottom of the pot with a wooden spoon to lift up any brown bits. Remove the herb stems.

Remove the pot from the heat and stir in the remaining 3 tablespoons butter until incorporated. Set aside.

continued . . .

3 cups (720 ml) Chicken Soup Stock (see Matzo Ball Soup, pg. 135)[3]

1 egg + 2 egg yolks

Packed 2 tablespoons chopped fresh parsley

Cranberry Sauce

⅔ cup (160 ml) water

⅓ cup + 2 tablespoons (110 ml) orange juice

3¼ cups (325 g) cranberries, fresh or frozen and thawed in a strainer

1 cup + 2 tablespoons (225 g) granulated sugar

Heaping ½ cup (60 g) chopped dried tart cherries

1 small cinnamon stick or ⅛ teaspoon ground cinnamon

¼ teaspoon salt

Assembly

Butter, for toasting

2 slices Honey Oat Bread (pg. 243)

1½ tablespoons House Mayo (pg. 218)

1 tablespoon Cranberry Sauce

5 to 7 slices House Turkey (pg. 161)

1 slice Stuffing

2 tablespoons Creamy Coleslaw (pg. 150)

---

3 By stock, we don't mean the boxed grocery-store stuff; that's basically soup-flavored water. Either make the real thing or buy it from somewhere you know does it well. Or use the box, but know it won't turn out quite the same.

In another large bowl, whisk together the whole egg and egg yolks. Whisking continuously, very slowly pour in the reduced chicken stock to avoid cooking the eggs.

Pour this mixture into the crouton bowl and add the chopped parsley. Mix everything together until it resembles a very chunky porridge. Season with salt and black pepper to taste. If you have the time, let it cool, then cover and place in the fridge overnight before baking (or for at least 30 minutes).

When ready to bake, preheat the oven to 400°F. Grease and line a 5×9-inch loaf pan with parchment paper.

Spread the Stuffing into the prepared loaf pan. Bake for 25 minutes. Raise the temperature to 425°F and bake for 5 more minutes, until the top is dark golden brown.

Let cool to room temperature, then place in the fridge to cool completely before slicing for the sandwich. If you don't want to wait, you can spoon it straight from the pan and spread it onto the sandwich warm. Store any leftovers in an airtight container in the fridge for 1 week or in the freezer for a few months.

MAKE THE CRANBERRY SAUCE

In a medium pot, combine the water, ⅓ cup (80 ml) of the orange juice, the cranberries, sugar, cherries, and cinnamon. Bring to a boil, then lower the heat and simmer for about 20 minutes, stirring frequently to avoid burning it. Remove from the heat, then blend with an immersion blender until the whole mixture is chunky. Place it back on low heat and cook until it reaches lava-like bubbles and the temperature measures 210°F, like jam. Stir in the remaining 2 tablespoons orange juice and season with the salt and a small pinch of black pepper.

Let cool to room temperature. Store in an airtight container in the fridge for a long time (since it's full of sugar, it will last forever). Stir it up again before using.

ASSEMBLE

Butter and toast only one side of the bread slices. The toasted side will serve as the INSIDE of the sandwich; this will form a sort of shell around the filling so that it doesn't fall out with every bite. More importantly, it will protect the bread from becoming soggy from the sauces while evenly absorbing the liquid so that it is infused into every bite.

Spread the mayo on one slice and the Cranberry Sauce on the other. On the mayo side, stack the turkey, stuffing, and slaw. Close it up with the cranberry-sauced slice of bread, and cut in half right before serving so that the liquids don't run out.

CAPUTO

A: This sandwich is not meant to be made at home. If you try it, you have way too much time on your hands. Even at Arthurs, we had to implement a daily cap so we wouldn't drive ourselves crazy.

The Caputo began in Chicago. I was in the city for two days and ate six Chicago beef sandwiches. I loved the harmony between the giardiniera, the tender beef, and the jus in which the sandwich had been baptized. Back in Montreal, I got to work on a sandwich that I hoped would dethrone the McArthur (pg. 94), which was outselling everything. My goal was to marry a Philly cheesesteak with a Chicago beef, to do something different from the standard steak and cheese sandwich found in Montreal (if anyone does know of a really good one in the city, I beg of you, let us know).

There were many obstacles to accomplishing that in Quebec, where we don't have access to the breads and cheeses specific to this sandwich. In lieu of a hoagie roll, I went for a Vietnamese baguette, which has a brittle, crackling crust and a soft, white interior. For cheese, I chose a white American style, which I would pick up by car in Vermont until border patrol caught me. I named the completed sandwich after Caputo's, the Italian grocery store in Chicago owned by the family of our former head of HR, Alessandra. Her grandfather, a prominent figure in Chicago's Italian community, continued to watch over his business with as much care and attention as possible into his 90s. He deserved a sandwich worthy of his name.

There are two cuts of beef in this sandwich. The top sirloin provides flavor, while the American provides the melt-in-your-mouth quality of a good Chicago beef. We cook them to rare, freeze them, slice them as thinly as possible, then sear them on the flattop to attain the mouthfeel of a crusted, seared, super-tender steak. Of course, you can make just one cut of meat or not make your own meat at all, just as you can buy pickled eggplant and giardiniera.

You would be insane to make this entire recipe as is, but that's just to say you would be like me.

continued . . .

White Wine Flavor Booster[1]

¾ cup (180 ml) cheap white
 wine

Scant ½ cup (100 ml)
 Worcestershire

5 large cloves garlic

1 large French shallot, diced

3 bay leaves

Heaping ¼ cup (20 g) dried
 thyme

1⅓ tablespoons black
 peppercorns

1⅓ tablespoons mustard seeds

1⅓ tablespoons dried oregano

½ teaspoon steak spice

Jus

2.9 lb (1.3 kg) veal bones

2.2 lb (1 kg) oxtail

1½ lb (700 g) bone marrow

2 tablespoons tomato paste

2 tablespoons milk powder[2]

10 stalks celery, finely diced

4 carrots, finely diced

2 large leeks, whites only, thinly
 sliced

1 lb (454 g) Roma tomatoes,
 halved

13.5 oz (380 g) cremini
 mushrooms

Heaping 2 cups (330 g) finely
 diced green bell pepper

¼ cup (100 g) Marmite

20 cloves (85 g) garlic

2 Spanish onions, finely diced

½ large bunch (15 g) fresh thyme

½ large bunch (15 g) fresh
 oregano

White Wine Flavor Booster

MAKE THE WHITE WINE FLAVOR BOOSTER

In a small pot, bring all ingredients to a boil. Reduce by half, about 20 to 30 minutes.

MAKE THE JUS

Preheat the oven to 475°F.

Defrost and rinse the veal bones, oxtail, and marrow, if frozen. Transfer to a sheet tray. Spread the tomato paste on only the veal bones and marrow. Sift the milk powder over everything.

In a bowl, mix together all remaining ingredients, minus the White Wine Flavor Booster. Spread on a separate sheet tray, using two if necessary to avoid overcrowding.

Roast the meat for 45 to 60 minutes, until dark golden brown, and the vegetables for 20 to 25 minutes, until lightly browned.

Transfer the roasted bones to a large stockpot. Add a small splash of water to the hot tray, scrape up all the browned bits, and add them to the pot along with the roasted vegetable mixture. Cover everything with cold water by 1 inch and bring to a boil. Lower the heat and simmer for 3 to 12 hours (the longer, the better).

Strain the stock. (Any oxtail meat can be reserved to use in the sandwich or to be eaten in fried rice or scrambled eggs.) Put the liquid back into the pot, along with the White Wine Flavor Booster, and reduce by one-quarter.[3]

Let cool. Freeze whatever you end up not using for the sandwich so you always have stock on hand.

---

1 There's probably a technical name for this, but we don't want to call it by that.

2 The milk powder is optional, but it helps facilitate the Maillard reaction—a favorite culinary term of all male YouTube chefs—to achieve a golden-brown crust more quickly.

3 Don't let it get too thick, as it will be further reduced during the assembly stage.

Roast Beef

1.3 lb (600 g) trimmed top sirloin[4]

12 oz (340 g) trimmed American cut/inside round

Granulated sugar, for seasoning

Clarified butter, for searing

Infused Butter (only for sous vide method, optional)

1 head garlic, cloves peeled and smashed

A few sprigs of fresh thyme

1 large French shallot, thinly sliced

¼ cup + 2 tablespoons (about 90 g) butter

1 tablespoon salt

MAKE THE ROAST BEEF

Season the top sirloin and American cut with salt and sugar until well covered. Wrap tightly in plastic wrap and cure overnight or up to 24 hours, flipping halfway through.

Heat a cast-iron skillet over high heat and slick it with clarified butter. Pat the meats dry and sear them on all sides in the pan until they are rare with a substantial crust.

You can roast the beef either by sous vide or in the oven. If going the sous vide route, let the meat cool completely before proceeding to make the Infused Butter, if using.

Method Option 1: Sous Vide

Place all the infused butter ingredients in the pan you used to sear the meat. Cook over low heat until the butter is slightly browned. Remove from the pan and let cool to room temperature.

Use one sous vide bag per piece of seared meat. Evenly distribute the cooled infused butter among the bags.

Let the bags fully cool in the fridge. Once cooled, seal the bags sous vide, and cook in a circulator: the top sirloin at 131°F for 6 hours and the American cut at 131°F for 3 hours.

Transfer the meat bags directly from the circulator into an ice bath. Once cold, transfer to the freezer. Reserve the infused butter for later use; you can add it back into the beef stock if desired.

Method Option 2: Oven-Roast

Preheat the oven to 150°F.

Roast the top sirloin for 5 hours and the American cut for 1½ hours. (If making this for the Bear's Roast Beef, pg. 117, roast the American cut for 3 hours, until medium-rare.) Let cool to room temperature, then transfer to the freezer.

SLICE THE BEEF

Once the meat has frozen, slice it as thinly as possible, using a meat slicer if you have one. The thinner the slice, the more it will melt in your mouth.[5]

continued . . .

---

4 This is the weight once the meat has been trimmed, so ask your friendly butcher to trim it first.

5 Do not re-sous vide the meat at this point, or it'll turn gray and weird.

Caputo Slaw

1 large head iceberg lettuce, shredded

1 medium head radicchio, shredded

1 Cascabella pepper or pepperoncini, diced[6]

¼ Vidalia or sweet onion, thinly sliced[7]

Chardonnay vinegar

Extra-virgin olive oil

Assembly

Butter, for toasting

1 Vietnamese baguette, halved like a hot dog, mie removed

Clarified butter, for cooking

2.2 oz (60 g) very thinly sliced top sirloin

2.2 oz (60 g) very thinly sliced American cut

4 to 5 slices Roasted Poblano Pepper Mix (pg. 226)

1 slice white American-style cheese

Jus, slightly warmed

Regular or spicy mayo of choice (see House Mayo, pg. 218), for spreading

1 to 2 tablespoons Giardiniera (pg. 158)

⅓ cup Caputo Slaw

MAKE THE CAPUTO SLAW

Combine all the vegetables in a bowl. Set aside. (The liquids will be added later.)

ASSEMBLE

Butter and toast only the exterior of the baguette. As the bread toasts, the interior will steam naturally.[8] Keep the bread covered while you prep the remaining components so that the bread doesn't dry out and the butter has time to soak into the crust, creating a crispy but malleable bun.

Slick a cast-iron skillet with clarified butter and bring it to medium-high heat.

Stack the sliced meats, alternating between the two types, being sure that the top and bottom outermost slices are top sirloin. (This is the fattier cut, so when you sear them, they'll crisp up better than the American.) Season these top and bottom slices with salt and black pepper, as you would a steak.

Once the skillet is hot, lay the meat in the skillet. Sear for 1 to 2 minutes, until a substantial crust has formed. Flip and repeat. By the end, it should resemble a well-seared steak. Crust is key!

With the meat still in the skillet, place enough Roasted Poblano Pepper Mix on top of the meat to cover it in an even sheet. Let cook for 1 to 2 minutes. Grab a straight-edged metal spatula or dough scraper and chop up the poblano mix about eight times, directly on the meat. This will help further tenderize the meat and make it easier to bite into. Slice the cheese in half and lay the halves side by side on top of the poblano mix.

Being careful not to splatter yourself, pour one ladleful of Jus over everything. The liquid should evaporate and thicken almost immediately.

Lightly spread mayo on the interior of the baguette. Open it up and press the interior into the pan so that it soaks up some of the Jus. Transfer the meat with everything on it into the baguette. Top with the Giardiniera, then the vegetables for the Caputo Slaw, and lightly splash with the Chardonnay vinegar and olive oil.

Serve with more warm Jus on the side for dipping.

---

6 Note that Cascabellas are four to five times spicier than pepperoncini. Reserve any juices that leak out of the peppers and reincorporate them into the slaw.

7 If making this in advance, rinse the onions with water so they don't make the whole slaw taste like onion the next day.

8 Keeping the inside of the bread untoasted will ensure that it doesn't absorb the juices from the sandwich too quickly and grow soggy. It will be cozy in there, like a slain Tauntaun.

BEAR'S ROAST BEEF

R: My dad was known as The Bear for two reasons. The first comes from the time he squeezed his friend too hard in a bear hug, accidentally breaking his rib. The second is slightly less believable but equally true: he was once thrown into a circus ring with a bear—albeit a declawed, toothless one—and made it fall to the ground by tickling its belly. (We don't condone animal cruelty, but hey, it was the '70s.)

The Bear loved beef in every form. He especially loved the roast beef sandwich at our favorite deli in Stowe, so much so that after he passed, they named it after him. With the help of our former chef, Luka Lecavalier, Alex took that version and added his usual complexity to it, but you can make your life easier by using store-bought ingredients.

MAKES 1 SANDWICH

1 pinch fried onion

1 pinch thinly sliced Vidalia onion

1 handful arugula

1 tablespoon drained Giardiniera (pg. 158)

1 big pinch freshly grated horseradish

Red Wine Vinaigrette (pg. 217)

2 slices Honey Oat Bread (pg. 243)

Butter, for toasting

4 oz (140 g) thinly sliced American cut roast beef (see Caputo, pg. 113)

Hot Honey Mustard (pg. 215), for spreading

House Mayo (pg. 218), for spreading

1 to 2 slices aged (no more than 2 years) white cheddar

1 thick-cut slice tomato (if in season)

1 slice Viens Beef Bacon (pg. 167) (optional)

Bear's BBQ Sauce (pg. 214), for spreading

In a small bowl, mix together the fried onion, Vidalia onion, arugula, Giardiniera, horseradish, a light drizzle of Red Wine Vinaigrette, and a pinch of salt. If preparing this salad in advance, be sure to rinse the Vidalia onion with water so the whole thing doesn't taste like onions by the time you serve it (and if using yellow instead of Vidalia onion, do the same regardless of when you make it).

Toast and very lightly butter the bread on both sides.

Unfold the roast beef and lightly season with salt, then fold it back up. On the bottom slice of bread, lightly schmear the Hot Honey Mustard and mayo. In order, lay down the cheese, tomato, roast beef, bacon, a few dots of BBQ sauce, the salad mix, and a bit more Hot Honey Mustard. Close the lid.

SALAD

R: My former boss once told me that I would end up "making salad for rich kids," and, well, he wasn't exactly wrong. Ever since I began my culinary career at Mandy's, Montreal's now-iconic salad bar, I've been obsessed with inventing big, bright, beautiful bowls

of greens. My love affair grew working at Joe Beef, stationed at the garde manger. Right before service, we would pick vegetables straight from the back garden to transform them into the freshest of dishes. Eventually, through our former catering company and my salad bar, Dirty Greens, I became known for my lavish salads, and now it seems I can't make anything else.

It was clear that Arthurs needed its own Seinfeldian "BIG SALAD" for my fellow Elaines. Over the years, Alex and I have created tons of them for Arthurs, but I've whittled down the list to the six I believe you need. They have all the elements of a lush, satiating salad: crisp veg, market-fresh produce, crunchy bits, healthy fats, and a salty-sweet finish. In all of them, the dressing (or sauce, see pg. 207 for more) is key. In my husband's words, which I can't say I fully agree with, "Salads are just a bunch of raw shit you don't wanna eat together until you put on a dressing."

With salad comes soup, and while we have only a few of those on our menu, they are made with just as much (if not more) love as our salads. It's true that a good soup can be nothing more than something you throw in a pot or blender and boil, but we've tried to take it a bit more seriously. The soups in these pages have been pulled from a place of nostalgia and history. They are all recognizable—matzo ball, cabbage, and split pea—but rightfully demand hours of your attention and care.

So, actually, I guess my boss was wrong; I've ended up making salad *and* soup for all kinds of people.

COBB SALAD

Besides its identifying ingredients—egg, avocado, bacon, tomato, lettuce, chicken or turkey, and a vinegar-based dressing—the only thing that makes a Cobb a Cobb is that it's laid out on a plate rather than tossed. If you toss it, it becomes a chopped salad, otherwise known as a Chobb. In fact, that would definitely taste better and be much more practical, but then we wouldn't be able to call it a Cobb.

Something we like about a Cobb is that it's a complete meal, packed with protein and good fat. Feel free to use a mix of homemade or store-bought ingredients, but don't tell anyone if you dumped it in a bowl instead of plating it nicely.

SERVES 1

French Dressing

1 small French shallot

Generous ⅓ cup (100 ml) reduced apple juice[1]

¼ cup (60 ml) apple cider vinegar

2¼ teaspoons honey

2 teaspoons Dijon

½ cup (120 ml) canola oil

Assembly

Loosely packed 3 cups (120 g) ribboned romaine[2]

8 to 10 cherry tomatoes, quartered

1 beet, roasted, diced

⅓ cup (60 g) diced House Turkey (pg. 161), shredded

¼ cup (35 g) sliced Lebanese cucumber (cut into small chunks)

1 avocado, sliced

2 to 3 slices Viens Beef Bacon (pg. 167), fried until crispy, finely chopped

1 hard-boiled egg, sliced

French Dressing, to taste

3 tablespoons roughly shredded Mimolette or cheddar

Bagel Chips (pg. 169)

1 teaspoon hemp seeds

MAKE THE FRENCH DRESSING

Place all ingredients, except the oil, into a blender and blend until smooth. With the blender on medium speed, gradually add the oil until emulsified. Alternatively, you can whisk everything by hand. Season with a generous pinch of salt to taste. Store in an airtight container in the fridge for up to 1 week (any longer and the onion flavor will get too strong).

ASSEMBLE

Lay out the romaine on the bottom of a shallow bowl. Arrange the tomatoes, beets, turkey, cucumber, avocado, bacon, and eggs on top in a linear fashion. Season everything with salt and black pepper. Drizzle the French Dressing over top, then scatter over the grated cheese, Bagel Chips, and hemp seeds.

[1] Buy high quality apple juice, and boil about ¾ cup (200 ml) until reduced by half. Let cool before using.

[2] A general note on salads: Don't feel pressured to follow exact quantities. Like, if you have a bit of leftover lettuce, please just put it in the salad. It won't change a thing.

PAPAYA SALAD

R: Right after Alex and I got engaged, we embarked on an eight-month voyage across South Asia. That makes it sound like an engagement trip, but it was more like a personal trip that he came along on. Well, years afterward, we were working on a summer salad for Arthurs. Because of our fondness for all the food we had throughout our travels, we thought it would be cool to do a papaya salad, very loosely based on the ones we ate in Thailand, although obviously much less spicy.

Alex never gave me a honeymoon (which I will hold over his head until the day he dies), but I have to give him most of the credit for how yummy this salad turned out.

SERVES 1

Fish Sauce Vinaigrette

½ cup (120 ml) freshly squeezed lime juice[1]

1½ tablespoons fish sauce

Packed 3⅓ tablespoons palm sugar or light brown sugar

2 large cloves garlic, roughly chopped

Assembly

4 to 5 florets (1 oz/30 g total) broccoli

1 cup (100 g) ribboned green papaya (ideally using a Kiwi Pro Slice Peeler)

½ cup (50 g) thinly sliced red cabbage

½ cup (50 g) shredded heirloom carrots

⅓ cup (50 g) diced or thinly sliced mango

½ avocado, diced

1 tablespoon pumpkin seeds, toasted + roughly chopped

Bird's eye chilies (preferably green and red), sliced (optional; we use 3 to 4 slices)

3 to 4 leaves fresh Thai basil, chopped

1 small handful fresh cilantro, chopped

2 tablespoons cooked quinoa

Fish Sauce Vinaigrette, to taste

Almond Buttah Drizzle (pg. 212), to taste

MAKE THE FISH SAUCE VINAIGRETTE

In a medium bowl, whisk together the lime juice, fish sauce, and palm sugar until the sugar is dissolved. Mix in the garlic.

Cover and let sit in the fridge for 24 hours. Strain and discard the garlic.

ASSEMBLE

In a pot of boiling water, blanch the broccoli florets, then transfer them to an ice bath.

In a salad bowl, lay down the papaya, cabbage, and carrots. Top with the mango, avocado, pumpkin seeds, chilies, herbs, and quinoa, then drizzle with the Fish Sauce Vinaigrette and Almond Buttah Drizzle as desired.

---

1 We know this is a lot of lime juice to squeeze by hand, but we're strongly against buying bottled lime juice, even if it's fancy and cold-pressed. To make your job easier, look for smooth limes, which usually contain the most juice.

#KGMTL POST-APOCALYPSE SALAD

R: This salad is dedicated to Katherine Garbarino, aka @kgmtl, one of my most supportive friends since the conception of Arthurs. Today she is a successful wellness guru and influencer, but when I met her she was a 17-year-old stoner at Dawson College, just like me. We created this bright, healthy salad in the midst of the COVID-19 pandemic, looking forward to the end of the apocalypse.

A: I was really hoping we'd get through this without saying the words "wellness" and "guru" in the same book.

Sumac Dressing

Scant ¾ cup (160 ml) extra-virgin olive oil

Scant ½ cup (100 ml) freshly squeezed lemon juice

3 tablespoons simple syrup (see note 1, pg. 69)

1 teaspoon sumac

½ teaspoon dried mint

¼ teaspoon salt

Assembly

Loosely packed 2 cups (80 g) sliced romaine

Loosely packed ½ cup (30 g) sliced radicchio

Loosely packed ½ cup (30 g) sliced kale

⅓ cup (40 g) diced cucumber

¼ cup (30 g) sliced radish

¼ cup (25 g) shredded carrots

¼ cup (25 g) peeled, shredded beets

2 tablespoons Pickled Turnips (pg. 153)[1]

1 tablespoon thinly sliced Cascabella pepper or pepperoncini

2 cherry tomatoes, halved

1 tablespoon pomegranate seeds

1 tablespoon finely chopped fresh parsley

1 tablespoon finely chopped fresh mint

Sumac Dressing, to taste

¼ cup (60 g) hummus[2]

Za'atar, to taste

Bagel Chips (pg. 169)

MAKE THE SUMAC DRESSING

In a medium bowl, whisk together all ingredients. Store in an airtight container in the fridge for up to 1 week.

ASSEMBLE

Lay the romaine, radicchio, and kale in a salad bowl, then top with the cucumbers, radishes, carrots, beets, Pickled Turnips, Cascabella, tomatoes, pomegranate seeds, parsley, and mint. Drizzle on the Sumac Dressing, then finish with the hummus, a good pinch of za'atar, and a small handful of Bagel Chips.

---

1 If you don't want to make your own, buy pickled turnips at a Middle Eastern grocery store.

2 We haven't given you a hummus recipe because you can find a million online. If you do go the homemade route, look for a recipe with dried chickpeas, whose taste and texture just turn out much better than canned. Our favorite "hummusier" in Montreal is Baba Hummus because they don't use neutral oils. Olive oil only!

CALIFORNIA SALAD

R: This recipe is inspired by the Chinese Chicken Salad from Joan's on Third in LA (even though I've never eaten it). We're aware that the origin of this dish has encountered quite a bit of skepticism in recent years. It's rumored that the late Sylvia Wu, of Madame Wu's Garden in LA, may have created it. Other accounts contend that the salad is a completely white American invention, which has proved to be an issue when it's been labeled distastefully, like "Chinese-y Chicken" or "Oriental Chop Chop." It may even have been the famous Austrian, Wolfgang Puck, who popularized it. We obviously have no idea what to believe, but "California Salad" seemed to be the most broadly respectful name we could give it. What we do know is that we love the way this salad tastes, especially the addictively salty-sweet (and pretty unhealthy) sugary almond butter dressing.

SERVES 1

Poached Chicken

2 medium (1.1 lb/500 g total) boneless, skinless chicken breasts

2 large green onions, twisted in half

2-inch piece peeled ginger, thickly sliced

3 tablespoons salt

Soy Mix

½ cup (120 ml) light soy sauce

½ cup (100 g) granulated sugar

Scant ¼ cup (50 ml) water

2 teaspoons salt

Almond Dressing

Generous ½ cup (135 ml) Soy Mix

1½-inch piece (½ oz/15 g) peeled ginger, minced

3 tablespoons almond butter

3 tablespoons rice vinegar

1 tablespoon sesame oil

2 teaspoons freshly squeezed lime juice

1½ teaspoons sambal oelek

Scant ½ cup (100 ml) neutral oil

MAKE THE POACHED CHICKEN

Place all ingredients in a medium pot. Fill with enough water to submerge the chicken by 1 inch. Bring to a simmer and cook for 10 to 15 minutes, until the chicken is fully cooked through. Alternatively, once the water is simmering, you can cover the pot and place in a 350°F oven for a similar amount of time.

Let the chicken cool slightly, then shred. Store in an airtight container in the fridge for up to 1 week.

MAKE THE SOY MIX

In a saucepan, bring the soy sauce, sugar, and water to a boil. Simmer until the sugar is melted. Transfer to a heatproof bowl and let cool. Taste, and add the salt a little at a time; the quantity you need will depend on how salty your soy sauce is. Store in an airtight container in the fridge for as long as your soy sauce lasts (longer than you).

MAKE THE ALMOND DRESSING

In a blender blitz all ingredients, minus the neutral oil, until combined. With the blender running, slowly drizzle in the oil until emulsified. Store in an airtight container in the fridge for up to 2 weeks.

continued . . .

Assembly

¾ cup (80 g) thinly sliced napa cabbage

Loosely packed 2 cups (80 g) thinly sliced romaine

Packed ⅓ cup (50 g) shredded carrots

Packed ⅓ cup (65 g) shredded Poached Chicken

⅓ cup (50 g) diced red bell pepper

Packed ¼ cup (50 g) diced mango or pear

1 tablespoon finely chopped green onion

1 tablespoon chopped fresh cilantro

½ avocado, diced

Almond Dressing, to taste

Fried shallots, for topping

Fried wonton wrapper strips, for topping

ASSEMBLE

Layer the cabbage, romaine, and carrots in a salad bowl, then top with the chicken, bell pepper, mango, green onion, cilantro, and avocado. Drizzle with some Almond Dressing, then top with a handful of fried shallots and wonton wrappers.

GRINGO SALAD

R: This salad was created by two men who love spoonable salads: my husband and our former chef, Luka Lecavalier. The idea was, quite simply, to create a Tex-Mex salad that didn't require a fork. In typical Alex fashion, they added as many seemingly unnecessary ingredients as possible, and in typical Alex fashion, it became an instant customer and staff favorite.

A: Fuck yeah.

SERVES 1

"Frito" Tortilla Chips

10 small corn tortillas

¼ cup (35 g) sweet paprika

1⅓ tablespoons onion powder

1⅓ tablespoons garlic powder

1 tablespoon ground Hatch green mild chili (optional)

2½ teaspoons masa harina

1 teaspoon white peppercorns, ground

½ teaspoon cinnamon

Neutral oil, for frying

Avo Crema

1 avocado

1 clove garlic

½ cup (120 g) 14% sour cream

2 tablespoons chopped fresh cilantro

2 teaspoons freshly squeezed lemon juice

Chili Lime Dressing

Generous ½ cup (125 ml) extra-virgin olive oil

½ cup (120 ml) freshly squeezed lime juice

2½ tablespoons granulated sugar

2 tablespoons sambal oelek

2¼ teaspoons salt

MAKE THE "FRITO" TORTILLA CHIPS

Cut the tortillas into ten strips (make four cuts one way and one the other way). In a small bowl, combine all remaining ingredients, minus the oil.

Heat about 1 inch of neutral oil in a cast-iron skillet set over medium heat. Once the oil is shimmering, fry the tortillas until lightly golden (they will continue cooking when removed). Transfer them to a bowl, then toss with salt and transfer to a paper towel–lined plate. Season with more salt, then toss with the spice mix. Store in an airtight container at room temperature for up to 1 week.

MAKE THE AVO CREMA

Combine all ingredients in a blender and blitz until smooth, adding water as needed to make it your desired thickness. Be careful not to overblend, as too much air will take away from the creaminess. Let rest at least 20 minutes before using. Season with salt and black pepper to taste. Store in an airtight container in the fridge for up to 3 days.

MAKE THE CHILI LIME DRESSING

In a medium bowl, whisk together all ingredients. Store in an airtight container in the fridge for up to 3 weeks.

continued . . .

Assembly

3 cups (120 g) chopped romaine

⅓ cup (40 g) thawed frozen corn or fresh blanched corn

⅓ cup (50 g) finely diced red bell pepper

⅓ cup (50 g) finely diced peeled jicama

2 tablespoons Pickled Turnips (pg. 153)

3 cherry tomatoes, halved

¼ nectarine, finely diced

Chili Lime Dressing, to taste

Avo Crema, to taste

2 tablespoons cotija

"Frito" Tortilla Chips

1 tablespoon finely chopped fresh mint

1 tablespoon finely chopped fresh cilantro

1 large pinch thinly sliced red onion

2 dashes tajin

ASSEMBLE

Lay the romaine in a salad bowl. In a separate bowl, toss the corn, bell pepper, jicama, Pickled Turnips, tomatoes, and nectarine with the Chili Lime Dressing and add it on top of the romaine. Top with a drizzle of the Avo Crema, and finish with the cotija, some "Fritos," fresh herbs, red onion, and tajin.

SMOKED SALMON PANZANELLA SALAD

This dish strikes the balance between smoky, salty, sweet, and slightly spicy. Any of the fresh ingredients can be substituted to suit the season, and it's an efficient way to use up any bagels going stale on your counter. The most important element is the Bulgarian feta, which is a bit pricey but significantly creamier than the standard grocery-store kind. It really makes the dish, so don't skip it.

SERVES 1

Butter, for toasting

1 sesame bagel

1 teaspoon sliced Cascabella pepper

1 tablespoon Bulgarian feta

1 large pinch thinly sliced Vidalia onion

½ teaspoon Pickled Mustard Seeds (pg. 154)

¼ avocado, diced

4 cherry tomatoes, halved

½ Lebanese cucumber, sliced into half-moons

¼ white nectarine, diced

¼ cup (60 ml) White Balsamic Vinaigrette (pg. 217)

14% sour cream, for dolloping

3 slices (2.6 oz/75 g total) Smoked Salmon (pg. 163)

Fresh dill, for garnish

Butter and toast the bagel. Cut it into ½-inch pieces. For one salad, use just a quarter of the bagel.

In a bowl, combine the bagel pieces, Cascabella, feta, onion, Pickled Mustard Seeds, avocado, tomatoes, cucumber, and nectarine. Drizzle everything with the White Balsamic Vinaigrette. Transfer to a serving dish and dollop the sour cream all over.

Drape the Smoked Salmon slices over the salad so that it blankets everything. Season with salt, black pepper, and a good pinch of dill.

MATZO BALL SOUP

R: Oh, matzo ball soup. Every Ashkenazi home has their own version, passed down from bubby to bubby, simmered on high holidays and chilly winter days.

There are two critical criteria by which this soup is judged. The first is the matzo ball, which we could call the closest thing Ashkenazis have to an American dumpling. It has to be tender and light enough to melt in your mouth, but still retain a firmness throughout, which has more to do with how you shape it than the recipe itself. The second is the chicken stock, which must be golden yellow and crystal clear, "clean" to the palate and the eye. So while roasting the bones or simmering the liquid for longer would actually give you a more intense flavor, that's not quite the point of this dish. Matzo ball soup is intentionally a bit muted, like something you eat when you're sick.

All this is deceptively difficult to accomplish, and we've done our best to explain how we go about it. But no matter how hard we try, whenever Alex sees a group of old Jewish women walk into Arthurs and order this soup, he runs away. He knows that, without fail, they're going to be drawing comparisons to their own recipe (it's the Ashkenazi version of Moroccan Salade Cuite, see pg. 222).

Unless you're trying to wow the bubby next door, don't stress about keeping the ball perfectly soft or the stock perfectly clear. It doesn't affect the taste whatsoever. All technique aside, the importance is that your soup brings you a feeling of heimish, of being at home.

SERVES 4

Chicken Soup Stock

4½ lb (2 kg) chicken carcasses, breast bones only[1]

1 medium boneless, skinless chicken breast (or bone-in and/or skin-on if that's what you find)

6 oz (170 g) chicken feet or wings

1 Spanish onion, roughly chopped

2 large carrots, roughly chopped

MAKE THE CHICKEN SOUP STOCK

Rinse all the chicken to remove any blood and impurities. Place in a large pot, then cover with all remaining ingredients, minus the fresh herbs. Add enough water to cover everything by 1 inch.

Bring to a soft boil, then lower the heat to a simmer. After about 30 minutes, impurities will rise to the top. Skim them off and discard, then cover and simmer on low for 2 hours and 15 minutes.[2] Do not stir, or the stock will become cloudy. After this simmering time, uncover the pot and gently submerge the herbs, leafy part first, agitating the stock as little as possible. Continue simmering, uncovered, for another 45 minutes without stirring.

continued . . .

---

1 If you can't find just the breast bones, buy the whole chicken. Thigh bones cloud the soup, but that doesn't matter if you care more about flavor than clarity.

2 Note that we are making a "soup stock," not a classic stock, and the liquid therefore shouldn't be too reduced or concentrated.

2 stalks celery, roughly
chopped

¼ green bell pepper, roughly
chopped

¼ small green cabbage, roughly
chopped

½ Granny Smith apple, roughly
chopped

2 cloves garlic

2 tablespoons salt

2½ teaspoons white
peppercorns

½ bay leaf

¼ teaspoon coriander seeds

A few sprigs fresh parsley

A few sprigs fresh dill

A few sprigs fresh thyme

Matzo Balls

1 cup (145 g) Streit's matzo
meal[4]

1 tablespoon salt

½ teaspoon baking powder

¼ sweet onion, finely diced

4 eggs, yolks + whites separated, at room temperature

Generous ¼ cup (65 ml)
Schweppes club soda, or
champagne if you're filthy
rich

3½ tablespoons melted
Schmaltz (pg. 169)

Neutral oil, for forming balls

Ladle the soup through a fine-mesh strainer lined with cheese-cloth.[3] For maximum clarity, ladle from only one side of the pot, then slowly pour in the rest. If desired, set aside the strained bits in the same pot and use it to cook the Matzo Balls later (the chef word for this is "remouillage").

MAKE THE MATZO BALLS

In a medium bowl, whisk together the matzo meal, salt, baking powder, onion, and a bit of black pepper.

In a separate bowl, whisk together the egg yolks, club soda, and Schmaltz.

In a third bowl, using a hand mixer, beat the egg whites to stiff peaks, being careful not to overwhip.

Make a well in the dry mixture, then pour in the liquid mixture. Working quickly, use your hands to mix the batter until no dry patches or lumps remain.[5] Still using your hands, vigorously fold in a third of the egg whites. Use a spatula to fold in another third, then the remainder.

Cover the mixture with plastic wrap so that it touches the surface of the batter. Refrigerate for at least 45 minutes, or preferably overnight.

Pour a bit of neutral oil into a bowl and rub a bit on your hands. Grab a piece of batter about 1 inch in diameter. Hold your hands together like you're cupping water, cradling the batter around, letting gravity shape it into a ball. Do not apply pressure, or the balls will turn out dense! Repeat with the remaining batter to make 6 to 8 balls in total. Store any balls you're not using immediately in an airtight container in the fridge for up to 1 week or in the freezer for up to 3 months.

---

3 The ladle method is used to avoid stirring up and clouding the soup.

4 We've tried this recipe with other brands of matzo meal and it hasn't worked, so we can't promise anything unless you use Streit's.

5 If you try to use a spatula, or wait too long before mixing, it'll be like mixing cement. As Freya and Abel Cohen's wise father once said, "If you used matzo ball mix to pave the streets of Montreal, we'd have no potholes."

Assembly

2 small carrots, halved

1 stalk celery, peeled and cut into bite-sized pieces

½ sweet onion, cut into bite-sized pieces

1½ to 3 cups (165 to 330 g) fine egg noodles (such as Streit's)

5 cups (1.2 L) Chicken Soup Stock

1 cup (195 g) shredded Poached Chicken (see California Salad, pg. 127)

4 Matzo Balls or more, depending on size

Fresh dill, for serving

Chopped chives, for serving

Extra-virgin olive oil, for drizzling

2 tablespoons Schmaltz (pg. 169) + more for drizzling

COOK THE MATZO BALLS

If you reserved the strained bits from the Chicken Soup Stock, fill that same pot with enough water to cover the Matzo Balls once they are added.[6] Bring it to a soft boil, then heavily salt.[7] Be sure to choose a pot with enough space for the balls to nearly quadruple in size—no one enjoys smashed balls.

With a spoon, individually lower each ball into the boiling water. Once all the balls are in, lower the heat to a simmer and cover the pot. Cook, covered, for 45 minutes to 1 hour. Don't touch them, don't look at them, don't talk to them, and don't even think about them during this time. It's just the way it's done and you're better off not asking questions. By the end, the balls should be almost quadrupled in size and fluffy.

ASSEMBLE

Meanwhile, bring 3 small pots of salted water to a boil. Boil the carrots in 1 pot until they are soft enough to be cut easily with a spoon. Boil the celery in the second pot until tender. Boil the onion in the third pot until translucent (ideally, you'll do this in 3 separate pots, but 1 pot is okay if you want fewer dishes). Alternatively, you can thinly slice the vegetables and simmer them in the Chicken Soup Stock in the next step instead.

Bring a medium pot of water to a boil. Add the noodles and cook until slightly overdone.

In a separate medium pot, heat the Chicken Soup Stock.

Using a spider, transfer the cooked noodles and vegetables to the pot with the Matzo Balls, then add the Poached Chicken. Taste and adjust seasoning if necessary. Distribute the Matzo Balls among four soup bowls, then ladle in everything else. Finish with a large pinch of dill, chives, cracked black pepper, and a drizzle of olive oil and melted Schmaltz.

---

[6] Alternatively, you can use regular water and add a bit of chicken broth powder, the neon yellow kind.

[7] Don't worry about oversalting the water. The balls are supposed to be on the salty side. If they turn out too salty, you can place them in warm, unsalted water, and the salt will release.

SPLIT PEA SOUP WITH BONE MARROW

R: Split pea soup was my dad's soup of choice. It was his pre-hockey meal that my whole family devoured together before he'd head out, slathering our super-fresh challah with bone marrow. Alex grew up with a slightly different version, soupe aux fèves, eaten with a side of braised beef or lamb and matzah at Passover. His mother burns it every single year while reheating it, but that doesn't make him like it any less. This recipe is a mix of these two fondly remembered childhood dishes. We've selected seared beef cheeks as the meat, but ham hocks, which my grandma from Quebec City put in her pea soup, would be a delicious (albeit non-kosher) replacement.

We do ask you to make the Chicken Soup Stock (see Matzo Ball Soup, pg. 135) for this recipe because it's healthy and flavorful, although you could buy it ready-made from your butcher or the grocery store. That's totally fine, but you'll sort of only get half the soup's potential, so do the most that your time and patience will allow.

SERVES 6

Soaked Split Peas

2¼ cups (450 g) dried green split peas

6¾ cups (1.6 L) water

Braised Beef Cheeks

2 medium (28 oz/800 g total) beef cheeks, cleaned by butcher

Heaping 2 tablespoons Schmaltz (pg. 169)

1 yellow onion, halved

1 stalk celery, halved

2 large carrots, halved

1 small head garlic, halved crosswise (skin on if desired)

2 sprigs fresh thyme

1 bay leaf

8 cups (2 L) Chicken Soup Stock (see Matzo Ball Soup, pg. 135) or water (enough to cover the beef by three-quarters)

SOAK THE SPLIT PEAS

Soak the split peas in the water for at least 12 hours and up to overnight, then drain.

BRAISE THE BEEF CHEEKS

Pat the beef cheeks dry and generously salt both sides. Let sit for 45 minutes at room temperature.

Preheat the oven to 350°F.

Heat the Schmaltz in a Dutch oven set over medium-high heat. Sear the beef cheeks on both sides until nicely browned, adjusting the heat as necessary to avoid burning them. Remove and set aside.

To the same pot, add the onion, celery, carrots, and garlic and cook until slightly softened. Do NOT season with salt![1] Return the beef to the pot, along with the the thyme, bay leaf and stock or water, ensuring the beef is three-quarters of the way covered. Bring to a boil, then lower to a simmer. Cover and cook in the oven for 2 hours, until the beef is fork-tender.

continued ...

---

[1] Salt makes a lot of dried legumes seize up and take an eternity to cook. Normally, we ask you to season at every step, but this (and Chickpea Cabbage Soup, pg. 141) is an exception.

Split Pea Soup

Schmaltz (pg. 169), for cooking

2 (1½-inch) pieces bone marrow (ask the butcher)

1 cilantro root, cleaned

1 large yellow onion, diced

2 carrots, peeled and diced

6 cloves garlic, chopped

½ teaspoon sweet paprika

½ teaspoon ground turmeric

½ teaspoon Aleppo pepper

Soaked Split Peas

8 cups (2 L) Chicken Soup Stock (see Matzo Ball Soup, pg. 135) or water

¾ cup (180 ml) braising liquid (reserved from the beef cheeks)

Grainy mustard, for serving

Buttered challah rolls, for serving

Remove the beef and set aside. Strain and discard the solids. Place the strained liquid back in the pot over medium-high heat and simmer to reduce by half; there should be about ¾ cup (180 ml) remaining.

COOK THE SPLIT PEA SOUP

Either transfer the reduced liquid to a container and continue with the same pot, or grab a new pot and heat a couple knobs of Schmaltz over medium heat. Sear the bone marrow until golden brown. Remove and set aside. Add the cilantro root, vegetables, garlic, and spices and cook for a few minutes to bloom them. Remove the cilantro root, then add the marrow back to the pot, along with the drained split peas and stock or water. Bring to a boil, then lower to a simmer. Cook for 2 to 3 hours, skimming off any impurities that rise to the top.

Once the peas are tender, remove the bone marrow, scraping the marrow into the soup or reserving to serve on the side. Add the reduced beef cheek braising liquid to the soup. Season with salt and black pepper to taste. Add the Braised Beef Cheeks to the pot and break them into chunks.

Serve with grainy mustard and a buttered challah roll.

CHICKPEA CABBAGE SOUP

A: Raegan came to me with the idea for a cabbage soup. Her notion of the dish was based on her grandma Zelma's rendition, a tomato-based cabbage soup that she would freeze in mass quantities and subsist off of as part of some fad diet. I transformed it into this, a soup that you'd actually want to eat.

Initially, this recipe was ridiculously long and complicated, with way too many ingredients. I always thought that it had to be that way and didn't want to risk compromising on any flavor. My staff despised making it so much that I would cook it myself to alleviate a bit of their workload. When we had to test it for this book, I was told by a number of people that there was no way any home cook would make it as is. I was forced to simplify and was surprised that the new technique produced the exact same results as the old. In short, apologies to all my former staff whom I ever tasked with making the original version.

SERVES 6

1¼ cups (200 g) dry chickpeas

½ cup (100 g) beluga lentils

1 medium head white cabbage, cut into 1-inch pieces

2½ tablespoons salt

1 tablespoon granulated sugar

2½ tablespoons dark brown sugar

3¾ cups (900 ml) water

1 pinch baking soda

2½ (14 oz/398 ml) cans crushed tomatoes

½ teaspoon fenugreek powder

½ teaspoon ground turmeric

1 tablespoon sweet paprika

2 teaspoons coriander seeds

2 teaspoons cumin seeds

1 teaspoon chili flakes

1 teaspoon fennel seeds

1½ tablespoons neutral oil

1½ tablespoons extra-virgin olive oil

¼ large Spanish onion, grated + ¼ large Spanish onion, finely diced

SOAK THE LEGUMES

Place the chickpeas in one large container and the lentils in another. Fill them both with water, stir thoroughly, then drain. Place them back in their respective containers and refill with enough water to cover them by 2 to 3 inches. Cover and let sit at room temperature for at least 12 hours and up to overnight. When ready, drain only the lentils and set aside (we have a slightly different method for the chickpeas).

PREPARE THE INGREDIENTS

Once the lentils and chickpeas are ready, transfer the cabbage to a large bowl. Add the salt, granulated sugar, and 1 tablespoon of the brown sugar and thoroughly massage them into the cabbage. It's okay if the cabbage pieces separate in the process. Let sit for at least 30 minutes and up to a few hours.

Roughly rub the soaked chickpeas in their soaking water between your fingers, so that some of their skins come off and float to the top. Discard the skins and drain the chickpeas, then add them to a large pot, along with the water. Add a pinch of baking soda and bring to a boil. Lower to a simmer and cook for 1 to 1½ hours, removing scum that accumulates at the top as necessary. When the chickpeas are cooked through, drain and set aside, reserving 1¼ cups (300 ml) of the cooking liquid for later use.

continued . . .

2 cilantro roots, cleaned, cut
    1 inch above the white root[1]

3 cloves garlic, minced

1 carrot, diced

2 tablespoons tomato paste

1 large vine tomato, grated

1 bay leaf

Waffle chips, for serving
    (optional)

14% sour cream, for serving
    (optional)

In a small bowl, stir together the crushed tomatoes and remaining 1½ tablespoons brown sugar and set aside. Place the fenugreek powder into a small bowl and mix with an equal amount of water. Set aside.

In a small skillet set over medium-low heat, toast all the spices. Grind all but the fennel seeds. Set aside.

MAKE THE SOUP

Heat both oils in a large pot over medium heat. Add the grated onion and cook until it begins to color. Continue cooking until the onion displays an uneven range of shades, from translucent to blackened (it will look as if some bits are burnt, but that is almost the goal). Add the diced onion, cilantro roots, garlic, and carrot, and cook for about 5 minutes, until softened. Add the drained lentils, then lower the heat to medium-low. Cook for 5 to 10 minutes to lightly toast the lentils. Add all the toasted spices, raise the heat to medium, and add the tomato paste. Cook for about 10 minutes, until the paste is a deep brick red. Do NOT add salt until the lentils are completely cooked through (see note 1 on pg. 139)!

Next, add the grated tomato and cook out for about 5 minutes. Add the cooked chickpeas and cabbage, along with its released liquid, and bring to a simmer. Cover and cook at a low simmer for 30 minutes, then uncover and continue cooking for another 30 minutes. Stir in the crushed tomato and brown sugar mixture, followed by the bay leaf, fenugreek slurry, and reserved chickpea cooking water. Simmer for about 10 minutes, until slightly thickened. Taste and adjust for sweetness, spiciness, and salt. Remove the cilantro roots before serving with waffle chips and sour cream, if desired.

If eating the soup the next day, you may need to rehydrate with water when reheating.

---

[1] If you can't find roots, just tie up fresh cilantro stems and use them instead. Remove them before adding the canned tomatoes, or leave them in longer for a more pungent flavor.

DELI

While the Jewish deli has become

widely known for items like lox, cold cuts, dill pickles, and bagels with schmear, these foods actually don't comply with the technical definition of the word "deli." Formally, a deli sells primarily meat. It is appetizing shops, or "appys," that have everything else, from smoked fish to prepared salads to cream cheese products. Back in the day, appys were vital to Jews observing kosher law, which basically doesn't allow for meat and dairy to be prepared in the same place. Most non-Jews, however, have never heard of appetizing shops because they're very rare today, rendered nearly obsolete by kosher-carrying grocery stores. Russ & Daughters in Manhattan is an example of an appy that's remained popular; if you've ever been there and wondered why "appetizers" is written in neon on their storefront, now you know. In Montreal, by contrast, there isn't a single appy left.

Don't get us wrong, we still have some awesome delis in town. Just like a boucherie or fromagerie, you can go to any of them and get a whole smorgasbord of mix-and-match foods. It's an incredibly convenient way to create a fully custom meal without doing any work or spending a lot of money, and without being that obnoxious customer at a restaurant who asks for a million modifications on their order. Snowdon Deli, for one, is mentioned numerous times in this book. When we were dating, we'd swing by and pick up four to six items. Raegan liked to stuff rolled-up turkey slices with eggplant and snack on them. By the time we got home, she'd be complaining of feeling sick—no kidding, she'd already eaten everything. It's a tradition we've never stopped, although now we tend to eat with one hand on the wheel, driving our kids back and forth like maniacs.

Arthurs obviously isn't kosher, but we still take pride in our deli/appy menu. You can come to us for a pound of house gravlax, a sesame bagel with schmear, a handful of vinegar coleslaw, or a scoop of chopped chicken. We'd like to act as more of a deli and sell slices of our roast beef and smoked turkey, but we know the demand isn't there for us. But maybe next time you're in, try ordering a few of the things from these pages to go, and see what you make of it.

A: You will never find gefilte fish on our deli menu. I just don't think it's something you should pay for at a restaurant (same goes for kasha and bowties, sorry!). The best way I can describe it is a watered-down log of fish paste. Even if you try to make it cool, like a gefilte taco (a real horrific thing I've seen in this city), you can't get over that sweet, wet, spongy quality. Listen, if someone invites me to their home and offers it with some horseradish, I'm not gonna turn away in disgust. I just can't bring myself to charge anyone for it unless I were to change it completely, in which case it wouldn't really be gefilte anymore. If you enjoy it, all power to you. Just don't put it in a damn taco.

Coleslaw

pickled
red chilies

egg salad

tuna
salad

Otto's
pickles

pickled
vidalia
onions

Rita's
eggplant

long hots

miami
chicken salad

TUNA SALAD

In our opinion, no proper tuna salad is complete without mayo. For this recipe, opt for a high-quality, sustainably sourced tuna, preferably whole white albacore in water.

MAKES 3 CUPS

2 small cans (9.9 oz/280 g total) high-quality tuna

½ cup (85 g) deveined, deseeded, brunoised jalapeño

Packed ½ cup (85 g) peeled, brunoised celery

⅓ cup (85 g) brunoised Otto's Dill Pickles (pg. 155)

Heaping ⅓ cup House Mayo (pg. 218)

Drain the tuna and flake it to oblivion in a bowl with a fork, until it practically becomes a paste. Add all the remaining ingredients and mix together until creamy and combined. Season with salt and black pepper to taste.

MIAMI CHICKEN SALAD

R: Although my family would visit Miami every year, it wasn't until I attended a wedding with Alex in my 20s that I finally tried out the famed Miami Juice. Their creamy, gluten- and mayo-free chicken salad is my inspiration for this recipe, which is undoubtedly worth the extra steps.

MAKES 3 CUPS

1.1 lb (500 g) boneless, skinless chicken breasts

1 cup (240 ml) Buttermilk Marinade (see Schnitzel, pg. 193)

Neutral oil, for cooking

1 cup (150 g) chopped carrots

1¼ cups (350 g) high-quality hummus (like Baba Hummus)

2 teaspoons Zhug Sauce (pg. 209)

1½ teaspoons freshly squeezed lemon juice

¼ teaspoon salt

Place the chicken in a medium bowl and cover completely with the marinade. Cover and refrigerate for 4 hours or up to overnight.

Get a grill or cast-iron skillet nice and hot, then slick it with neutral oil. Remove the chicken from the marinade with a slotted spoon to drain as much excess marinade from the chicken as possible. Cook for about 5 minutes, flipping halfway through, until charred and fully cooked. Set aside to cool.

Blend the carrots in a juicer (or a food processor or grater) until pulpy. Place them in a cheesecloth and wring out the liquid with your hands—there should be 3 oz (90 g) of pulp remaining. Take a shot of carrot juice for some beta-carotene.

Shred the cooled chicken. Place it into the bowl of a stand mixer fitted with the paddle attachment, along with the carrot pulp and remaining ingredients. Mix on low speed for a few minutes, until creamy. Don't overmix or it'll become a paste.

Taste and season with more salt, pepper, and lemon juice if necessary.

FLUFFY EGG SALAD

A: I eat egg salad by the liter; it is literally my favorite snack in the whole world, especially the one from Snowdon Deli. But a lot of egg salads are heavy and overly creamy, so one day, I sought out a homemade alternative. I boiled eggs, whipped the yolks, and passed the whites through a ricer. When I folded the whites into the yolks, I saw that the ricing had created air pockets in them, resulting in a light, bouncy egg salad that held its texture for days.

The key to any good egg salad, like a good potato or pasta salad, is to cool the eggs just enough to be able to peel them, then immediately assemble the dish. For some reason, hot eggs seem to absorb flavor better than cold ones. And if you plan on eating the salad the next day, don't put in any sort of onion, or it'll just become egg-flavored onion salad. Besides overcooking the eggs, it's the only way you can mess up.

MAKES 4 CUPS

7 eggs

2 tablespoons House Mayo (pg. 218)

1½ teaspoons Dijon

½ teaspoon salt

1 pinch granulated sugar

White pepper, to taste

Maldon salt, for finishing

Cook the eggs to a perfect hard boil. We like to start them in cold water and bring to a boil. Then, cover the pot, remove from the heat, and leave them alone for 8 to 10 minutes.

Peel them while they're still hot, then separate the yolks and whites. Pass the yolks through a ricer or sieve into a bowl. Vigorously stir in the mayo, Dijon, salt, sugar, and white pepper until all mashed up and homogeneous.

Rice the egg whites into the same bowl and gently fold them in. Garnish with a bit of Maldon.

RITA'S EGGPLANT

R: My grandma Rita always had this Romanian eggplant dish around. She was a very particular woman who maintained an immaculately organized and well-stocked home, gave generously, and taught me all there is to know about the finer things in life. We recreated her recipe and put it on the menu in her honor, although we seem to have ended up *dis*honoring her. Anytime she came by Arthurs, she was so disappointed in ours that she eventually stopped ordering it altogether. It may not have been her favorite, but its taste still reminds me of her.

MAKES 2 CUPS

4 medium eggplants (preferably Japanese)

2 tablespoons salt

¼ cup (35 g) brunoised sweet or Vidalia onion

2 cloves garlic

2 tablespoons freshly squeezed lemon juice

1 tablespoon white vinegar

2 tablespoons canola oil

¼ red bell pepper, brunoised

¼ green bell pepper, brunoised

Cut the eggplants in half lengthwise and pierce the skin with a fork. Place the eggplants, flesh side up, on a sheet tray, and sprinkle with the salt. Let sit for 30 minutes to 2 hours (the bigger your eggplants, the longer they need to help remove bitterness and acidity).

Preheat the oven to 325°F.

Bring a small pot of water to a boil. Place the onion in a sieve and dunk into the water for 45 seconds. This will ensure that the finished dish doesn't taste all oniony by the second day.

Place the salted eggplant, flesh side down, on a new rimmed sheet tray lined with parchment paper. Roast for about 1 hour, until it feels soft when you poke it with your finger. Remove from the oven and allow to cool a little.

Peel the eggplant and scoop out the top layer of seeds. Place the remaining flesh into a nonreactive strainer set over a bowl. Cover and refrigerate for at least 6 hours, or preferably overnight.

In a small bowl, mash together the garlic and lemon juice. Let sit for 10 minutes to allow the garlic to infuse. Pass through a fine-mesh strainer and discard the garlic. This way, the garlic flavor will be evenly distributed in the finished product and the garlic itself won't have the chance to ferment.

In a food processor, pulse together the eggplant flesh, infused lemon juice, and white vinegar. With the food processor running, slowly add the oil. Pulse until the mixture is mostly smooth.

Transfer to a bowl and gently mix in the onion and bell peppers by hand. Season with salt to taste, and adjust vinegar as desired. Store in an airtight container in the fridge for up to 3 days, and longer if you don't mind a stronger onion and garlic flavor. It tastes even better the next day.

CREAMY COLESLAW

R: I'm more of a vinegar slaw kind of girl, but this recipe is almost enough to change my mind. It came about from my request to Alex for a creamy sandwich, to which he obediently obliged by creating the Vermont Thanksgiving Turkey (pg. 107). We had some pumpkin seeds left over from Halloween, and to avoid wasting them, he threw them into this slaw, which ended up tasting really good. We made it even better through the recipe testing for this book, adjusting it so that it releases less water than the Vermont sandwich, has better depth of flavor, and tastes good enough to stand on its own.

MAKES 8 CUPS

Ranch Powder

½ cup + 2 tablespoons (80 g) buttermilk powder

¼ cup (25 g) sour cream powder

1¾ teaspoons salt

1½ teaspoons dried parsley

1½ teaspoons powdered sugar

¼ teaspoon mustard powder

¼ teaspoon granulated garlic

⅛ teaspoon black pepper

Creamy Dressing

3 tablespoons 14% sour cream

3 tablespoons House Mayo (pg. 218)

1 heaping tablespoon Bulgarian or other soft feta

1½ tablespoons Dijon

1½ tablespoons apple cider vinegar

2 teaspoons granulated sugar

2 teaspoons Ranch Powder

¾ teaspoon salt

Coleslaw

2 tablespoons pumpkin seeds

Extra-virgin olive oil, for toasting

6⅓ cups (630 g) shredded green cabbage

¾ cup (75 g) shredded carrots

MAKE THE RANCH POWDER

Combine all ingredients in a bowl. Store in an airtight container at room temperature for a very long time.

MAKE THE CREAMY DRESSING

In a medium bowl, mix together a small amount of the sour cream with all the mayo to smooth out the feta. Add the remaining sour cream and all other ingredients and mix together until homogeneous. Store in an airtight container in the fridge for up to 3 days.

MAKE THE COLESLAW

In a small skillet set over medium heat, toast the pumpkin seeds with a bit of olive oil and salt. Let cool, then roughly chop. Set aside.

Prepare a tray with three layers of paper towel.

Combine the cabbage, carrots, onion, sugar, and salt in a large bowl and let sit for 5 minutes to cure.

Transfer the mixture to a strainer and rinse with cold water. Wring out all the water with a kitchen towel. Spread out on the prepared tray. Leave in the fridge for 10 to 15 minutes to dry.

½ cup (50 g) thinly sliced white onion

¼ cup + 3 tablespoons (85 g) granulated sugar

¼ cup (32 g) salt

Packed 2 tablespoons chopped fresh dill

Packed 3 tablespoons shredded 3- to 5-year aged cheddar

Transfer to a bowl. Add the toasted pumpkin seeds, dill, and cheddar. When ready to serve, toss with the Creamy Dressing. Store in an airtight container in the fridge for up to 3 days.

VINEGAR COLESLAW

R: This coleslaw is inspired by the great Moishes, Montreal's famed steakhouse institution since 1938. As the good friend of the original owner's son, Lenny Lighter, my dad loved taking us there to eat. They'd bring vinegar coleslaw, dill pickles, and assorted bread and butter to the table, which I'd assemble into a sandwich and gorge on before the real meal. When we opened Arthurs, I'd drive over in a pickup truck and fill the bed with barrels of their pickles, listening to them slosh around as I swerved around potholes. When I think of coleslaw, Moishes' classic version is still what comes to mind.

MAKES ABOUT 12 CUPS

9 cups (900 g) very thinly sliced cabbage (from ½ large head)

3⅓ cups (330 g) grated carrots, very thinly sliced

1½ teaspoons salt

1¾ cups (350 g) granulated sugar

½ cup + 3 tablespoons (165 ml) red wine vinegar

½ cup + ⅓ cup (200 ml) white vinegar

3 tablespoons + 1 teaspoon water

¾ cup + 2 tablespoons (210 ml) neutral oil

3 cloves garlic, crushed

1½ tablespoons dried parsley

½ teaspoon coarsely ground black pepper

In a large bowl, mix together the cabbage, carrots, and salt. Set aside.

In a medium pot, bring the sugar, vinegars, and water to a boil. Remove from the heat, then stir in the oil and let cool.

Lightly squeeze the excess water out of the cabbage and carrots. Transfer the vegetables to a container, and stir in the garlic, parsley, and black pepper. Pour the cooled liquid over the slaw, and mix to combine. Cover, then refrigerate for a minimum of 48 hours before eating.

MARINATED LONG HOTS

This is a great base recipe for pickling nearly any spicy pepper. The mild heat of long hots makes them ideal for our purposes, as we keep the peppers whole and serve them as a side dish. Nosh with caution—some long hots are hotter than others!

MAKES 12 PEPPERS

12 Italian long hots or peppers of choice

3 cups (720 ml) white vinegar

2 cups (400 g) granulated sugar

6 cloves garlic

1 tablespoon pickling spice

1 tablespoon salt

5½ cups (1.3 L) water

Extra-virgin olive oil, for finishing

Garlic, thinly sliced, for finishing

Lemon juice, for finishing

Maldon salt, for finishing

Get a cast-iron or grill pan hot over medium-high heat, and lightly char the peppers.

In a large pot, combine the vinegar, sugar, garlic, pickling spice, salt, and water. Bring to a boil and then remove from the heat.

Add the charred peppers to the pot, then place a heavy heatproof plate on top of the peppers to submerge them in the liquid. Let the pot cool to room temperature. Once cooled, place the whole pot in the fridge for 24 hours. To ensure maximum pickling, make sure the peppers remain submerged.

Transfer the peppers to airtight containers and fill with enough of the pickling liquid to fully cover them. Store in the fridge for up to 3 months.

To serve, lightly cover the peppers in good olive oil, then top with thinly sliced garlic, lemon juice and Maldon.

PICKLED RED CHILIES

A: These finely sliced chilies, given to us by our former cook Charlotte Mofford, are how we top any dish that could use a hint of spice, like a side of sliced avocado. If you don't tolerate spice well, the oil alone is enough to impart a very subtle heat. For no heat at all, you can try replacing the red chilies with mini bell peppers; for crazy heat, use bird's eye.

MAKES 1½ CUPS

8 oz (225 g) Holland red chilies, finely sliced

2 tablespoons salt

Scant ½ cup (100 ml) white vinegar

Scant ½ cup (100 ml) neutral oil

2 small cloves garlic, smashed

1 tablespoon dried oregano

In a large bowl, mix together the chilies and salt. Cover and let sit overnight at room temperature.

Wring out the chilies with a cloth to remove as much liquid as possible. Add the vinegar. Once more, cover and let sit overnight at room temperature.

Wring out the chilies again, then mix in the oil, garlic, and oregano. Store in an airtight container in the fridge for up to a few months.

PICKLED TURNIPS

R: I ate a lot of Lebanese food growing up, so pickled turnips are a natural part of my diet. They also remind me of my years in the fine dining scene in the early 2000s, during the inexplicable gastropub–pickled turnip–hummus–octopus craze. Alex, on the other hand, never bought into it; he's stayed away from octopus ever since he learned they have "alien" DNA (and since he watched *Penguins of Madagascar*). Chef-y trends and crazy husbands aside, pickled turnips work well in most salads and spreads, or all by their lonesome as a crunchy little snack. I've been known to eat them by the handful.

MAKES 8 CUPS

1 medium beet, sliced[1]

1 medium turnip, finely diced

3 cups (720 ml) water

3 cups (720 ml) white vinegar

1 French shallot, halved

1 bay leaf

4 black peppercorns

1¼ cups (250 g) granulated sugar

1½ tablespoons salt

Place the beets and turnips in a large bowl.

In a large pot, bring the water and vinegar to a boil. Add the shallots, bay leaf, peppercorns, sugar, and salt and stir until the sugar is dissolved.

Pour the hot liquid over the beets and turnips. Let cool to room temperature, then cover and place in the fridge for 48 hours before using.[2]

Store in an airtight container in the fridge for up to 3 weeks.

---

[1] The more beets you use, the pinker the turnips will become. You could also replace fresh beet with beet juice.

[2] You can leave the beets in the container, or remove them once it looks like they've stopped releasing their pigment into the liquid. The beets make a good snack on their own; better yet, grill them and pair with some labneh.

PICKLED VIDALIA ONIONS

R: Pickled onions, and really pickled anything, are always good to have on hand. They keep for an eternity in the fridge and can contribute a briny, tangy sweetness to a wealth of dishes, especially fatty and spicy ones—creamy soups, rich salads, sandwiches, cured salmon plates, etc. Depending on how you plan to use them, any onion will work in place of Vidalia, from French shallots to the whites of green onions.

MAKES 8 CUPS

1 cup (240 ml) white vinegar

1 cup (240 ml) water

2 black peppercorns

½ bay leaf

⅓ cup (66 g) granulated sugar

1 tablespoon salt

1.1 lb (500 g) Vidalia onions, thinly sliced into half-moons

Place all ingredients, minus the onion, in a medium saucepan. Bring to a boil, then remove from the heat and add the onion.

Set aside to cool, then pour into one or more containers (mason jars work well), and cover with an airtight lid. Store in the fridge forever.

PICKLED MUSTARD SEEDS

MAKES 2 CUPS

1¼ cups (300 ml) champagne vinegar

Scant ½ cup (100 ml) apple juice[1]

3⅓ tablespoons white balsamic vinegar

3½ tablespoons water

¼ cup + 1 tablespoon (60 g) granulated sugar

1 tablespoon salt

1½ teaspoons mustard powder

Scant 1 cup (200 g) yellow mustard seeds

1 large French shallot, halved

In a large bowl, stir together all ingredients, minus the mustard seeds and shallot.

Place the mustard seeds in a medium pot and cover generously with water. Bring to a boil, then drain and discard the water. Repeat another six times. The repetitions are optional, but it will soften the bitter tannins of the mustard seeds and remove their gumminess.

Stir the mustard seeds into the bowl with the other ingredients, then add the shallot. Cover and let sit overnight in the fridge before using. Store in an airtight container in the fridge for up to 3 months. Keep the residual liquid to use, with or without the seeds (it works great as a vinaigrette ingredient).

1 For a non-apple-y taste, replace the apple juice with a scant ½ cup (100 ml) water and increase the sugar by 3 heaping tablespoons.

OTTO'S DILL PICKLES

R: During WWII, my grandpa Otto fought for the Jewish Brigade Group, part of the British Royal Air Force. He was positioned as a ball turret gunner, the most vulnerable target on the aircraft. When I was a kid, he'd sometimes send me into the basement of his cottage to fetch a fresh batch of his dill pickles. There, hanging in the basement, were his hard helmet, his gold medals, and his tattered, army-green uniform speckled with badges. Brush them aside, and there were the glass jars nestled in neat rows on a shelf, filled with unbelievably crunchy and juicy pickles. With bated breath, we begged him to make a fresh batch every summer, and he always did.

Grandpa Otto replicated the exact same pickles every year, but we encourage you to add any spices or aromatics you want.

MAKES 24 PICKLES

3 tablespoons salt

1 cup (240 ml) cold water

2 tablespoons pickling spice

2 cloves garlic, cut in half vertically, germs removed

3 sprigs fresh dill

24 small Kirby cucumbers

Prepare a wide-mouthed 1-gallon (4 L) mason jar for canning: Preheat the oven to 275°F and bring a large pot of water to a boil. Wash the jar and lid in hot water. Carefully lower them into the boiling water, and leave them there for 5 minutes. Transfer to a sheet tray covered with a rag. Place in the oven for 10 minutes. Remove and set aside on a clean rag. Discard the boiling water, refill the pot with fresh water, and bring to a boil again.

In a large bowl, dissolve the salt in the water. Add the pickling spice, garlic, and dill.

Use tongs to place the cucumbers upright into the sanitized jar while it's still hot. Pour in the seasoned water, then fill the jar the rest of the way with regular cold water, leaving ½ inch of headspace at the top. Seal the jar with the lid, not screwing it too tightly shut.

Place the jar into the boiling water. The water should cover the jar by 2 inches. Boil for 15 minutes. Remove, set aside on a clean rag and let cool for 12 hours. You should hear the seal pop, at which point you can twist it more tightly shut. Be sure to wear gloves and avoid touching any inner parts of the jar throughout this process, to avoid contaminating it.

Leave the jar in a cool, dark area for at least 2 weeks, until the cucumbers are pickled: they should darken in color and basically taste like pickles. If they don't, throw them out. We're not responsible if you get sick.

GIARDINIERA

A: I've devoured a lot of beef sandwiches in Chicago (see Caputo, pg. 111, for more), and one thing they've all had in common is some historic giardiniera. It was obvious that our own beef sandwich had to have one, but in Montreal, it's super difficult to find a canned version that's not heavily oil-based. We went ahead and made our own vinegar-based version, keeping it on the subtle side so as not to compete against everything else going on, especially in the Caputo. Go ahead and try this recipe with different vegetables, so long as they're hearty enough to retain their crunch throughout the brine.

MAKES ABOUT 6 CUPS

Fermented Vegetables

1¼ cups (200 g) diced Spanish onion

2¼ cups (200 g) diced celery

1½ cups (150 g) cauliflower cut into tiny florets (same size as diced vegetables)

1 cup (140 g) diced red bell pepper

¼ teaspoon black peppercorns

¼ teaspoon coriander seeds

3% salt solution (see method for amount)

Fermented Chilies

3% salt solution (see method for amount)

6 chilies of choice (jalapeño, bird's eye, habanero, etc.)

Giardiniera

Fermented Vegetables

2 cups Pickled Eggplant (pg. 159)

3 to 6 Fermented Chilies, to taste

2 teaspoons dried Mexican oregano

White vinegar, for finishing

Neutral oil, for finishing

MAKE THE FERMENTED VEGETABLES

In a big bowl, combine the onion, celery, cauliflower, bell pepper, peppercorns, and coriander seeds, then use a funnel to distribute among wide-mouthed fermentation jars with airlock seals for burping.

Using a scale, weigh out enough water in a bowl to cover the vegetables. This is by eye; start with about one and a half times the total weight of the vegetables, about 5 cups (1200 ml). Don't worry if it might be too much; you can always remove it. Multiply the water weight by 0.03; this is the amount of salt you need in grams. Add that amount of salt to the water, whisking to dissolve. This is your 3% salt solution.

Distribute the salt solution among the jars so that the liquid covers the vegetables by 1 inch. Place something heavy on top of the vegetables, such as a tiny plate; push it down so that some of the liquid rises up and covers the plate, which will help weigh it down further (you could also try to do this with just a circle of parchment paper). Just make sure the vegetables stay submerged. Close the jars and leave to ferment in a cool, dark place for 8 to 14 days (depending on your room temperature).

MAKE THE FERMENTED CHILIES

Follow the same instructions for 3% salt solution and fermentation as laid out in the Fermented Vegetables method above, using the chilies instead of vegetables. (If you'd like, you can use a covered plastic container rather than fermentation jars.) If you have leftovers, you need to cook them soon or they'll continue to ferment. One cool thing you can do is blend them into a chili mush and use them like a spicy condiment.

MAKE THE GIARDINIERA

After 2 weeks, the liquid of the Fermented Vegetables should look a bit cloudy, like pickle juice. When in doubt, taste it. If it tastes fizzy or makes you sick, consult the internet. Remove the Fermented Vegetables from the liquid (reserving the liquid) and mix together with the Pickled Eggplant, Fermented Chilies, and oregano. Transfer all that into a very large jar (or a few small ones), sterilized if desired. Pour in the liquid from the Fermented Vegetables just until it covers everything, leaving about 1½ inches of space at the top of the jar. Stir in a sprinkling of vinegar (which stops the fermentation), then fill the jar ½ inch more with neutral oil and close or seal (there should be about 1 inch of empty space between the oil and the lid). If you've chosen to seal it, go lighter on the oil (¼ inch instead of ½ inch), as any vegetables that are in contact with the oil won't stay crunchy for long (this is inevitable, but by using less oil, less of the veg will soften over time). Sealed, it will last for a few years in a cool, dark place; closed (but not sealed), it will last for up to 3 months in the fridge.

PICKLED EGGPLANT

A: This was made for our Caputo (pg. 111), but there's a lot you can do with pickled eggplant: put it on a meat and cheese platter, use it as a sandwich condiment, dump it over potatoes and call it "loaded fries," or even wrap it in cheesecloth and wedge it under your mattress to ward off evil.

MAKES 6 CUPS

4 large eggplants, peeled and sliced into short strips

¼ cup (32 g) salt

1½ teaspoons granulated sugar

¾ cup (160 ml) neutral oil

2¼ teaspoons red wine vinegar

½ fresh Scotch bonnet chili, deseeded and sliced

Place the eggplant strips in a large nonreactive bowl. Sprinkle with the salt and sugar, and toss until evenly incorporated.

Place something heavy, like a plate, on top of the eggplant and press down. Let sit in the fridge overnight or up to 24 hours.

Working in batches, squeeze out as much liquid as possible from the eggplant. Alex recommends putting it into a small pillowcase, twisting it tightly closed, stepping outside, and swinging it around like a wild animal while the liquid sprays everywhere.

Transfer the eggplant to a sealable container, along with the oil, red wine vinegar, and Scotch bonnet. The eggplant should be fully submerged in the liquid and be light in color (if not, you probably messed up the cure). Cover, and let sit in the fridge for a couple days before consuming. It will last for up to 3 months. If making a larger batch, you can also jar it.

HOUSE TURKEY

R: This is our standard, deli-style turkey, reminiscent of the kind your mom put in your school sandwich (at least so I hear . . . my lunch was always some odd mélange of takeout leftovers). At the restaurant, we use a circulator to sous vide the turkey. If you have one, you can set it to 145°F and cook the turkey for three hours in a bag. It's not necessarily the better way, though; in general, the only time we believe in using a circulator is for making deli-style sandwich meats, but it's never a requirement. At home, using the slow roasting method may not result in a turkey as consistent in flavor as the sous vide version, but it'll be just as tasty.

MAKES 8.8 LB (4 KG)

12½ cups (3 L) cold water

1 cup (240 ml) water

1⅓ cups (170 g) salt

Packed ⅓ cup (70 g) light brown sugar

⅓ cup + 1 tablespoon (25 g) dried thyme

3½ tablespoons chili flakes

7 cloves garlic, minced

½ sweet onion, chopped

2 (4.4 lb/2 kg) boneless, skinless turkey breasts

Extra-virgin olive oil, for rubbing (optional)

Spice rub of choice, for rubbing (optional)

Fill a large container with the 12½ cups (3 L) cold water.

In a small saucepan, combine the 1 cup (240 ml) water with the salt and brown sugar. Bring to a boil to just dissolve the sugar. Remove from the heat and add the thyme, chili, garlic, and onion.

Pour the mixture into the large container with cold water. Add the turkey breasts and cover. Let sit in the fridge for 24 to 48 hours.

When ready to roast, preheat the oven to 250°F.

Remove the turkey breasts from the brine and pat dry. If desired, rub them with a bit of oil and cover with a spice rub of choice. Place in a roasting dish and roast for 2 to 2½ hours, until the internal temperature reaches 150°F. (For drier turkey, you can of course cook it for longer.) Remove from the oven and tent with aluminum foil. Let cool to room temperature, then tightly wrap each breast individually in plastic wrap and twist into a log-like shape. Leave in the fridge overnight.

The next day, slice the turkey to your desired thickness.

SMOKED SALMON & GRAVLAX

R: Arthurs isn't a full-blown deli, but when it came to Smoked Salmon, we knew we would be making ours in-house. Alex called up his best friend's little brother, a novice welder, to put together a smoker on a budget. With two old oil barrels, he built us a majestic smoker, which, after years of service, is now held together by aluminum foil.

Alex played around for weeks with salt and sugar ratios and smoking methods, eventually settling on this recipe. Compared to some other places, we cure the fish more lightly so that you can still taste the fish itself. The only downside is that it lasts a bit shorter than a stronger-cured fillet, but luckily our diners like it enough that we have to make it three times a week anyway. We still use our old oil barrel smoker, and she has treated us very kindly.

I also thought it would be good to give the option of Gravlax, which is for anyone who likes cured salmon without the smoky flavor. It's a tiny bit sweet and lends itself well to fresher, springtime dishes.

MAKES 1 (8 LB/3.5 KG) FILLET

Smoked Salmon

8 lb (3.5 kg) skin-on salmon fillet

4⅓ cups (1.3 kg) coarse salt[1]

3⅓ cups (665 g) granulated sugar

Packed 3 cups + 2 tablespoons (665 g) light brown sugar

2 teaspoons juniper berries

1½ teaspoons black peppercorns

Whole or chipped cherry, maple, and apple wood, for smoking[2]

Gravlax

3⅓ cups (330 g) peeled, shredded red beets

½ ruby red grapefruit, cut into 1-inch pieces

⅓ cup (80 ml) London dry gin

½ bunch fresh dill

MAKE THE SMOKED SALMON

Trim off any fatty, white pieces around the sides and surface of the fillet (you can use them for curing, candying, grilling, and more). On the wide end of the fillet, cut a small slit in the skin so the cure can penetrate through.

In a bowl, mix together all remaining ingredients, minus the wood; this mixture is the cure. Lay a generous piece of plastic wrap in the bottom of a large, shallow pan. Coat the plastic with a thin layer of the cure. Lay the fillet on top, skin side down. Blanket the flesh with the remaining cure so that none peeps through. Wrap the fillet with the plastic wrap.

Cover the pan and leave it in the fridge for about 36 hours, depending on the thickness of the salmon—if you are using a very thick fillet, leave for 48 hours; for a very thin fillet, such as the tail end, leave for only 12 hours (although we don't recommend the tail, as it doesn't contain much fat). It'll look about as appetizing as a Montreal street that's been salted after a snowstorm, but it will eventually taste a whole lot better.

continued ...

---

1 Do not use kosher salt for this. Coarse salt is necessary for curing because it dissolves slowly (plus it's cheaper). To get your product as close as possible to ours, use the same salt we do, Sifto No. 8, which has a pebble-like texture and size.

2 We recommend you don't use hickory, which is too smoky for this recipe.

Rinse off the cure with water, then pat dry. Place the fillet, skin side down, in a smoker. Cold-smoke for 2 to 3 hours with a mix of cherry, maple, and apple wood.[3] Transfer the salmon to a tray and let air-dry in the fridge for a few days before consuming (this is optional, but it intensifies the flavor and makes slicing easier).

MAKE THE GRAVLAX

Complete the Smoked Salmon recipe up until the fish has been blanketed with the cure.

Before wrapping with the plastic, blend the beets, grapefruit, gin, and dill in a blender until a smooth puree forms. Coat the salmon flesh with the mixture. Wrap the fillet with plastic wrap.

Cover the pan and leave it in the fridge for 48 hours. If you prefer a well-cured salmon, press it with something heavy as it cures.

Rinse off the cure with water, then pat dry. Transfer the salmon to a tray and let air-dry in the fridge for a few days (again, this is optional, but it intensifies the flavor and makes slicing easier).

SERVE

To serve either the Smoked Salmon or Gravlax, grab the longest and sharpest knife you can find. Position your knife at about a 45-degree angle. Using the whole length of the blade, slice the salmon crosswise as thinly as possible, transferring the slices to a plate as you go, and stopping when you hit the skin.

3 If you don't have a smoker, you could do this recipe with a smoke gun. Another option is to brush the salmon with a mix of molasses, coconut aminos, and liquid smoke, although most liquid smoke uses hickory and can be overpowering.

VIENS BEEF BACON

Everyone agrees that Phillip Viens is one of the best charcuterie guys in the city. We approached him at the start of Arthurs to find an alternative to pork bacon. (While we're definitely not a kosher restaurant, we do have a lot of loosely observing kosher and halal customers. For their peace of mind, we decided to keep a pork-free kitchen.) Phil had also just opened his storefront, Aliments Viens, where it was just him and about half an employee. In one night, he conjured up this 100% beef bacon for us, and we have yet to find another that comes close to comparison. It gives you all the textural variation you want from its pork counterpart, but tastes like the crispy bits of a steak. Start to finish, the process takes about one week but is surprisingly simple. If you're still intimidated whatsoever, no problem—go get it on St-Laurent from the man himself.

MAKES 50 TO 60 SLICES

Beef Bacon

10 cups (2.4 L) water

1⅔ cups (210 g) salt

1 tablespoon curing salt #1 (we use Prague Powder)

Packed ½ cup + 2 tablespoons (125 g) dark brown sugar

1⅔ tablespoons black peppercorns

1⅓ tablespoons chili flakes

2 lb (900 g) fat-on beef brisket flat, cut square (ask your friendly butcher to do this)

Spice Rub

¼ cup (15 g) coriander seeds

¼ cup (30 g) black peppercorns

Pure maple syrup, for serving

MAKE THE BEEF BACON

In a stainless-steel pot, combine all ingredients, minus the brisket. Boil until the salts and sugar have dissolved, about 3 minutes. Transfer the brine to a large airtight container or mason jars. Allow to cool slightly, then cover and refrigerate until completely chilled.

Place the brisket in a plastic or glass container large enough to hold the brine. Pour in the brine and submerge the brisket, using a weighted object, like a plate, to keep the meat fully submerged.

Leave the meat to brine in the fridge for 5 to 7 days, checking it periodically to ensure it remains submerged, and turning it over every second day. The thickness of your brisket determines the brining time: 1 to 1½ inches will be suitably brined in 5 days, and 2 inches will be closer to 7 days. If the cut is 3 or more inches, don't hesitate to leave it in a little longer. Once brined, the exterior of the meat will become slightly translucent, but there is no true way to know if the meat is fully ready until you cook it!

Lightly rinse the brisket under cold running water and pat dry. Discard the brine.

Transfer to a plate or nonreactive dish. Leave uncovered in the fridge overnight to rest and to allow the cure to settle throughout.

The next day, preheat the oven to 275°F.

continued . . .

Place the brisket in a casserole dish. Roast until the internal temperature of the meat registers 185°F, about 3 to 4 hours. The meat should look only slightly browned, with a few caramelized juices pearling on the surface.

Allow the meat to cool to room temperature before covering and refrigerating overnight to chill completely.

With the longest, sharpest knife you have, slice the cold meat as thinly as possible, using long, slow, deliberate, gentle sawing strokes. (The bacon we get from Viens is sliced less than 1⁄16 inch thick. It'll be hard for you to get it as thin and crispy as we do, but it will taste the same.) It will keep in an airtight container in the fridge for up to 3 weeks or in the freezer for up to 6 months.

MAKE THE SPICE RUB

Grind the coriander seeds and black peppercorns, preferably using a mortar and pestle. Store in an airtight container in the pantry for up to 3 months.

FRY THE BACON

When ready to fry, sprinkle the Spice Rub on both sides of the bacon slices. Place in a pan set over medium heat and fry until it reaches your desired crispiness. Serve with maple syrup on the side.

SCHMALTZ

A: Enough has been said about schmaltz, dubbed "liquid gold" for a reason. It is wildly unused in restaurants but unquestionably worth the money and effort. With a high smoke point, you can cook nearly anything in it, and it has this inimitable back note of caramelized onion chicken soup essence. We've found the best chicken fat from a kosher butcher, so that's a good place to start if you know one.

MAKES ABOUT 3 CUPS

2.2 lb (1 kg) chicken fat, cubed
Scant ½ cup (100 ml) water
2 large Spanish onions, diced

Place the chicken fat and water in a large pot and bring to a boil. Cook at a high simmer until all the chicken fat is rendered; the fat will liquefy, and any remaining bits will begin to fry.

Once the fat is amber and the chicken bits are crispy, add the onion. Cook until dark brown and crispy.

Strain out the crispy fat and onion (these bits, called gribenes, can be saved and used as crunchy toppings for a variety of dishes). Store the Schmaltz in a sealed container in the fridge for up to 3 months or in the freezer for up to 6 months. Use it in place of butter or oil to cook practically anything!

BAGEL CHIPS

Here's the perfect way to make sure your stale bagels don't end up in the trash. For the #KGMTL Salad (pg. 125) we only ask for a handful, but you'll wanna bake much more than that for snacking.

MAKES ANY AMOUNT

Stale bagels
Extra-virgin olive oil
Za'atar

Preheat the oven to 350°F.

Using a serrated knife, slice the bagels into rounds as thinly as possible. Spread the slices on a parchment-lined sheet tray. Drizzle them with a bit of oil, a pinch of salt, and a good amount of za'atar. Bake for 7 to 10 minutes, depending on the thickness of your slices, until golden brown. Stir halfway through to ensure even browning. Store in an airtight container for a long time; if they get stale, just quickly re-crisp them in the oven at a low temperature.

schmear:

from the Yiddish *shmirn*, meaning "to grease, smear"

SCHMEARS

A: When I envision schmear, it looks a lot like a Magnolia Bakery pudding. By all appearances, it should seem as if its components have been hastily layered into a pan, then scooped and spread directly onto your bagel. Every bite should look and taste a little different from the last—some more cream cheesy, some more sweet, some more chunky, and so on. You could be practical and stir in your add-ins, which would get you a totally fine schmear, but I find that layering the ingredients makes it much more exciting to eat.

Some ideas to get you started:

- Strawberry jam and jalapeño jelly
- Blueberry jam with a candied dukkah topping
- Caramelized onion (see Gravlax Sandwich, pg. 102)

Hell, you can even make cake or buttered popcorn schmear. Ever since the world thought it was okay to turn a perfectly good bagel into a fucking rainbow, apparently anything is possible!

nosh

from the Yiddish *nashn,* meaning "to nibble" or "to snack,"
taken from the Middle High German *nashchen,* in certain
contexts meaning to consume sweets in hiding

To be read with a Seussian rhythm

We're noshers by nature.
We're noshers by nurture.
When do we nosh?
We're happy you asked:
When we're hungry
          Hormonal
             Hungover
                Heartbroken
Or anything else a mere human can be.
What do we nosh?
Flip through this book, and surely you'll see.

Our daughter Freya
Will surely be sneaking
Salami with syrup and sweets on the sly.
Our baby Abel
Is bound to be taking
Big bites of beef bacon or Boston cream pie.

You can nosh with your hands,
With a fork or a knife,
You can chow chicken liver
Or chew on malt fries.
Whatever your nosh is,
Half-eaten or whole,
The world is less hangry and bellies are full.

From sprinkle cookies to coleslaw,

almost anything in our restaurant, and in this book, could be called a nosh. For the sake of organization, we've narrowed down "nosh" to comprise savory snacks, like latkes, chicken liver toast, malt vinegar fries, and schnitzel. The best kind of nosh can be eaten with your hands, but we equally value more substantial ones, like lobster pierogies. Although, if you're as ruthless as Alex, you can find a way to eat anything with your hands.

The only thing a nosh really needs to do is satisfy you. And if your idea of satisfaction is to smash together scrambled eggs, guac, fries, tuna salad, waffles, caper mayo, and pickled chilies, your nosh is probably disgusting, but still valid. Unless you order something deconstructed—in which case, fuck off—we're not gonna turn you down. Your nosh is your nosh. Who are we to tell you otherwise?

GRAVLAX PLATE

R: I created this dish for a friend working at our neighboring bakery, Rustique. My intention was to make a light, pretty, market-fresh plate on a whim. It's a joy to assemble and has ended up being one of the few dishes that hasn't budged since it hit the menu.

SERVES 1

1 generous tablespoon brunoised green apple

1 tablespoon brunoised yellow or Chioggia beet

1 teaspoon brunoised French shallot

3 tablespoons extra-virgin olive oil

1 teaspoon freshly squeezed lemon juice

½ teaspoon caviar

½ teaspoon mustard seeds

4 slices (about 3½ oz/100 g total) Gravlax (pg. 163)

14% sour cream, for topping

3 cherry tomatoes, halved

1 small pinch fresh dill

1 big pinch sprouts (sunflower, pea shoots, etc.)

Red Wine Vinaigrette (pg. 217)

1 slice black Russian bread or bread of choice, toasted and buttered, for serving

In a small bowl, combine the apples, beets, and shallots, and toss with the olive oil and lemon juice. Season with salt and black pepper, then gently stir in the caviar and mustard seeds. This is your Gravlax "dressing."

To assemble, drape the Gravlax on your serving plate. Season with salt. Generously spoon on the dressing. There should be enough that it coats the entire plate and makes it glisten.

Drop six baby dollops of sour cream around the plate. Top each dollop with a cherry tomato half, and season each one with salt. Scatter the dill over everything.

Lightly coat the sprouts with the Red Wine Vinaigrette. Scatter them over the plate without concealing the other components, so that the fish peeks through.

Serve with the bread.

Latkes

A: When we were first conceiving the Arthurs menu, we knew the latke, a staple in any Jewish restaurant and at most Hanukkah feasts, had to be on it. As Raegan and I weren't raised eating them (my Hanukkah latke was a Spanish omelet), finding our perfect recipe required research. With meager funds, we ate our way through every latke joint in New York, Toronto, and Montreal. A select few, like Russ & Daughters, made me realize that we had to take this seriously.

Anyone can make a good latke at home, but a restaurant complicates everything. It is the single most ongoing item on our menu; we've gone through about 20 recipes and 100 methods. Unlike the home cook, we have to make 200 to 800 latkes at a time, as it's impossible to know how busy we'll be on any given day.

Most places that care strongly about their latkes have a designated staff and station for them. Let me tell you, that was not, and likely never will be, in our budget. When we were still a new restaurant, we didn't know how to handle the demand. To get enough latkes prepped before service, my staff and I would start working at 4 a.m. Twice during service, we would pause all orders and clear the flat-tops and stovetops just to fry latkes. The potato took precedence over all.

Since then, we've learned to prebake and deep-fry our latkes in manageable quantities throughout service. Here, we instruct you to individually fry each latke in a skillet, which we would still do if we had the means.

Feel free to riff on this recipe, but riff with prudence. If your base is off, you will inevitably find yourself in a pickle. And yes, you can add pickles to latkes.

I could write you a novella on the latke. Here are just a few things to consider:

Oxygen: To avoid a gross, gray-black latke, fry your latkes immediately after shaping. Lemon juice, citric acid, or onion juice help but alter the final taste. If you want to prep the potatoes in advance, grate, cook, dry, freeze, and strain them before using.

Starch: Let your grated potatoes sit in water for at least 15 minutes, enough time for the starch to settle to the bottom of the bowl, before using. Then dispose of the water and mix the starch into the potatoes. This way, your latkes retain the crispiness and flavor that come from the starch, but not its excess moisture.

Time & Smell: The bigger the batch of latkes you have to fry, the longer their intense, oniony odor will reside in your home. If making a large quantity, you can bake the latkes for 20 to 25 minutes, then reverse-sear them for only about 2 minutes per side. But either way, expect your kitchen to stink.

Gluten: Our gluten of choice is matzo meal because it has a toasted flavor and, compared to all-purpose flour, leaves less room for error. Saltines, Ritz, and almost any other dry cracker would be a good replacement. For a gluten-free latke, you can remove the matzo entirely and have a fine result, or play around with various flours.

Flavor: Whatever you add to a latke—be it zucchini, jalapeños, apples, cheese, or pickles—be wary of water content. Consider pre-salting the ingredient to draw out as much moisture as possible (but also consider the saltiness of the ingredient and reduce the seasoning of the actual latkes accordingly). You may also need to add additional matzo meal.

LATKES

MAKES 15 LATKES

2.4 lb (1.1 kg) peeled russet potatoes

1 (about 8 oz/225 g) Spanish onion

2 eggs, yolks + whites separated, at room temperature

¼ cup + 2 tablespoons (40 g) matzo meal (preferably Streit's)

3¾ teaspoons salt

Clarified butter and/or Schmaltz (pg. 169), for frying

14% sour cream, for serving

Roasted Applesauce (pg. 216), for serving

Chives, finely sliced, for serving

Freshly grated horseradish, for serving

Roughly grate the potatoes into a bowl filled with cold water. The water will slow oxidation and help with crispiness later on. Set aside while you grate the onion into a separate bowl.

Remove the grated potato from the water with your hands and transfer to the bowl with the grated onion. Reserve the water.

Working in batches, use your hands, a cheesecloth, or a kitchen towel to squeeze the potato and onion together, removing as much liquid as possible. Discard the liquid and transfer the strained potato and onion to a clean bowl as you go.

By now, the starch will have settled in the bowl with the potato water. Carefully pour out the water; you'll clearly see the starch remaining at the bottom.

To the bowl with the wrung potato and onion, add the reserved starch, egg yolks, matzo meal, and salt. Mix together until well combined.

In a separate bowl, using a handheld or stand mixer, whip the egg whites to semi-stiff peaks. Do NOT overwhip—once you hit soft peaks, whip for an extra 5 to 10 seconds, then stop. Delicately fold them into the potato mixture.

Fill a large cast-iron or nonstick skillet about ¼ inch deep with clarified butter and/or Schmaltz. Set over medium-high heat.

Once the fat is hot, use a ⅓-cup measurement or #10 (3¼ oz) cookie scoop to scoop the batter in a mound-like shape into the pan. Repeat, working in batches to prevent crowding. Lower the heat to medium. Using a spatula, lightly flatten each mound. Generously salt the side facing up. Fry until golden brown, about 3 to 5 minutes, then flip each latke and salt the other side.[1] Each side of the latke should be a deep golden brown.[2]

Place the latkes on a paper towel–lined plate to absorb excess fat, then transfer to a wire rack set over a sheet tray.

To serve the Arthurs way, top the latkes with a dollop each of sour cream and applesauce, a sprinkling of chives, and some freshly grated horseradish.

---

1 If you add the salt before frying, it may create a puddle of water on your latkes.

2 If preparing a large number of latkes in advance, you can keep them warm on a wire rack in an oven at low heat for a maximum of 1 hour.

MALT VINEGAR FRIES

R: I link malt vinegar to long winter days I spent outside skating and skiing as a kid, ending with a vinegar-soaked brown paper bag of fries. Later in life, I picked up a similar snack habit after my shifts at Joe Beef, heading across the street to Burgundy Lion for a pint and a basket of their house potato chips sprayed with vinegar.

You need to set aside a good chunk of time to make these fries, but the complexity pays off, especially if you have a tabletop fryer. They're roughly based on Heston Blumenthal's triple-cooked chip technique: boil, freeze, fry, freeze, and fry again. Every step contributes to their glass-like quality, transparent when held to the light and shattering to reveal a creamy interior when bitten into.

SERVES 4 TO 6

25 cups (6 L) water

⅓ cup + 2 tablespoons (60 g) salt

¼ cup + 2 tablespoons (75 g) granulated sugar[1]

⅓ cup (80 ml) white vinegar

1 teaspoon black peppercorns (optional)

1 handful fresh parsley stems (optional)

4 cloves garlic, crushed (optional)

5 lb (2.3 kg) russet potatoes, peeled

Neutral oil, for frying

Malt vinegar, for finishing

PARBOIL THE FRIES

In a large pot, combine the water, salt, sugar, white vinegar, peppercorns, parsley, and garlic. Bring to a boil.

Meanwhile, cut the potatoes lengthwise into ⅓-inch rounds, then cut each round into ⅓-inch batons, transferring them to a bowl of cold water as you go so they don't oxidize.

Once the pot of water is boiling, use a spider to remove the solids (you could also put them all into the water in a cheesecloth first for easier removal). Prepare two sheet trays with a wire rack set on top of each.

Add the potatoes to the boiling water and cook for 5 minutes at a low boil, until the potatoes are just starting to bend and look slightly translucent and veined when held up to the light.[2] Work in batches if necessary to avoid crowding the pot. Using a spider, transfer the potatoes to the racks, separating them out as much as possible to cool and air-dry.

DO THE FIRST FRY

Fill a large heavy-bottomed pot halfway with neutral oil (do not fill it any higher, unless you like hot oil in your face). Set over medium heat and bring the oil to 400°F.

Working in batches to avoid crowding the fries or overflowing the pot, fry the potatoes for 45 seconds to 1 minute, making sure they don't darken in color. The exterior of the fry should

continued . . .

---

1 If you live in an area with sweeter russet potatoes, you may be able to lower the sugar amount, or omit entirely.

2 Check frequently for doneness. The larger your batch of fries, the longer the cook time will be.

still be firm. Transfer the fries back to the racks, spreading them out evenly. Between batches, return the oil to 400°F.

Allow the fries to cool to room temperature, then cover and freeze overnight on the sheet trays.[3] Strain the oil and set aside for reuse.

DO THE SECOND FRY

When ready to finish the fries, fill a large heavy-bottomed pot halfway with neutral oil, and heat it to 350°F. Prepare a sheet tray lined with paper towels. Working in small batches, drop the fries into the oil straight from the freezer.[4] Begin with a small quantity, as the frozen fries will cause the oil to bubble intensely. Fry the potatoes for 4 to 6 minutes, until golden brown. Using a spider, transfer the fries to the prepared tray. Between batches, return the oil to 350°F.

Transfer the fries to a large bowl and toss with a small amount of salt and malt vinegar while they're still hot. Serve with Fried Egg Aioli (pg. 219) or put them in a tuna sandwich.

---

[3] From this point, the fries will keep, covered, in the freezer for up to 3 months.

[4] This is very important! If the fries are thawed, they will not become crispy.

PIEROGIES

A: For the longest time, I really only ate pierogies when I was sick and would ask Raegan to pick up the frozen grocery-store variety, along with packets of Lipton instant chicken noodle soup to boil them in. I recall gaining about 40 pounds during that period (in truth, I ate this even in perfectly good health). That all changed one evening at Impasto in Little Italy. They served me a gnudi dough folded like a steamed bun, stuffed with something slightly sweet, and drizzled with a very light cream sauce. The dish left such an impression on me that I still remembered it three years afterward, when we opened Arthurs. I went to every pierogi joint in the city to come up with my own recipe, and ended up with this: a cross between a pierogi, gnocchi, and gnudi dough that is filled with a classic mix of potato and cheese. Sephardic Jews eat a Passover charoset of dates, spices, and nuts, so we also added a dose of date puree as a nod to that. The great thing about pierogies, and really any dumplings, is that they can be stuffed and dressed however you want, with all kinds of meats, vegetables, cheeses, and more. Here, we do it a little on the fancy side, with lobster and a summer corn sauce.

Perogies are labor-intensive, but this makes them an ideal project to try with your kids. Not with ours, though; I tried this with our daughter and it was a fucking disaster, albeit a fun one. Make the dough, filling, and date puree one day, and then just assemble them the next. They freeze well, so you might as well make the full batch.

MAKES 40 PIEROGIES

Pierogi Dough

1½ lb (700 g) Yukon gold potatoes (to yield 1.1 lb/500 g cooked)

2¼ cups (500 g) 70% moisture ricotta

3 cups (250 g) grated parmesan

4 egg yolks

1 egg white

Zest of ½ lemon

1 tablespoon salt

2⅓ cups (325 g) flour

MAKE THE PIEROGI DOUGH

Bring a large pot of water to a boil and salt it heavily. Peel the potatoes and add both the potatoes and skins to the boiling water.[1] Cook the potatoes until a knife inserts easily into them.

Discard the water and peels. Let the potatoes dry and cool to room temperature. Pass the potatoes through a ricer into a large bowl.

In a medium bowl, mix together the ricotta, parmesan, egg yolks and white, lemon zest, and salt. Fold in the riced potatoes.

Sift the flour over the mixture, then gently fold it in, being careful not to overmix. Feel it out, adding more flour as needed, until the dough is tacky (but not sticky) and holds together.

Form the dough into two rectangles and wrap in plastic wrap. Let rest in the fridge overnight.

continued . . .

---

1 The peels are added for enhanced flavor, but you can leave them out if desired.

Potato Filling

14 oz (400 g) peeled Yukon gold potatoes

½ cup + 2 tablespoons (135 ml) whole milk

3 tablespoons butter

Heaping ⅓ cup (70 g) shredded aged cheddar

1 teaspoon salt

Date Puree

10 large, plump (about 8 oz/225 g total) Medjool dates, pitted[2]

1 cinnamon stick

1 teaspoon salt

1 pinch freshly grated nutmeg

4 tablespoons (56 g) butter, cubed, at room temperature

2 teaspoons freshly squeezed lemon juice

Assembly

Clarified butter, for searing

14% sour cream, for serving

Date Puree, for serving

Chives, finely chopped, for serving

Mimolette (preferably aged 1 year), for serving

Caviar (optional), for serving

---

2 Don't use the old, super-dried-out dates you found in the back of your cupboard. They'll turn the puree gritty and dry.

MAKE THE POTATO FILLING

Bring a large pot of water to a boil and salt it heavily. Cook the potatoes until a knife inserts easily into them.

Meanwhile, in a large saucepan, gently warm the milk and butter until the butter is melted.

Once the potatoes are cooked, remove them from the water and pass them through a ricer into the saucepan with the milk and butter. Stir until the potatoes have warmed through. Remove from the heat and fold in the cheese until melted. Season with the salt and some black pepper to taste. Set aside to cool.

Once cooled, transfer the mixture to a piping bag for easier assembly.

MAKE THE DATE PUREE

Place the dates in a small pot with the cinnamon stick. Fill with just enough water to cover the dates three-quarters of the way. Bring to a boil, then immediately remove from the heat. Cover the pot and let steam for 5 to 10 minutes.

Discard the cinnamon stick, then transfer the dates and water to a food processor. Add the salt, nutmeg, and half of the butter. Blend until all the butter has been incorporated. Add the remaining butter and the lemon juice and blend once more.

If there are still date skins in the puree, pass it through a fine sieve to get it extra smooth.

ASSEMBLE

Bring a large pot of water to a boil and salt it.

Meanwhile, lightly flour a clean work surface. Roll out one rectangle of the chilled Pierogi Dough to ⅕-inch thick. Using a 3-inch ring mold or round object, cut out circles of dough (each one should be about 1 oz/30 g). Gather and reroll the scraps until all the dough is used (but don't do this too many times or it will become tough).

Squeeze 1 tablespoon Potato Filling into the middle of each round, leaving a ¾-inch border around the perimeter (you can use a spoon, but piping is neater).

Close the pierogies by hand, folding them in half and crimping the edges shut. Transfer to a lightly floured sheet tray. Repeat with the second rectangle of dough. At this point, you can freeze the pierogies if desired for up to 3 months (you can boil

continued . . .

them directly from frozen, but don't cook and then freeze them, as there will be too much water in the dough).

Drop the pierogies into the boiling water, working in batches to avoid overcrowding the pot. They are done when they float to the top.[1]

Use a spider to remove the cooked pierogies from the water, and transfer them to an ice bath then to a paper towel–lined plate.

Slick a skillet with clarified butter and place it over medium-high heat. Working in batches, sear the pierogies on one side until you're sure they're golden brown, then flip and remove the pan from the heat. If you flip too early, the pierogies will stick to the pan and tear.

To plate, grab a bowl and schmear it with a generous amount of sour cream and a small dollop of the Date Puree. Add the pierogies to the bowl and finish with finely chopped chives, grated Mimolette, and cracked black pepper. If you wanna get fancy, I guess you could put a fucking dollop of caviar on top.

Summer Corn Pierogies with Lobster

40 PIEROGIES

Pierogies, cooked and seared

Summer Corn Sauce

2 small cobs corn

2 cups (480 ml) heavy cream

Cloves of ½ head garlic, peeled

1 teaspoon granulated sugar (optional)

Clarified butter, for cooking

¼ yellow onion, thinly sliced

Lobster

8 oz (225 g) cooked, shucked lobster (see Lobster Sandwich, pg. 105)

Extra-virgin olive oil, for serving (optional)

Lemon, for serving (optional)

MAKE THE SUMMER CORN SAUCE

Remove the kernels from the corn and set aside. Chop the cobs into quarters.

Place the cobs, cream and garlic in a small saucepan. The cream should fully cover the cobs. Bring to a boil, then lower to a simmer. Reduce by one-third, until the garlic is very soft; if it's not soft enough, keep cooking, adding more cream as necessary to compensate. Remove the cobs and season the sauce with salt. Blend with an immersion blender until smooth. Set aside and keep warm.

Bring a small pot of water to a boil and salt it. Briefly cook the corn kernels until al dente. If your corn isn't very sweet, add a bit of sugar to the water. Strain and set aside.

continued . . .

1 If you want a softer pierogi, you can skip the pan-frying and plate them now.

Add a knob of clarified butter to a small pan set over medium-high heat. Fry the onion until the edges are a very dark golden brown. If there is any remaining clarified butter in the pan, pour it out and set aside for serving.

Stir the cooked corn kernels and onion into the warm sauce.

ADD THE LOBSTER & ASSEMBLE

Once the pierogies are ready to be plated, stir the lobster into the cream—you don't want the lobster to sit so long in the sauce that it infuses too much of its flavor.

Plate the pierogies as instructed on pg. 188. Finish the lobster sauce with a drizzle of the reserved clarified butter and spoon the sauce on top of everything. Alternatively, add the sauce to the same pan as the seared pierogies and simmer for 1 minute before plating. Another option is to serve the lobster how Alex prefers it: cold, sitting on top of the sauce, with a bit of olive oil, lemon juice, salt, and black pepper.

BAVARIAN POTATO SALAD

A: During our "engagement trip" around Asia, Raegan and I had a brief layover in Frankfurt. Like the good tourists we were, we ate sausages and potato salad in an airport restaurant. It wasn't the most epiphanic meal of our travels, but it was the first time I had eaten a potato salad without mayo. When I got home and needed to throw together a side for our grand opening, I remembered that salad, and I found out about a related one from Bavaria. It's chunkier than the American version and creamy in a lighter way, thanks to the absence of mayo and the addition of warm broth. Normally it doesn't have bacon, but we needed a way to use up leftover bits and this became our way of doing it. You can eat the assembled salad as is, but if you're a crispy person like Raegan, we strongly suggest you sear it.

SERVES 6 TO 8 AS A SIDE

5 lb (2.3 kg) Yukon gold potatoes, skin on

1 cup (160 g) finely diced red onion

About 10 slices (8 oz/225 g total) Viens Beef Bacon (pg. 167) or bacon of choice

2 tablespoons finely chopped fresh parsley

1 teaspoon dried dill

1 teaspoon dried parsley

2 teaspoons granulated sugar

Scant ½ cup (100 ml) red wine vinegar

¾ cup (180 ml) unsalted vegetable stock or Chicken Soup Stock (see Matzo Ball Soup, pg. 135), hot

Clarified butter, for frying

Maldon salt, to taste

Yellow mustard, for serving

Schnitzel Plate (pg. 197), for serving (optional)

Place the potatoes in a large pot and add enough water to submerge them by at least 1 inch. Bring the water to a boil, then season generously with salt. Boil the potatoes until a knife inserts easily into them. When they're just cool enough to handle, peel them to release some steam, then chop into large chunks; they should be big enough so that they're not completely reduced to mush by the end of the recipe. Set aside.

Meanwhile, bring a small pot of water to a boil and salt it. Blanch the red onion for 1 minute. Drain and set aside. Do NOT skip this step or the whole thing will taste like raw onions the next day.

Cook the bacon in a pan until crispy. Place on a paper towel–lined plate to absorb excess fat. Let cool, then finely chop.

In a large bowl, combine the potatoes, red onion, bacon bits, fresh and dried herbs, and sugar. Mix together vigorously with a wooden spoon until the mixture is well combined but still chunky. There should be a combination of mashed and intact potato pieces. Stir in the vinegar and hot stock. Season with salt and black pepper. Let cool and sit overnight or for at least 30 minutes.[1]

Set a large cast-iron skillet over medium-high heat and coat it with clarified butter. Using a ⅓-cup measurement or large ice-cream scoop, scoop the potato salad into the skillet in rounds, working in batches to avoid crowding the pan. After about 3 minutes, flip the mixture and continue frying until both sides are a deep golden brown. Add more clarified butter to the pan as needed.

Sprinkle with a pinch of Maldon and cracked black pepper. Serve warm or cold with some yellow mustard and the Schnitzel Plate.

---

[1] At this point, the salad could be eaten as is, but we like the added crispiness of pan-frying.

SCHNITZEL

A: A lot goes into crafting an exceptional schnitzel. Each step contributes to the attainment of a perfectly crunchy, golden crust. Since our schnitzel needs to withstand the weight of the McArthur (pg. 94), we went with a sturdier version of the delicate German schnitzel, which is typically characterized by a small air pocket between the chicken and the crust. For extra structure and durability, we closed that pocket and made a scraggly crust that wouldn't break when cut into. To accomplish this, we made a breading of three components performing three separate tasks: matzo meal for toasty flavor, breadcrumbs for crunch, and potato flakes for airiness and potato chip essence. But to tell you the truth, you can follow our method to a T and end up with a subpar schnitzel if you do not adequately season your components. When it comes to fried chicken, there is nothing more important than salt. Say it with me—*there is nothing more important than salt.*

MAKES 4 PIECES

Seasoning

4 medium (about 2.2 lb/1 kg total) boneless, skinless chicken breasts, butterflied[1]

Garlic powder

Granulated sugar

Buttermilk Marinade

2 cups (480 ml) buttermilk

1 cup + 2 tablespoons (250 g) full-fat yogurt

2 tablespoons steak spice

1 tablespoon salt

1 tablespoon grated yellow onion

1 clove garlic, grated

1 teaspoon sesame oil

SEASON THE CHICKEN

Season both sides of the butterflied chicken with a generous amount of salt, some garlic powder, and a touch of sugar (in a ratio of 12:4:1). Cover with a sheet of parchment paper. Pound the chicken to ¼ to ½ inch thick.

MARINATE THE CHICKEN

Combine all marinade ingredients. Place the chicken in a plastic bag or covered container and pour in the marinade. Evenly coat the chicken in it, then place in the fridge overnight or for at least 4 hours.

BREAD THE CHICKEN

Set up your assembly line: mix together the Spiced Flour ingredients in one large, shallow dish; whisk together the Egg Wash ingredients in another; and combine the Breading ingredients in another.

Remove the chicken from the marinade and brush it against the side of the container to remove the excess. Very lightly dredge each breast in the Spiced Flour and shake/pat off as much excess as possible. Let sit for 5 minutes to ensure the flour sticks to the chicken.

continued . . .

---

1 If making this for the McArthur (pg. 94), halve the butterflied chicken and use one half-breast per sandwich (so this recipe would make enough for eight sandwiches).

Spiced Flour[2]

2 cups (280 g) flour

2 tablespoons onion powder

1⅔ tablespoons ground mace

1 tablespoon garlic powder

1½ teaspoons salt

1¼ teaspoons sweet paprika

¾ teaspoon cayenne

Egg Wash

8 egg whites[3]

2 tablespoons cornstarch

¼ teaspoon salt

1 generous pinch black pepper

Breading

2 cups (172 g) potato flakes

2 cups (224 g) breadcrumbs

½ cup (73 g) matzo meal
   (preferably Streit's)

½ teaspoon salt

Frying & Finishing

Neutral oil, for frying

Schmaltz or clarified butter, for
   frying

Creamy honey, for finishing

Zhug Sauce (pg. 209), for
   finishing

Lemon wedges, for serving

Next, dunk each breast in the Egg Wash, checking that each crevice is coated. Let the chicken sit in the Egg Wash for 10 to 30 seconds. This ensures that the Spiced Flour has time to combine with the egg so that the breading won't absorb all of it. It's hard to explain, but this is basically how we avoid forming an air pocket between the chicken and the crust.

Lastly, lay each breast into the breading. Scoop the breading onto the exposed part of the chicken. Using your hands, scrunch up the chicken, almost as if you're crumpling paper. Flip and rotate the chicken 90 degrees. Repeat the breading and scrunching process. This method creates crevices and ridges to which the breading will adhere and become ultra-crispy when fried. You've done it properly if the chicken looks like Badwater Basin.

FRY THE SCHNITZEL

Fill a large cast-iron skillet with enough fat to submerge the chicken halfway (we like a mix of 80% neutral oil and 20% Schmaltz or clarified butter). Heat the fat over medium-high until it reaches 350°F, or quick bubbles form around the end of a wooden spoon. Place one to two pieces of chicken in the skillet, facing away from you. Lower the heat to medium. Fry for 3 to 5 minutes, then flip and generously season the exposed side with salt. Fry for another 3 to 5 minutes, then transfer to a paper towel–lined plate or sheet tray and season the other side. Remember that salt is the most important part, so don't be stingy with it! The Schnitzel should be fractured, like a Montreal sidewalk, with varying shades of light to dark golden brown. Repeat with the remaining chicken breasts, adding more oil as needed.[4]

Let the chicken rest for 5 minutes before serving. After resting, the internal temperature should be around 165°F. Drizzle the chicken with creamy honey and schmear with Zhug Sauce. Serve with lemon wedges.

---

[2] If you plan to make the Spiced Flour in advance, be sure to remix it right before using.

[3] We've tried it with whole eggs and yolks and, for reasons I can't explain, the whites work best. In conjunction with the cornstarch, the whites help the crust maintain crunch, even once other ingredients are added. It's also a good way to use up leftover whites in your fridge.

[4] If you wish to deep-fry, heat the oil in a large pot to 350°F. When you add the chicken, do so slowly, lowering it into the oil in a waving motion away from you. The waving gets you crispier edges.

SCHNITZEL PLATE

A: The very first day we opened, the one fryer we had refused to work. We resorted to pan-frying all our schnitzel and latkes, which could have been only a minor pain in the ass had all our burners been working properly, but of course they were not. In that moment, it made no sense to go through the hassle only to put the schnitzel on a plate with some honey and sprouts. So I came up with a quick Smashed Cucumber Salad to serve it with on the spot, inspired by the one from *This Is Camino*. By the end of the week, we also had a Thai Basil Wedge Salad and a Szechuan Cabbage Slaw, plus a Bavarian Potato Salad to go with all three. The beautiful thing about this plate is that every variation works in every season, and none of them over-whelms the signature lemon-honey-zhug flavoring of the schnitzel itself.

SERVES 1

1 piece Schnitzel (pg. 193), hot

1 lemon wedge, for squeezing

Creamy honey, for drizzling

Zhug Sauce (pg. 209), for
    schmearing

Bavarian Potato Salad, hot
    (pg. 191)

Fried capers, for garnish

Chives, finely chopped, for
    garnish

For Serving

Szechuan Cabbage, Thai Basil
    Wedge Salad, or Smashed
    Cucumber Salad (recipes
    below)

Grated horseradish (optional)

Place the Schnitzel on a plate and drizzle it with a squeeze of lemon juice and the honey, then schmear with Zhug Sauce. Add a scoop of Bavarian Potato Salad on the side, then top every-thing with the fried capers and chives.

In the winter, serve with hot Szechuan Cabbage. In the summer, serve with grated horseradish and either the Thai Basil Wedge Salad or Smashed Cucumber Salad.

Szechuan Cabbage

SERVES 4

1 medium head (2.2 lb/1 kg) red
    cabbage, chopped in 1-inch
    cubes

1 medium head (2.2 lb/1 kg)
    white cabbage, chopped in
    1-inch cubes

3 tablespoons salt

⅓ cup (80 ml) neutral oil

Rinse the red cabbage in a strainer until the water runs clear. Place the red cabbage in one large bowl and the white cabbage in another. Divide the salt between the two bowls and mix to distribute. Let cure for 1 hour, then rinse both cabbages sepa-rately. If you want, you can cure the cabbages together, but the colors will bleed.

Heat a couple glugs of the neutral oil in a Dutch oven set over medium heat.

continued . . .

¼ cup (60 ml) apple cider
    vinegar

¼ cup (60 ml) Chinese vinegar

Scant ¼ cup (50 ml) Chinese
    rice wine

Packed 1 tablespoon light
    brown sugar

1½ teaspoons Maggi Liquid
    Seasoning

1½ teaspoons sesame oil

⅓ cup (75 ml) Chicken Soup
    Stock (see Matzo Ball
    Soup, pg. 135)

1-inch piece peeled ginger,
    finely grated

3 cloves garlic, finely grated

7 dried Tien Tsin chilies[1]

1 teaspoon Szechuan
    peppercorns

Meanwhile, in a small bowl, whisk together the remaining neutral oil, apple cider vinegar, Chinese vinegar, rice wine, brown sugar, Maggi seasoning, sesame oil, and chicken stock.

Sauté the ginger and garlic in the Dutch oven until aromatic. Add the chilies and Szechuan peppercorns and cook until fragrant. Stir in the cabbage and season with salt, then add about half of the oil mixture. Bring to a boil, then cook on high until done to your liking. Continue adding the oil mixture as you see fit; this is meant to be on the oilier side, but if you prefer less, that's fine. Remove the cabbage with a spider and taste the broth. If you find it needs more flavor, continue reducing until it tastes good to you.

Smashed Cucumber Salad

SERVES 4

6 Lebanese cucumbers

7 to 8 fresh leaves anise hyssop

¾ bunch fresh cilantro

3 fresh leaves sorrel

1 tablespoon chopped Pickled
    Red Chilies (pg. 152)

½ clove garlic, minced

Lemon wedge, for squeezing

Lime wedge, for squeezing

Red Wine Vinaigrette (pg. 217),
    for finishing

3 tablespoons toasted,
    chopped almonds

High-quality extra-virgin olive oil,
    for finishing

Honey or mirin, for finishing
    (optional)

Rub the cucumbers with salt, then lay them on a cutting board. Whack them with the palm of your hand to break them up, then tear them into pieces. Transfer to a bowl.

Tear up the anise hop and cilantro. Twist the sorrel leaves to break them up, then thinly slice. Transfer the herbs to the same bowl as the cucumbers. Add the chilies, garlic, and a squeeze of the citrus juices. Finish with a small splash of Red Wine Vinaigrette and the almonds. Toss everything together and season with salt and black pepper to taste, then drizzle on the olive oil. If not serving with the Schnitzel Plate, drizzle with a tad of honey or mirin.

1 These are those little red chilies that you can find in bulk at any Asian grocery store.

Thai Basil Wedge Salad

SERVES 4

Buffalo Sauce

1½ cups (360 ml) Frank's RedHot

1½ teaspoons pickle juice

½ teaspoon honey

½ cup + 2 tablespoons (136 g) butter, cubed

Ranch

2.8 oz (80 g) Bulgarian feta

1¾ cups (400 g) full-fat yogurt

¾ cup House Mayo (pg. 218)

½ cup + ⅓ cup (200 ml) evaporated milk or buttermilk

1½ tablespoons freshly squeezed lemon juice

2 teaspoons Ranch Powder (see Creamy Coleslaw, pg. 150)

2 teaspoons mustard powder

¼ teaspoon granulated garlic

Pinch dried dill

Pinch onion flakes

Assembly

¼ cup (6 to 8 slices) chopped Marinated Breakfast Salami (pg. 34) or bacon of choice

3 to 4 Lebanese cucumbers

3 to 4 leaves fresh Thai basil, torn

3 to 4 leaves fresh mint, torn

Lemon, for squeezing

Ranch

1 head iceberg lettuce, quartered

Red Wine Vinaigrette (pg. 217), for splashing

Extra-virgin olive oil, for splashing

Buffalo Sauce

Otto's Dill Pickles (pg. 155), for serving (optional)

MAKE THE BUFFALO SAUCE

In a small saucepan, bring the Frank's to a boil and simmer until reduced by almost half.[1] Stir in the pickle juice and honey. Remove the pot from the heat and gradually stir in the butter until fully combined. Let cool to room temperature, then cover and leave in the fridge overnight. Store any leftovers in an airtight container in the fridge for up to 1 month.

MAKE THE RANCH

In a bowl, use a spatula to stir together the feta with a scant ½ cup (100 g) of the yogurt until well combined. Mix in the remaining yogurt and all remaining ingredients (if you have a baby or toddler at the ready, get them to do the pinch of dried dill and onion flakes by grabbing a fistful). Salt to taste. Store leftovers in an airtight container in the fridge for 1 to 2 weeks.

ASSEMBLE

Fry the salami in a small pan until nice and crispy. Set aside to cool.

Smash the cucumbers, using the same method as for the Smashed Cucumber Salad (pg. 198). Place them in a bowl, then stir in the herbs, a squeeze of lemon juice, and a bit of salt. Add to the Ranch and stir to combine.

Lightly season the iceberg with salt and black pepper, opening up the leaves to ensure each layer of leaves is seasoned (or at least the top, middle, and bottom ones). Splash the layers with Red Wine Vinaigrette and a bit of olive oil.

Drizzle the Buffalo Sauce and Ranch over the iceberg. Top with the crispy salami or bacon. If desired, throw in a few slices of Otto's Dill Pickles or some bread-and-butter ones.

---

[1] If you accidently over-reduced and find that it tastes too salty by the end, gently reheat the sauce, add water as needed, then re-emulsify with a bit of butter.

NOSHVILLE CHICKEN

A: The rub, marinade, dredge, and frying of this hot chicken all come from tons of research and testing (and reading J. Kenji López-Alt). I looked at fried chicken from literally every U.S. state, as well as various Asian styles, and played around with all sorts of flours before settling on plain old all-purpose and cornstarch. Lucky for you, it's also the easiest to replicate from the pantry, even if it does still take at least 12 to 24 hours to complete.

MAKES 10 TO 12 PIECES

Nosh Dry Brine

1½ teaspoons black peppercorns

¼ cup + 3 tablespoons (50 g) white peppercorns

¼ cup + 2 tablespoons (50 g) sweet paprika

¼ cup + 1 tablespoon (10 g) dried oregano

Scant ¼ cup (30 g) salt

2½ tablespoons dried thyme

2½ tablespoons dried basil

2½ tablespoons mustard powder

1½ tablespoons granulated garlic

1½ tablespoons ground ginger

1½ tablespoons chicken broth powder

1 to 2 tablespoons granulated sugar

Chicken

10 to 12 boneless, skin-on chicken thighs

Buttermilk Marinade

2 cups (480 ml) buttermilk

½ cup + ⅓ cup (200 ml) pickle juice

2 eggs

MAKE THE NOSH DRY BRINE

In a spice grinder or mortar and pestle, grind the peppercorns. Transfer them to a bowl and mix in all remaining ingredients, minus the sugar. Combine 1 cup (130 g) of the spice mix with 1 tablespoon sugar (adding the remaining tablespoon if you like a sweeter flavor). Set aside the rest of the spice mix for later in the recipe.

Rub each chicken thigh all over with roughly 2 tablespoons of the spice-sugar mix. Cover with plastic wrap and leave in the fridge for 6 to 12 hours.[1]

MAKE THE BUTTERMILK MARINADE

Combine all ingredients in a bowl. Place the brined chicken in a shallow baking dish or large plastic bag. Pour enough marinade onto the chicken so that each piece is completely covered, setting aside 3 tablespoons for the Dredge. Cover the dish or seal the bag and leave in the fridge for another 6 to 12 hours.

MAKE THE NOSH DREDGE

Combine all ingredients, except the Buttermilk Marinade, in a large, shallow dish. Drizzle in the Buttermilk Marinade and toss it together until cornflake-looking clumps form in some places.

Shake off any excess marinade from the chicken, then lay each piece in the dredge. Thoroughly scrunch the flour into every crevice of the chicken, using the same method as for Schnitzel (see "Bread the Chicken," pg. 193).

---

1 If brining for the shorter amount of time, add a bit more salt to compensate.

1 tablespoon vodka

1 large bay leaf, crushed

1 cup + 2 tablespoons (250 g) pressed whole milk yogurt

Scant ½ cup (60 g) grated Spanish onion

2 teaspoons Crystal or Louisiana hot sauce

1 large clove garlic, grated

Nosh Dredge

4 cups + 2 tablespoons (577 g) flour

1 cup + 3 tablespoons (190 g) cornstarch

4¼ teaspoons baking powder

3⅓ tablespoons roasted soy-bean powder (optional)[2]

1 tablespoon Nosh Dry Brine

3 tablespoons reserved Buttermilk Marinade

Frying

Neutral oil, for frying

Ground dry spaghetti sauce mix, for finishing (optional)[3]

Nosh Sauce (pg. 213), for serving (optional)

FRY THE CHICKEN

Fill a large cast-iron skillet with enough neutral oil to submerge the chicken halfway. Heat the oil over medium-high until it reaches 325°F, or quick bubbles form around the end of a wooden spoon.

Working in batches, fry the chicken until it's deeply golden and has an internal temperature of 165°F, about 5 to 8 minutes, flipping halfway through. Place on a paper towel–lined sheet tray to absorb excess oil. Lightly season with the dry spaghetti mix. (Depending on the salt content of the mix, you may need to add a bit of salt as well.) Between batches, bring the oil back up to temperature.

Brush with Nosh Sauce (pg. 213), if desired.

---

2 Roasted soybean powder is more for looks; it helps the crust look golden without overcooking the chicken. It also adds a subtle nutty flavor, but you don't need to go out of your way to buy it.

3 You can find this at the grocery store; it's just a mix of spices that happens to work really well with fried chicken. Casse-croûtes often use it to enhance the flavor of their spaghetti sauce, like how you'd use powdered poutine mix.

CHICKEN LIVER SPREAD

A: Chicken liver was always done on the chunky side in my home. It was lightly sweetened and looked like whoever made it had chewed up a bunch of liver and spat it into a bowl. In terms of taste, though, it was great, and I've liked liver ever since. Each time Raegan and I went to Schwartz's, which was a lot in our dating period, I didn't order smoked meat—I ordered steak with a slice of liver and a hot dog.

The style of chicken liver here is a cross between the textured one of my childhood and the buttery one found in French-inspired Montreal restaurants. Sadly, our clientele has not shared my enthusiasm for liver. Save for myself and the same 10 senior citizens who ordered it every week, no one mourned its removal from the menu. It's a real shame. You can eat it with Schnitzel (pg. 193), with Fluffy Egg Salad (pg. 148), or cold with a side of warm peas. Just don't eat it raw, like those kids on TikTok!

Well, shit. Maybe it's true that only old people like liver.

MAKES 1 TO 2 CUPS

7½ oz (215 g) chicken livers, deveined

Whole milk, for soaking

1 medium French shallot, finely diced

¼ cup (56 g) butter, at room temperature

2 large cloves garlic, minced

2 tablespoons ruby port

2 tablespoons dry Madeira

¾ teaspoon sherry vinegar

1 tablespoon Schmaltz (pg. 169), at room temperature + more for drizzling

Sprinkle of smoked or regular Maldon salt, for finishing

Place the livers in a shallow dish, cover them in milk, and let sit for 20 minutes. This will remove some of their bitterness and blood.

Place the livers on a sheet tray lined with paper towel and pat dry. Season with salt and black pepper.

In a pan set over medium-low heat, sauté the shallots in 1 tablespoon of the butter until golden, but not browned. When the shallots are about halfway done, add the garlic. Deglaze the pan with 1 tablespoon each of the port and Madeira, watching carefully to avoid overbrowning.

Remove the shallots and garlic, set them aside, and wipe out the pan. Raise the heat to medium-high and add another tablespoon of butter. Working in batches if necessary, sear the livers on both sides until the exterior is browned but the interior is still pink.[1] Transfer to a plate and discard any blood that is released. (If working in batches, divide the tablespoon of butter between them so as not to add extra butter.) Deglaze the pan with the remaining port and Madeira.

Transfer the contents of the pan to a food processor, along with the shallots, garlic, liver, sherry vinegar, and Schmaltz. Pulse until the mixture is slightly chunky, gradually adding the remaining 2 tablespoons butter. If you like it very chunky like Alex, smash everything on a cutting board with a fork instead. Or, if you like it extra smooth, pulse until a mousse forms, then strain through a fine-mesh strainer. Season with salt and black pepper to taste.

---

1 Browning the livers is more important than preserving a pink interior. If your livers are smaller, for example, and you can't brown them without browning the insides, that's perfectly fine.

Place the liver spread in a bowl and cover with plastic wrap so that it makes contact with the surface (this prevents a yucky skin from forming). You can pour a layer of melted Schmaltz over top, but only do this if you plan on eating it on something warm, like toast, because the congealed fat is kind of gross. Refrigerate until cold. [2]

Finish with a light flurry of Maldon and a crack of black pepper, if desired. If you made the chunky version, we recommend you eat it warm. Serve with a smorgasbord of crackers, rye bread, browned or fried onions, jam, and radishes.[3]

[2] The liver will turn gray the next day, but this is no reason to worry; most restaurants keep theirs pink with nitrates.

[3] For a crazy delicious dinner, use an immersion blender to incorporate leftover liver into nearly any warm sauce (an idea I owe to Leigh Roper, a much better chef than I am).

KARNATZEL IN A BLANKET

R: This isn't a recipe so much as an idea, which is basically just fun pigs in a blanket. If you don't already have a karnatzel dealer's number saved, you can find a hookup at your local Jewish deli. You could be a douche and make your own puff pastry, or you could save your time and go buy it at the store. In total, you should only be spending about 15 minutes putting this together for your kids and/or your next Jewish aperitivo.

MAKES 24 BITES

1 package puff pastry (about 14 oz/400 g)

1 egg, for brushing

2 extra-long karnatzel

Sesame seeds or topping of choice (like steak spice, everything bagel seasoning, etc.)

Hot Honey Mustard (pg. 215), for serving

Preheat the oven to 450°F.

Roll out the puff pastry and slice it lengthwise into three strips. Cut each strip into eight isosceles triangles, like slices of pizza. They should be about 5 inches long, with a base of 1½ inches.

In a small bowl, whisk the egg and brush it on the entire surface of the triangles. Line a sheet tray with parchment paper.

Cut the karnatzel into 24 (2½-inch) pieces. Place one piece on the base end of each triangle and roll it up. Repeat with the remaining karnatzel, transferring to the prepared sheet tray as you go. Brush the tops with the egg and scatter with sesame seeds or whatever you desire.

Bake according to the directions on your puff pastry box, until puffed and golden. We baked ours for about 15 minutes. Serve with Hot Honey Mustard.

THE GREAT SAUCE

A: # What makes a sauce a sauce?

As in, what is the definition of the word? We can't figure it out. Schmears (pg. 171) are not in this chapter, but then isn't a schmear more of a spread than a sauce? But is a spread not a sauce? If you can swipe mayo on a piece of bread and call it a "special sauce," then why can't you say the same of flavored cream cheese on a bagel?

CONUNDRUM

Is it a matter of consistency? Roasted Applesauce (pg. 216) is a spoonable sauce, which we could just as easily call baby food. Then is all baby food sauce? And is soup just spoonable sauce? Zhug Adom (pg. 209) is a solid that forms the base of a paste that only formally becomes sort-of sauce when you add a fat or liquid. Not sure if that's relevant.

Maybe it's about *how* you use it. If I heat up garlic, fat, and salt, it's a sauce. If I leave it cold and throw it over a salad, now it's a dressing (and therefore not in this chapter). But have we made a grave mistake? Is a dressing actually a cold sauce? What if I leave the warm sauce out for too long and it's at room temp the next day? Has it then evolved, or *de*volved, into a vinaigrette? Or if I don't eat my ice cream fast enough and it melts, is it a cold sauce? How about if I pour it over a brownie? None of this seems right.

Are you still reading? Are you lost in the saucy spirals of an existential crisis? Congratulations. We have no answers for you.

R: Dear god. This is all insane. Everything falls under the sauce umbrella. End of story.

Whatever you define sauce as, Alex is phenomenal at making them. He goes through all his own research, testing, and techniques to reach the pinnacle of sauce-making, combining methods and flavors from various cuisines. His Nosh Sauce (pg. 213), for example, is mainly inspired by the American South but also includes schmaltz and South American chilies. He may resent me for saying this, but they truly don't call him the Sauce Boss for nothing!

A: That's the first time I've ever heard you say such nice things about me—thank you, but next time say it to me in person. It's true that I hate the nickname Sauce Boss; I'd really rather you just call me The Boss. Eh, you'd never do that.

Roasted apple sauce

Zhug

Salsa

Amba

Nosh sauce

Schmaltz

Habanero hot sauce

Bear's BBQ sauce

House Mayo

ZHUG

A: Zhug is one of the many ways that we incorporate the heat of the Middle East into Ashkenazi dishes. Originally from Yemen, zhug is now a recognized element of Israeli cuisine. It comes in two main forms: zhug adom and zhug sauce. The former is red, pasty, and spicy, while the latter is green, loose, and chimichurri-esque. I consider it as more of a spiced, rather than a spicy, condiment. Regardless, it's become known as Arthurs' staple house "hot" sauce, used in sandwiches, avo toasts, and more (it makes a fantastic meat marinade as well). Plus, my wife hates it, which is reason enough to keep it on the menu.

MAKES 1½ CUPS

Zhug Adom

½ teaspoon salt

¼ cup (28 g) chili flakes

4¼ teaspoons cumin seeds, toasted[1]

1½ teaspoons coriander seeds, toasted

1 teaspoon black peppercorns, toasted

½ teaspoon cardamom seeds[2]

½ teaspoon whole cloves (optional)

6 cloves garlic

½ bunch (1.8 oz/50 g) fresh cilantro, ends trimmed

¼ bunch (1 oz/30 g) fresh parsley, ends trimmed

Zhug Sauce

Zhug Adom

About 4 large (6 oz/170 g) jalapeños, deseeded

½ bunch (1.8 oz/50 g) fresh cilantro, ends trimmed

7 cloves garlic

¼ teaspoon ground cumin (preferably toasted whole then ground)

¼ teaspoon salt

¼ cup (60 ml) extra-virgin olive oil

MAKE THE ZHUG ADOM

Grind together the salt and all spices in a spice grinder or mortar and pestle.

Transfer to a food processor and add the remaining ingredients. Pulse until the ingredients are very finely chopped and everything holds together. If not making the Zhug Sauce immediately, store in an airtight container in the fridge for up to 3 weeks.

MAKE THE ZHUG SAUCE

Add all ingredients to the food processor with the Zhug Adom and pulse until it reaches a spreadable, chimichurri-like consistency. Adjust salt to taste.

For a more liquid sauce, add a little more olive oil (as we do for the Avo Toast, pg. 42) or water and adjust the salt. Store in an airtight container in the fridge for up to 1 week; after that, it will start to brown (it's still good, just not as pretty).

---

1 If you only have ground spices on hand, begin with one-third of all spice quantities listed here, then increase according to taste.

2 You can use de-podded seeds to cut down on prep, but their flavor will be less pungent (don't increase the quantity, though).

AMBA

A: I've always been fascinated by finding ways to merge Indian cooking techniques with Middle Eastern and Israeli flavors; naturally, I was attracted to amba. Like Zhug (pg. 209), there are a million versions of it. (Amba was brought from India to Iraq by Baghdadi Jews, then taken to Israel during the Zionist movement.) It's a fermented, tangy sauce that pairs well with other condiments. Two of my preferred ways to use it are by drizzling it over roasted endives or mixing it into homemade mustard to make a honey mustard–esque condiment.

An alternative recipe is to replace a little under half of the ripe mango with fermented papaya. Yet another option is to fully ferment, rather than simply cure, the mango for up to two weeks. This longer fermentation would probably make the amba better, but we've gone the shorter route to minimize prep time and the chances of messing up.

MAKES 2 CUPS

1 unripe mango

1 ripe mango

1 Scotch bonnet chili or habanero, deseeded + deveined

3⅓ cups (800 ml) water

½ cup (120 ml) apple cider vinegar

1⅓ tablespoons harissa

1 tablespoon light brown sugar

1 teaspoon fenugreek seeds, ground

1 teaspoon mustard seeds

½ teaspoon chili flakes

¼ teaspoon ground cumin (preferably toasted whole then ground)

⅛ teaspoon ground turmeric

Peel, pit, and chop the mangoes. Place them with the Scotch bonnet chili in a strainer set over a bowl. Sprinkle with salt and let sit overnight, or for up to 2 days, to cure. Be sure to leave them in a warm spot where the sun can reach them. Drain and discard the liquid.

In a large pot, combine the water with all remaining ingredients. Bring to a boil and remove from the heat to cool.

Once cooled, stir in the mangoes and chili. Cover and let sit in the fridge overnight. This gives the flavors time to mingle and meld.

Blend the mixture in a blender until smooth. Transfer to a medium saucepan, bring to a simmer, and reduce by one-third. Taste and adjust the seasoning as needed. Store in an airtight container in the fridge for up to 3 weeks or in the freezer for up to 3 months; if it splits after being defrosted, simply reblend it.

SALSA

A: I think something about my Moroccan-ness has given me an adoration for Mexican food. If you look from a distance, the celebratory dinner tables of these cultures' cuisines are almost indifferentiable, as if they were set in the same home. Both have a rich array of braised meats, warmly spiced stews, grains, salsas, purees, fresh herbs, and an abundance of vegetables—makes sense, given the long history of culinary exchange between the Ottoman Empire and South and Central Americas. Today, many aspects of Latin American cuisine resemble those of their North African and Middle Eastern counterparts; if we consider C-letter spices alone, they share at least cumin, coriander, cloves, and cinnamon.

I wanted to come up with a salsa made in the "proper" way, with a calculated balance of chilies and vegetables seared on cast iron (or a plancha, if you have one). While we don't use a mortar and pestle for the sake of ease, we encourage you to do so (just boil your chilies after toasting them so they get soft). I'm making a big deal of it, but in the end this is really just a basic ranchero salsa.

MAKES 2 CUPS

5 Roma tomatoes

½ jalapeño

Neutral oil, for drizzling + cooking

½ large sweet or white onion, skin on, halved

3 large cloves garlic, skin on

2 morita chilies

2 chile de árbol

1 chipotle chili

1 New Mexico chili

2 tablespoons apple cider vinegar

⅛ teaspoon chicken broth powder

Granulated sugar, to taste[1]

Freshly squeezed lime juice, to taste

Fresh cilantro, finely chopped, to taste

Place the tomatoes and jalapeño in a bowl and lightly drizzle with the oil, then lightly sprinkle with salt. This will help draw out some of their juices after they've been seared.

Place a layer of aluminum foil in a cast-iron skillet set over medium-high heat. Working in batches if necessary, sear the tomatoes on all sides until browned all over and blackened in some spots. They should be very soft. Remove and set aside.

Sear the jalapeño, onion, and garlic on all sides. They should be slightly tender on the inside and blackened in spots. Watch closely to prevent burning, as the ingredients will be finished at different times. Set everything aside to cool.

Add all dried chilies to the hot pan, then immediately lower the heat to prevent burning. Sear for 30 seconds to 1 minute on each side, depending on the size of the chili. Transfer the chilies to a small saucepan, then cover with just enough water to barely submerge them. Bring to a boil, then remove from the heat and cover. Let sit for a few minutes to slightly rehydrate.

Peel the onion and garlic. Devein and deseed the jalapeño and discard the stem.

continued . . .

---

1 You want just enough sugar to bring out the sweetness of the tomatoes. This will depend on the ripeness and seasonality of your tomatoes.

Place the rehydrated chilies in a blender. Blend until pureed, adding a seared tomato and its juices as necessary to help the blending along. Gradually add all the charred ingredients, using a combination of pulsing and blending until thick and slightly chunky. Take your time to make sure you don't overblend. Alternatively, you could do this with a mortar and pestle or mol-cajete, beginning in the same way and slowly adding the charred ingredients until the salsa is a coarse consistency.

Set a skillet over medium-high heat and add a splash of oil. Once the oil is hot, slowly pour in the salsa. It should sizzle and bubble. Lower the heat and simmer until reduced by 10%, about 15 minutes. Remove from the heat and season with the apple cider vinegar, the chicken broth powder, and some sugar and salt.[2]

Right before serving, stir in the lime juice and cilantro to taste. Store in an airtight container in the fridge for up to 1 week or in the freezer for up to 3 months.

ALMOND BUTTAH DRIZZLE

R: This sweet and savory, addictive drizzle pairs extra well with our Papaya Salad (pg. 123), but it's good to have around at all times, especially when grilled chicken thighs and spring rolls are on the table. Be sure to use fresh lime juice.

MAKES 1 CUP

½ cup (175 g) almond butter

¼ cup (60 ml) freshly squeezed lime juice

Scant ¼ cup (75 g) pure maple syrup

Scant ¼ cup (50 ml) water

2 cloves garlic

1½-inch piece (½ oz/15 g) peeled ginger

1⅔ tablespoons soy sauce or tamari

1 teaspoon sesame oil

Place all ingredients in a blender and blend until completely smooth. It should be quite watery, as it will firm up as it sits in the fridge.

---

2 Wait for the salsa to cool down before retasting and adjusting the salt and vinegar. You should, however, perfect the sugar while the salsa is hot so it can dissolve.

NOSH SAUCE

A: Seeing as our Noshville Chicken (pg. 200) is dubbed after one of the spiciest varieties of fried chicken varieties you can encounter, its accompanying sauce obviously isn't allowed to be subtle. This is a HOT hot sauce, and I refuse to tell you exactly how to tone it down.

This is also a fat-based sauce, which means that it won't turn the chicken crust soggy. Schmaltz, already chicken-based, is the natural fat choice, but you can use 100% butter or oil for a vegan and shelf-stable version. After the sauce is made and reheated for the chicken, it will split—this is intentional! When you brush it on the chicken, most of the crust will absorb the fat component, which keeps it crispy for longer, while other spots will absorb the liquid component, which is where the sauce's tangy-sweet flavor can come through.

It's cheesy to say, but this sauce is very dear to me, and I have yet to find a way to bottle it. If anyone figures it out, send me a sample!

MAKES 2 CUPS

Habanero Hot Sauce

2⅓ cups (170 g) destemmed and halved fresh habanero or Scotch bonnet chilies

Neutral oil, for cooking

1¼ cups (200 g) diced Spanish onion

3 cloves garlic, chopped

5 cherry tomatoes

½ cup (75 g) diced carrot

2 teaspoons salt

Scant ½ cup (100 ml) water

1 green onion, whites only, cut into 1-inch pieces

¼ cup (60 g) yellow mustard

1½ tablespoons light brown sugar

¼ cup (60 ml) white vinegar

Nosh Sauce

7 dried habanero chilies, destemmed, or 1½ teaspoons ground habanero

MAKE THE HABANERO HOT SAUCE

Deseed the habaneros according to heat preference. We like to deseed half, but deseed all for a milder sauce.

In a large heavy-bottomed pot or Dutch oven, heat two glugs of neutral oil over medium-low heat. Sweat the onion and garlic, stirring regularly, until lightly golden. Add the cherry tomatoes, carrots, salt, and water. Cover the pot and cook until the carrots are soft.

Add the habaneros, green onion, mustard, sugar, and vinegar. Stir to combine, then cover and cook for about 10 minutes over low heat, stirring occasionally to prevent sticking.

Transfer to a blender and blend until very smooth; because it's hot, leave the top open and place a rag over top, holding it in place with your hand and gradually increasing the speed from low. Store in an airtight container for up to 2 weeks in the fridge or up to 3 months in the freezer.

MAKE THE NOSH SAUCE

In a spice grinder or mortar and pestle, blitz the dried habanero and Tien Tsin chilies until they are dust. Transfer to a small bowl and add the cayenne, garlic powder, and black pepper.

Place in a medium saucepan set over medium heat, along with the Schmaltz and butter. When the mixture starts to bubble, lower the heat and cook for 5 minutes, watching carefully and

continued ...

5 dried Tien Tsin chilies (see note 1, pg. 198) or chile de árbol[1]

2 tablespoons cayenne

2 teaspoons garlic powder

1 teaspoon black peppercorns, ground

½ cup + 1 tablespoon (125 g) Schmaltz (pg. 169)

½ cup + 1 tablespoon (129 g) butter

Packed 1 tablespoon dark brown sugar

½ cup (120 ml) Frank's RedHot

2 tablespoons pickle juice

½ cup (120 ml) Habanero Hot Sauce

stirring often to avoid burning the spices. Turn off the heat and stir in the brown sugar to dissolve. Transfer to a large bowl and let cool for 20 minutes.

With an immersion blender or whisk, gradually mix in the Frank's hot sauce and pickle juice, then the scotch bonnet sauce. Store in an airtight container in the fridge for up to 2 weeks or in the freezer for up to 3 months.

If making Noshville Chicken (pg. 200), return the sauce to the heat and keep it hot at a very low simmer. It will separate, but this is what we want.

---

1 At the restaurant, we also include dried habanero powder. If you have it, replace 1 Tien Tsin/ chile de árbol with a pinch of it.

BEAR'S BBQ SAUCE

Not every recipe needs some joke or fable introducing it. This is simply an amazing BBQ sauce that goes well with everything, and especially well with our roast beef sandwich (pg. 117). It requires about 5 minutes of prep time and 30 minutes of cook time, meaning you can pull it off by the time your ribs, pulled pork, beef sandwich, or whatever you're serving it on is ready.

MAKES 4 CUPS

1 medium dry ancho chili, destemmed and deseeded

1 tablespoon black peppercorns

1 tablespoon coriander seeds

4 cups (768 g) ketchup

Neutral oil, for cooking

1⅓ tablespoons mustard powder

1¼ teaspoons cayenne

1 yellow onion, finely diced

3 medium French shallots, finely diced

8 cloves garlic, minced

Packed ½ cup + 1½ table-spoons (125 g) dark brown sugar

3⅓ tablespoons Worcestershire

In a small saucepan, dry-toast the ancho, peppercorns, and coriander seeds over medium heat, watching carefully to avoid burning. Remove the peppercorns and coriander, and grind them.

Cover the ancho halfway with water (use at least ½ cup water; you'll need it in a few minutes). Bring to a boil, then remove from the heat, cover, and let steep for 5 minutes. Transfer the ancho and ½ cup of its steeping water to a deep container. Add half of the ketchup, and blend with an immersion blender.

In a large pot, heat a splash of oil over medium heat. Add the toasted spices, mustard powder, and cayenne. Toast until bubbling. Stir in the onion, shallots, and garlic and cook until soft and lightly colored. Add the brown sugar and bring to a slight bubble, then add the Worcestershire, ancho-ketchup mix, and remaining ketchup. Simmer for 15 to 30 minutes, until you reach your desired consistency. Store in an airtight container in the fridge for up to 1 month or in the freezer for up to 3 months.

HOT HONEY MUSTARD

A: Sad to say, but to make an exceptional honey mustard, you must start off by making mustard from scratch; using store-bought just won't get you the ideal thickness. Yes, it'll take a bit more time, but there's nothing technically difficult about it. Plus the base lasts for ages, so you can put off making the actual honey mustard for as long as you want. Another thing to be aware of is that this specific recipe was made to be paired with the already-sweet Bear's BBQ Sauce (pg. 214) in the Bear's Roast Beef sandwich (pg. 117). This means that it's a bit less sweet than it should be, so add more sugar to the base and more honey at the end if you want a truer honey mustard. Or, for a non-hot mustard, replace the spicy mustard powder with regular.

The final, most important note I can give you is to not taste anything until the finished product has sat for 24 hours because, until then, it tastes like toxic waste. But who am I kidding? Now you're probably more curious than ever. Go ahead. Like I say, you should always try everything once. Especially acid.

MAKES 1 CUP

Base[1]

Heaping ⅓ cup (40 g) mustard powder

Heaping ⅓ cup (40 g) spicy mustard powder (preferably Keen's)

⅓ cup (80 ml) apple cider vinegar

2 tablespoons dark brown sugar

1 tablespoon honey

⅓ teaspoon salt

¼ teaspoon granulated garlic

⅛ teaspoon onion powder

Hot Honey Mustard

3½ tablespoons dark brown sugar

2 tablespoons water[2]

2½ tablespoons white vinegar

2 teaspoons apple cider vinegar

¾ teaspoon salt

Scant ¼ cup Base

3 tablespoons neutral oil

MAKE THE BASE

In a large bowl, stir together all ingredients. Cover and let sit at room temperature for 24 to 48 hours. Store in an airtight container in the fridge for up to 6 months.

MAKE THE HOT HONEY MUSTARD

In a small saucepan, combine the sugar, water, vinegars, and salt. Heat over low heat until the sugar is dissolved, then whisk the mixture into the Base. Let cool to room temperature, then gradually whisk in the oil as you would for a mayo. Store in an airtight container in the fridge for up to 6 months.

---

1 This makes about double what you need for the full recipe. This way, you have some extra to play around with the consistency of the final product. It also keeps for an extremely long time.

2 If you'd like a more spreadable honey mustard, reduce the water and vinegar quantities.

ROASTED APPLESAUCE

This applesauce is super velvety thanks to butter and super pink thanks to the unpeeled apples. If you want to get the rose color extra vibrant, leave the foil on for the whole roasting time to avoid browning. And if you'd like to explore more possibilities, there are many ways to turn this sauce into something fancy, such as caramelizing the apples whole, adding chilies, whipping the end product with butter and sugar, and so forth. If you're making a large quantity, you could even reserve the cores, cover them with water and some sugar, and make a jelly, or use them for homemade apple cider vinegar (just google it). Take this recipe as a universal base sauce and do what you will with it.

MAKES 2 CUPS

2 tablespoons cubed butter

1½ lb (700 g) Cortland apples, cored and quartered

2 tablespoons granulated sugar

2 tablespoons apple cider vinegar

Preheat the oven to 325°F.

Break the butter up into small bits. Add it to a large bowl, along with all remaining ingredients, and stir to combine. Transfer to a deep roasting dish, sized so that the apples are layered on top of each other. Cover tightly with aluminum foil and bake for 15 to 20 minutes, stirring halfway through, until the apples are soft.

Remove the foil and continue baking for 10 minutes to darken the top layer of apples.

Let cool until warm, then blend until smooth. If desired, strain out any remaining bits of apple skin. Store in an airtight container in the fridge for up to 3 months.

SAVORY TAHINI SAUCE

A: This sauce is one of the most versatile recipes in the book. To name just a few ideas, you can drizzle it over fish, meat, and veg; add it to a salad; and stir it into thick yogurt to form a tangy dip. Tahini texture and taste can vary significantly from brand to brand, so shop around to find the best one your wallet allows (we love Almazara). Don't forget to mix up the tahini very, very well before using, stirring from bottom to top. It'll take more effort than you'd like, sort of like churning cement, but you've gotta do it well to get all the flavor. You could get intense and make your own tahini, but we'll leave that decision to you.

MAKES 1 CUP

⅓ teaspoon cumin seeds

⅓ teaspoon caraway seeds

¾ cup (180 ml) freshly squeezed lemon juice + more as needed

In a small skillet, dry-toast the spices until fragrant. Let cool, then coarsely grind with a spice grinder or mortar and pestle. Transfer to a bowl.

Add in the lemon juice and all the garlic. Use an immersion blender to blend thoroughly. Let sit for 10 minutes to allow the

1 clove garlic

1 teaspoon roasted garlic (see Harissa Mayo, pg. 219) (optional)

½ cup (120 ml) ice water

½ cup (125 g) high-quality tahini

1 teaspoon salt

1 teaspoon extra-virgin olive oil

flavors to infuse—all you want is the essence (sorry, douchebag word) of the garlic and spices, plus the garlic will start to ferment if you leave it in for too long. Pass through a fine-mesh strainer and discard the solids.

Meanwhile, prepare the ice water. Place the tahini in a bowl. Drizzle in one-third of the ice water and whisk. The tahini should stiffen up significantly. Pour in the strained lemon juice and keep whisking until smooth. Gradually add more ice water until you reach your desired consistency; ideally, the sauce should coat the back of a spoon.

Stir in the salt and olive oil for some extra smoothness. Taste and adjust lemon and salt to your liking. Cover and leave in the fridge for a few hours before using. It will keep for a maximum of 3 to 5 days. Give it the ol' whiff if you're not sure.

VINAIGRETTES

These vinaigrettes are a pantry must. Store them in a squeeze bottle at room temperature (they solidify in the fridge) and throw them over any fresh dish lacking acidity.

Red Wine Vinaigrette

MAKES 1¼ CUPS

1 cup (240 ml) extra-virgin olive oil

¼ cup (60 ml) red wine vinegar

1 teaspoon water (to make the vinegar less sharp)

Pour all ingredients in a bottle and shake it up. Store at room temperature until the day you die.

White Balsamic Vinaigrette

MAKES 1½ CUPS

½ cup + 2 tablespoons (150 ml) white balsamic vinegar

¾ cup + 2 tablespoons (210 ml) extra-virgin olive oil

2 tablespoons water

1 generous teaspoon white vinegar

⅓ teaspoon salt

Follow the above method for Red Wine Vinaigrette.

HOUSE MAYO

A: While you can always buy mayonnaise, nothing compares to homemade. (That is, unless you're making a BLT. I can't explain it, but store-bought is better then.) A well-executed mayo is velvety and unctuous in texture, rich and lightly acidic in taste, and smooth and cream-colored in appearance. As you'll see, it's much easier to do than people think. This recipe provides the foundation for any desired mix-ins but is also superb as is, eaten with a solid batch of fries (like the ones on pg. 183).

MAKES 2¼ CUPS

3 egg yolks

1½ tablespoons Dijon

2 cups (480 ml) neutral oil[1]

1½ tablespoons freshly squeezed lemon juice

1½ teaspoons white vinegar

1½ teaspoons red wine vinegar

1½ teaspoons salt

---

1 Alternatively, you can substitute 50% of the neutral oil for avocado or extra-virgin olive oil. Any more than that, however, and the flavor of the oil will be too apparent.

In a large bowl, whisk together the yolks and Dijon. Whisking constantly and vigorously, very slowly stream in the oil until emulsified.

Whisk in the lemon juice, vinegars, and salt. To loosen and whiten the mayo, add a tablespoon of warm water. If your mayo is jiggly, whisk in a bit more water until smooth. Season with black pepper, if desired. Store in an airtight container in the fridge for up to 4 days.

VARIATIONS

Caper Mayo

MAKES 1 CUP

⅓ cup (60 g) capers, drained

Neutral oil, for frying

1 cup House Mayo (recipe above)

Pat the capers dry with a paper towel.

Heat a generous amount of neutral oil in a small pan set over medium-high heat. Add the capers and lower the heat to medium. Fry until darkened but not burnt, about 5 to 7 minutes.

Once the capers have cooled, lightly crush them with a fork. Stir the crushed capers into the mayo. Store in an airtight container in the fridge for up to 4 days.

Harissa Mayo

MAKES 1 CUP

1 head garlic

Extra-virgin olive oil, for roasting

1½ to 3⅓ tablespoons harissa[1]

1 cup House Mayo (recipe opposite)

Preheat the oven to 350°F.

Cut the little root nub off the garlic. Rub the head all over with a bit of olive oil and salt, then wrap in aluminum foil. Roast for 15 minutes, until tender and golden. Let cool, then squeeze the head of garlic from the top so that all the cloves pop out from the root end.

Transfer half the cloves to a bowl and mash them to a paste with a fork. (Reserve the remaining cloves for future cooking, like the Fried Egg Aioli below.)

In a small bowl, mix together the roasted garlic with the harissa. Whisk the mixture into the mayo, then taste and add more harissa if you want it spicier. Store in an airtight container in the fridge for up to 4 days.

Zhug Mayo

MAKES 1 CUP

1 to 2 teaspoons Zhug Sauce (pg. 209)

1 cup House Mayo (recipe opposite)

In a bowl, whisk together the Zhug Sauce and mayo until combined. Taste and add more Zhug Sauce, according to your spice preference. Store in an airtight container in the fridge for up to 4 days.

Fried Egg Aioli

MAKES 2 CUPS

1 small Yukon gold potato[2]

1 teaspoon white vinegar

1 hard-fried egg[3] (pg. 29)

2 cups House Mayo (recipe opposite)

Cloves of ½ head roasted garlic (see Harissa Mayo, recipe above)

1 clove garlic, minced

Boil the potato in cold, salted water until fork-tender. Let cool slightly, then peel. Drizzle with the vinegar, then roughly chop and pass through a ricer.

Place the fried egg into a blender with the riced potato, mayo, and all the garlic. Blend until smooth. Store in an airtight container in the fridge for up to 4 days.

---

[1] A high-quality harissa should resemble a thick chili paste. When you look at the jar, the oil should be separated from the solids, which should not be uniform in texture. Try to stay away from anything in a tube or can, which usually has a pureed form of harissa mimicking the consistency of tomato paste.

[2] Alternatively, you can use 2 tablespoons instant mashed potatoes. You can also use about ½ cup (100 g) of canned, drained, and mashed white or kidney beans, using more for a looser texture and less for a stiffer one.

[3] You can use a normal fried egg, but the egg flavor won't come across as strongly. Whatever method you use, be sure to get some browning on the edges and to not cook the yolk past medium.

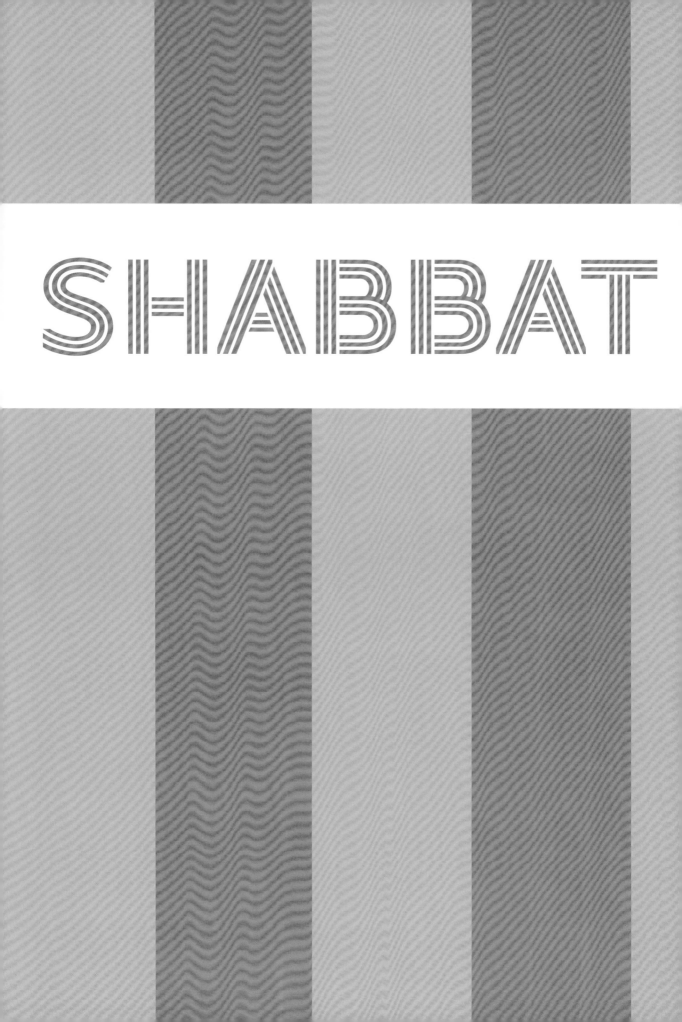

SHABBAT

R: # The Steinbergs did Shabbat by

ditching town to drive into the glorious state of Vermont. After school on Friday, we packed up the minivan with all our bags, family members, and dogs to make the two-hour road trip across the border. That way, in the winter, we were on time for 7 a.m. Saturday ski school in Stowe. For Shabbat dinner, we'd stop at our favorite casse-croûte or eat once we reached the countryside.

A: The Cohens did Shabbat somewhat more normally: lots of food and arguing.

Every Friday, my mom brought out her best servingware and invited up to 20 people to partake in a grand, multicourse affair. We began with what felt like a four-hour aperitif of nuts, cheese, olives, and drinks served by my father. Against his command, my siblings and I would duck in and out of the dining room, leeching off the cold salads my mom had already laid out. By the time we got around to the hagafen (kiddush), we were starving and itching to get the meal over with so we could go hang out with our friends.

At last, my mom would scream throughout the house, calling us down to the table. Our cups filled with kosher wine (or plan B, Diet Coke), we chanted the kiddush with zero harmony whatsoever. Then my dad performed the hamotzi by tearing apart the challah, dipping it in salt, and tossing it at us in a game of catch.

We then dug into the cold salads—grilled eggplant dressed with garlic and coriander, hummus, baba ghanoush, salade cuite, devilled eggs, roasted Hungarian peppers, and carrots coated in cumin and fresh herbs, at minimum. Next came soup and fish in some form, white fish cooked in peppers and olives or salmon glazed with honey and spices. Conversation always began in a civil manner, then swelled at about the same violent rate as our stomachs.

As we changed out our plates and cutlery for the meat course, the table talk tensed up. In between bites of braised lamb shoulder, veal roast, or a large cut of beef, we'd pair off: my dad and younger brother cracking jokes, my sister and youngest brother fighting incessantly, and my mom worrying over me and my quietness. Any guests fortunate enough to partake in the spectacle were faced with my father's generous insistence to refill their plates at the slightest sign of emptiness.

Having stuffed ourselves with food and talk, we topped off the night with something sugary: fresh fruit or apple pie with Häagen-Dazs and a lightly sweetened mint tea.

At the very end, we all rolled onto the couch to watch TV, then slept like babies with mild indigestion.

SALADE CUITE

A: Every Moroccan household has their own version of salade cuite, and everyone's mother makes it best. Whenever I made it, my mother always let me know that I had screwed it up. She thus took it into her own hands to make it for Arthurs out of her home, eventually passing that tradition on to our housekeeper, who is now the expert. It was served at every Shabbat, alongside fresh bread, hummus, baba ghanoush, and salads. Maybe it's because we've been overfed by it, but for reasons unknown, every Ashkenazi I've met loves it even more than us Moroccans. It takes a few attempts to figure out how much oil to use, but the more you make it, the more instinctual it becomes.

MAKES 4 CUPS

Paprika Oil

Scant ½ cup (110 ml) neutral oil

1 tablespoon sweet paprika

Salade Cuite

3 red bell peppers

2 green bell peppers

2 (28 oz/796 g) cans crushed or whole peeled tomatoes

Paprika Oil, for cooking

6 cloves garlic, chopped

1 tablespoon granulated sugar (or more, depending on the sweetness of your tomatoes and peppers)

⅓ teaspoon chili flakes

MAKE THE PAPRIKA OIL

In a bowl, whisk the oil with the paprika until combined. Store in an airtight container at room temperature for up to 3 months (or more, just keep checking it).

MAKE THE SALADE CUITE

Preheat the oven to broil.

Broil the peppers whole until they are tender and their skin is charred. Transfer to a container, and cover with plastic wrap or a kitchen towel. Let the peppers steam until they are soft but still have bite. Peel and deseed them then thinly slice lengthwise. Discard any liquid that the peppers release.

Remove the tomatoes from the cans, leaving the juices behind, and place them in a saucepan. If using whole tomatoes, crush them by hand until they're in bite-sized pieces. Add the juice of one can and bring to a boil. Lower the heat to a simmer. As the tomatoes simmer, use a wooden spoon to further crush them, still keeping them chunky. Use a wooden spoon through the sauce and leave a trail that lasts a few seconds. Lower the heat.

Meanwhile, in a separate stainless-steel pan set over low heat, warm about 3 tablespoons of Paprika Oil. Add the garlic and cook for 2 to 3 minutes until softened, being careful to not color it at all. Raise the heat to medium, and stir in the sliced peppers. Cook for another 5 minutes, stirring to ensure the garlic doesn't burn.

Transfer the contents of the pan to the pot with the cooked tomatoes. Add another tablespoon of Paprika Oil, the sugar, and the chili flakes. Simmer on low for about 30 minutes to 1 hour, until reduced by about half and well thickened. As it reduces, add Paprika Oil in ½-teaspoon increments as needed so it always looks glossy.

Adjust sugar and chili flakes as desired. Refrigerate for a few hours or overnight before using.

LILIANE'S OMELET ESPAGNOLE

A: Even though he's no less Moroccan than my Casablancan mother, my father has always considered himself Spanish. He's kind of got a point; he comes from Tangier, situated on the northern tip of Morocco, right across the Alboran Sea from southern Spain. Down there, the main language is Spanish, which is how this omelet got the "espagnole" part of its name. When my parents got married, my father's mother taught my mom, Liliane, how to make this for our family. It's a true pantry meal, and everyone in the house was happy when it made its weekly appearance on the table. We always ate it at room temperature with a cold topping, like mayo or salade cuite, and made a hot pita sandwich out of it the next day.

I've mentioned before how much I hate browned eggs in most contexts (see The Scramble, pg. 38), so it might seem hypocritical of me to include this recipe. This omelet *will* take on color in the pan, but I want to emphasize that that color should come mainly from the caramelization of the onions and potatoes rather than from the eggs themselves. The only tricky thing about this recipe is getting the egg texture down; it should be creamy, not runny, when you cut into it. To help make this easier, we've borrowed a trick from Mandy Lee's "Magic 15-Second Creamy Scrambled Eggs," in which she uses starch and milk as binding agents to obtain that perfect consistency.

SERVES 2

14 oz (400 g) peeled Yukon gold potatoes

2 tablespoons extra-virgin olive oil

2 cups (200 g) thinly sliced Spanish onion

8 eggs + 1 egg yolk

3 teaspoons potato starch

3½ tablespoons whole milk or water

3 tablespoons neutral oil[1]

Chives, finely chopped, for garnish

Salade Cuite (pg. 222), for serving

House Mayo (pg. 218), for serving

Fresh pita or challah, for serving

---

1 This may seem like a lot of oil, but it's meant to be a fatty dish. You can reduce the oil if you really want to, though.

Thinly slice or nick the potatoes. To nick them, use a paring knife to chip away at the potato, turning it into small, uneven pieces.

Heat the olive oil in a 6-inch nonstick skillet set over medium-low heat. Add the potato slices or pieces. Once they begin to soften, add the onion and raise the heat to medium. Stir continuously until golden brown. Season with salt and black pepper, then transfer the entire contents of the pan to a bowl.

In a medium bowl beat the eggs and egg yolk with a fork or immersion blender until no streaks remain. (Do not use a whisk, as the goal is not to incorporate air.) In a small bowl, whisk together the potato starch and milk and then whisk it into the eggs. Season with salt and black pepper, then stir in the warm potato and onion mixture, along with any oil left in the bowl.

Turn the heat down to low, and add the neutral oil. Pour everything into the skillet, and raise the heat to medium. Slowly cook the eggs, occasionally running a spatula around the edge of the pan to make sure the edges don't stick.

continued . . .

5 to 8 minutes in, lower the heat to low, cover the pan, and cook for 1 minute. Shake the pan a bit to get everything to cohere and ensure nothing is sticking to the sides and bottom. Uncover the pan. Using a spatula, circle around the edge one time, then flip the omelet onto a flat plate and slide it back into the pan to cook the other side (simply flipping with a spatula directly in the pan will break the omelet).[2] Increase the heat to medium, and cook on the other side for about one-quarter of the time you cooked the first side (so 2 to 3 minutes).

Remove the omelet from the pan, and let rest for at least 15 minutes—the inside should be runny, so it needs to firm up a bit to become creamy, like a lasagna. Honestly, you probably won't get the texture right on the first go, but it will still be tasty.

Serve at room temperature or cold garnished with chives, and with Salade Cuite, mayo, and fresh pita or challah on the side (just don't reheat it, it's weird).

2 We've given you an approximate time to help, but knowing when to flip the omelet is really a feeling; it comes with practice.

ROASTED POBLANO PEPPER MIX

A: This is one of a range of salads my mom always had on the Shabbat table. It tastes best when made one day in advance, and you can use any kind of pepper you want, including spicy ones. Keep leftovers for making sandwiches, such as the Caputo (pg. 111).

MAKES ABOUT 3 CUPS

1 large bell pepper

1 medium poblano pepper

1½ tablespoons extra-virgin olive oil + more for drizzling

1½ teaspoons red wine vinegar

½ clove garlic, minced

Preheat the oven to broil.

Lightly drizzle the peppers with a bit of olive oil and season with salt. Broil them on both sides until charred. Transfer to a container, and cover with plastic wrap or a kitchen towel. Let the peppers steam until they are soft but still have bite. Once steamed, peel and deseed the peppers and thinly slice lengthwise.

While the peppers are still warm, mix with the remaining ingredients and season with salt and black pepper to taste. Store in an airtight container in the fridge for up to 10 days.

KUZBARA FISH

A: What has stuck with me most about this meal is a fear of fish bones. Every damn time, this dish arrived at the table with a panicked warning from my father, "Attention aux arêtes!!" My brothers and I would basically ignore him, chewing the fish with mild paranoia and hacking up life-ending bones every now and then.[1] My younger brother (the same one who has been conditioned to carry Diet Coke at all times, pg. 242) has been so traumatized that he now refuses to eat it.

The dish itself is comforting, simple, and quick, suited to a weeknight dinner. What distinguishes it is the method of completely covering the fish in kuzbara, or cilantro, right before serving. This adds a subtle earthiness that doesn't overwhelm the other flavors, plus it disperses the aroma throughout the house. Use a firm, slightly fatty fish, such as grouper, swordfish, or—my least favorite—salmon. Just don't use a leaner fish, like cod, or it will release too much water as it cooks, diluting the sauce. At the very least, pick a deboned one.

SERVES 4

1½ lb (700 g) firm, fatty white fish fillets or steaks (my preferred cut)[2]

¼ teaspoon granulated sugar

3 red bell peppers

Cloves of 1 head garlic, skin on

3 tablespoons extra-virgin olive oil

2 to 3 tablespoons Paprika Oil (see Salade Cuite, pg. 222)

1 chile de árbol

1 guajillo or New Mexico chili

¼ confit lemon

6 green olives of your choice

4 Moroccan olives

½ large bunch fresh cilantro (kuzbara)

Juice of ½ lemon

1 teaspoon olive brine (from the jar)

Preheat the oven to 425°F (if using the oven method; see next page).

Place the fish on a rimmed sheet tray and season both sides with the sugar and a bit of salt (the amount of salt you need will vary based on fish type). Leave in the fridge while you prepare the sauce.

Char the whole peppers on a grill or in a very hot pan. Transfer to a container and cover to let them steam. Once they've cooled enough to handle, remove their skin, seeds, and veins. Thinly slice lengthwise and season with a pinch of salt. Set aside.

Remove the skin from three of the garlic cloves and mince thoroughly. Set aside.

In a medium pot set over medium heat, combine the olive oil and 1 tablespoon of the Paprika Oil. Fry the remaining whole, unpeeled garlic cloves for about 5 minutes. They may look too dark, but that's just the skin, so don't worry.

Lower the heat to medium-low. Stir in the sliced peppers, minced garlic, dried chilies, confit lemon, and olives. Cook for about 10 minutes, stirring occasionally. Remove the confit lemon and discard. Season with salt to taste.

continued . . .

---

1 Do not attempt at home.

2 If you know you'll have leftovers, we suggest using salmon because it tastes better cold.

COOK THE FISH

There are two ways to cook the fish:

1. Oven method: Place the fish in a shallow baking dish. Brush with 1 tablespoon of the remaining Paprika Oil and bake in the oven for 6 to 8 minutes. Remove from the oven and pour the hot sauce over top. Place back in the oven for about another 5 minutes, depending on how well done you like your fish.

2. Skillet method: Add 1 tablespoon of the remaining Paprika Oil to a skillet and get it nice and hot over high heat. Lower the heat to medium, then sear the fish on both sides to crisp the skin and caramelize the flesh. Continue cooking the fish through to your desired doneness, about 8 minutes total. Pour the sauce over top; it'll bubble, so be careful. Remove from the heat.

Either method is great, just don't serve the sauce on the side. This is meant to be a long-term relationship between fish and sauce, not a one-time fling.

PREPARE THE CILANTRO

There are also two ways to prepare the cilantro, the most important part. In both methods, the cilantro must be kept whole!:

1. Right after you remove the fish from heat (or right as you take it out of the oven), drape the fish with the cilantro and drizzle with the lemon juice and olive brine (as shown in the photo on pg. 228). Cover the fish for just a moment. When you uncover it, all those good aromas will be unleashed.

2. Place the fish on a serving platter and the cilantro on a separate plate. Place the remaining 1 tablespoon of Paprika Oil into a small pot and get it super hot. Carefully pour it over the cilantro, preferably in front of a group of people easily impressed by a sizzle. Finish with the lemon juice and olive brine.

Some rice and potatoes would make a great side. And faites attention aux arêtes!!

DAFINA

A: Dafina is a weekend staple among Moroccan Jews. To avoid using any appliances, my family would turn the oven on low Friday afternoon, then load up the racks with beef, eggs, grains, potatoes, and stock. By Saturday lunch, it was ready to be eaten with Shabbat leftovers. To uphold Cohen tradition, the first thing we had to do was grab an egg, salt it, and take a bite. Once that was out of the way, I'd proceed to mash up everything on my plate and eat it bathed in stock like a toothless child. It was a moment of relative peace, the family brawl having already run its course at the previous night's dinner.

While dafina is typically served with meat cooked in the same pot, our preferred pairing is Prime Rib (pg. 240). Another change we've made is shortening the cook time, so even you nonobservers might be willing to make it.

SERVES 6

2 cups (320 g) dry chickpeas

¾ cup (135 g) pearl barley

½ calf foot (ask an old-school butcher; request a high-collagen replacement if they don't have it)

1- to 2-inch piece bone marrow

2 tablespoons Schmaltz (pg. 169)

⅓ teaspoon Ceylon cinnamon

1 pinch ground turmeric, for color

1 small pinch cumin seeds, toasted

1 large yam (preferably Japanese), peeled and quartered lengthwise[1]

12 small red bliss potatoes or other waxy potatoes, peeled

4 eggs in the shell, washed

½ large Spanish onion

The night before, cover the chickpeas with a little more than twice their volume in water. Cover and leave at room temperature.

The day of, heat the oven to 300°F.

Rinse the barley under cold water until it runs clear. Place in cheesecloth and loosely tie it up into a bag, allowing enough room for the barley to expand as it cooks. Set aside.

Rinse the calf foot and bone marrow with cold water and pat dry.

In a large oven-safe pot,[2] melt the Schmaltz over medium-high heat. Thoroughly sear the calf foot and bone marrow on all sides. Remove from the pot and set aside.

Lower the heat to medium, then add the cinnamon, turmeric, and cumin seeds. Toast for about 1 minute. Return the calf foot and bone marrow to the pot. Place the yam and potatoes in the pot and shake them around. Add the bag of barley, and the eggs, onion, garlic, and dates, being sure to nuzzle in the barley and eggs nicely. Next, add the Chicken Soup Stock. Pour in enough water to cover everything fully. Cover and bring to a boil over medium-high heat, nudging (not stirring) the mixture around occasionally to be sure the bottom doesn't burn.

---

1 If you can only find small yams, simply leave them whole.

2 You really need a big Dutch oven for this recipe. If you only have something smaller, we suggest halving the recipe.

1 medium head garlic, top snipped off and a few layers of skin peeled off[3]

5 Medjool dates, pitted

4 cups (960 ml) Chicken Soup Stock (see Matzo Ball Soup, pg. 135)[4]

Once it has come to a boil, place in the oven. Cook, covered, for 5 to 6 hours. (It can be done in 4 hours, but the flavor will be much lighter. It can also be done overnight, for Shabbat purposes, if you set the oven to its lowest temperature.) Taste and adjust salt.

In the last hour of cooking, make the chickpeas. Strain them and place in a large pot. Cover with cold water, then bring to a boil. Lower to a soft boil and cook for about 30 to 40 minutes, until they are soft but still hold their shape. We recommend you don't add salt until they are fully cooked or they might become tough. Feel free to add aromatics to the water, such as chilies or carrots. Drain the cooked chickpeas and reserve the cooking water.

To serve, take a bit of the dafina liquid from the Dutch oven and mix it with chickpea cooking water, so you have a mixture of 75% dafina liquid and 25% chickpea liquid. For a thinner sauce, use more chickpea liquid; for a more concentrated sauce, reduce it on the stovetop.[5] Stir the sauce into the chickpeas.

Lay out all components of the Dafina on the table and let everyone serve themselves as they like.

---

3 If in doubt, call up your mohel and ask for him to circumcise your garlic. He'll know what to do.

4 If using store-bought stock, be sure to adjust the salt accordingly.

5 You can keep any leftover chickpea cooking liquid to use as a thickener in any soup base.

LILIANE'S ROASTED LAMB SHOULDER WITH SAFFRON

R: Alex's mom always says that to make this recipe she just "rubs garlic" over the lamb. Seven hours later, we've got a miraculously delicious roast on the table. Turns out, there's a bit more technique involved, but nothing you can't get done by dinnertime. His family serves it with a side of canned "desert truffles," about three pounds per one pound of meat. If bouncy, somewhat tasteless spheres sautéed in olive oil is what you're into, then give the Cohen way a go. Otherwise, you might enjoy it with rice or couscous. The next day, pull any leftover meat off the bones, warm it up, and fold it into creamy scrambled eggs. If it's Passover, eat with a size of matzah and mayo.

SERVES 4 TO 6

¼ cup (32 g) salt, for brining

1 tablespoon granulated garlic

1 tablespoon granulated sugar

3.3 lb (1.5 kg) lamb shoulder, cut into 2-inch pieces (ask your butcher to do this)

1.1 lb (500 g) lamb leg and belly, cut into 2-inch pieces (ask your butcher to do this)

Beef tallow or Schmaltz (pg. 169), for searing

2½ tablespoons extra-virgin olive oil

2 large Spanish onions, thinly sliced

½ cup (50 g) dried apricots

1½ teaspoons tomato paste

½ teaspoon peeled + grated ginger

1 cinnamon stick

¼ teaspoon ground turmeric

2 cups (480 ml) Chicken Soup Stock (see Matzo Ball Soup, pg. 135)[1] or water

1 large pinch saffron

Cloves from 2 heads garlic

In a small bowl, combine the salt, granulated garlic, and sugar (for a ratio of 4:1:1). You can use any additional spices you like; just be sure they won't burn when seared. Generously rub the lamb all over with the rub, and reserve any excess for future use. Place the lamb on a wire rack and refrigerate, uncovered, for at least overnight and up to 48 hours.

When ready to roast, preheat the oven to 400°F.

In a large heavy-bottomed pot, heat a thin layer of tallow over medium heat. Sear the lamb on all sides until dark golden, being careful not to burn it. Remove the lamb and set aside, keeping any released fat in the pot.

Raise the heat to medium-high, then add the olive oil, onion, dried apricots, tomato paste, and ginger. Cook for at least 10 minutes, until the edges of the onion become dark. Immediately lower the heat to low. Add the cinnamon and turmeric and cook for 3 to 5 minutes. Return the lamb to the pot and season with black pepper.

In a separate pot, bring the Chicken Soup Stock to a simmer, then add the saffron. Let sit for 1 minute to bloom, then strain out the saffron. Add the stock to the lamb pot along with the garlic. Season with a bit of salt, then cover and bring to a boil.

Place the pot in the oven, covered, for a minimum of 4 hours.[2] The liquid should reduce almost entirely so that the lamb is dry and crispy on the outside but moist on the inside. You should be left with enough highly concentrated braising liquid to pour over the lamb at the table.

---

[1] If using store-bought, be sure to adjust salt accordingly.

[2] If you don't want your lamb to be crispy, cook it at a lower temperature for a bit less time.

You can also baste the lamb a few times as it cooks to help soften up the exterior.

FREYA BONES

R: Our daughter, Freya, seems to love to munch on bones even more than our dog did. Thanks to Alex's Moroccan descent, those bones tend to be from lamb, which we like because, compared to beef, the fat-to-meat ratio is lower, which allows the fat to render and crisp up more easily.

We set out to make a lamb dish just for her. Yang Rou Chuan (Beijing lamb skewers) served as our inspiration, but we swapped the chilies for sugar and ground the spices more finely to make it more tolerable for a child. With chewy, fatty meat; succulent, tender bones; and a crispy, sugary coating, this dish is a bone fiend's paradise. Needless to say, Freya adores it.

SERVES 2 ADULTS PLUS 1 DOG/CHILD

1 unfrenched rack of lamb

1 tablespoon cumin seeds

2 teaspoons fennel seeds

2 teaspoons turbinado sugar or 1 teaspoon granulated sugar

1 teaspoon ground turmeric

Neutral oil, for cooking

5 Lebanese cucumbers, thinly sliced

Balsamic vinegar

Chinese black vinegar

Extra-virgin olive oil

With a sharp knife, remove about ½ inch from the top of the fat cap on the rack of lamb. Discard, then score the remaining fat (or ask your butcher to do this). Season generously with salt all over. Place in the fridge overnight, uncovered.

One hour before you're ready to cook, remove the lamb from the fridge to bring it to room temperature.

Preheat the oven to 200°F.[1]

In a small skillet, toast the cumin and fennel seeds until aromatic. Set aside to cool, then grind as finely as desired with a spice grinder or mortar and pestle. Transfer to a small bowl and mix in the sugar and turmeric. Set aside.

Roast the lamb in a cast-iron pan or roasting dish for 15 to 20 minutes, depending on your desired level of doneness. We like to pull it when it has an internal temp of 135°F so that it comes to medium for Freya. Once out of the oven, season the lamb all over with the spice mix.

Heat a generous glug of neutral oil in a large cast-iron pan set over medium-high heat. Once the pan is hot, sear the lamb on all sides until it's golden and some of the fat has rendered. Remove from the pan and cover with aluminum foil to rest for 10 minutes. (Any pan fat can be drizzled on top before serving or stirred into your dog's food.)

Meanwhile, toss the cucumbers with a drizzle of balsamic vinegar, black vinegar and olive oil then season with salt and black pepper.

Slice the rack into chops. Grab it with your hands and BLOW BLOW BLOW so you don't burn yourself!

---

1 Alternatively, to grill the lamb, first sear it all over in a pan, then rub it with oil and the spice mix. Grill with one side on direct heat and the other on indirect, with the grill closed, for about 6 to 8 minutes. Open the grill and sear it on direct heat until you get a nice crust all over. Let rest then serve.

239

SHABBAT

PRIME RIB

R: Prime rib holds a special place in my heart. Passed down from my grandma Rita, this recipe was my dad's favorite meal on holidays and special occasions. It was also supposed to be the centerpiece of the meal that I made for Alex on our first Valentine's Day together, but I completely botched it, tying together two steaks and overcooking the hell out of them. He married me anyway, proof that a terrible "prime rib" is still better than no prime rib at all (although he's since been put in charge of the holiday roast).

In my mind, this was always a meal of love, slow-cooked, slathered in mustard, and blanketed with sweet onions. Alex, however, changed all of that for this book, deciding to make it taste more like a steak. No surprises there. Serve it with our Dafina (pg. 231) and then appreciate the next day's leftovers; they make a mighty fine sandwich with yellow mustard, especially if you cooked the prime rib to medium. Don't forget the post-prime-rib nap.

SERVES 4 TO 8, DEPENDING ON YOUR GUESTS' STOMACHS

2 tablespoons salt

2 teaspoons black pepper

1½ teaspoons granulated sugar

6.6 lb (3 kg) bone-in prime rib[1]

In a small bowl, mix together the salt, black pepper, and sugar. Rub it all over the prime rib until well coated. Place on a wire rack and leave in the fridge, uncovered, for 12 to 48 hours, flipping halfway through.

The day of cooking, let the meat come to room temperature.

Preheat the oven to 150°F with a rack in the center. If your oven doesn't go below 200°F, reduce the cooking time by 1 to 2 hours.

Place the meat bone side down on a wire rack set over a sheet tray. For rare, roast for 5 hours, until the internal temperature reaches 120°F (it will rise to 125°F as it sits). For medium-rare, roast for 6 to 6½ hours, until the internal temperature reaches 128°F (it will rise to 135°F as it sits).

Remove from the oven and tent the meat lightly with aluminum foil. Let rest for 45 minutes, enough time for the prime rib to reabsorb all its juices without the interior getting too cold. Don't just stand around while you wait—start the Shabbat aperitivo or whatever you do.

Raise the oven to 500°F. Place the meat back in for 5 minutes for a great crust.

Let rest for an additional 5 minutes before slicing. Make sure to serve Mom first; she gets the part with the bone, the best part.

---

1 Alternatively, you can ask the butcher to debone it and tie it back up, which will make it easier to slice in the end.

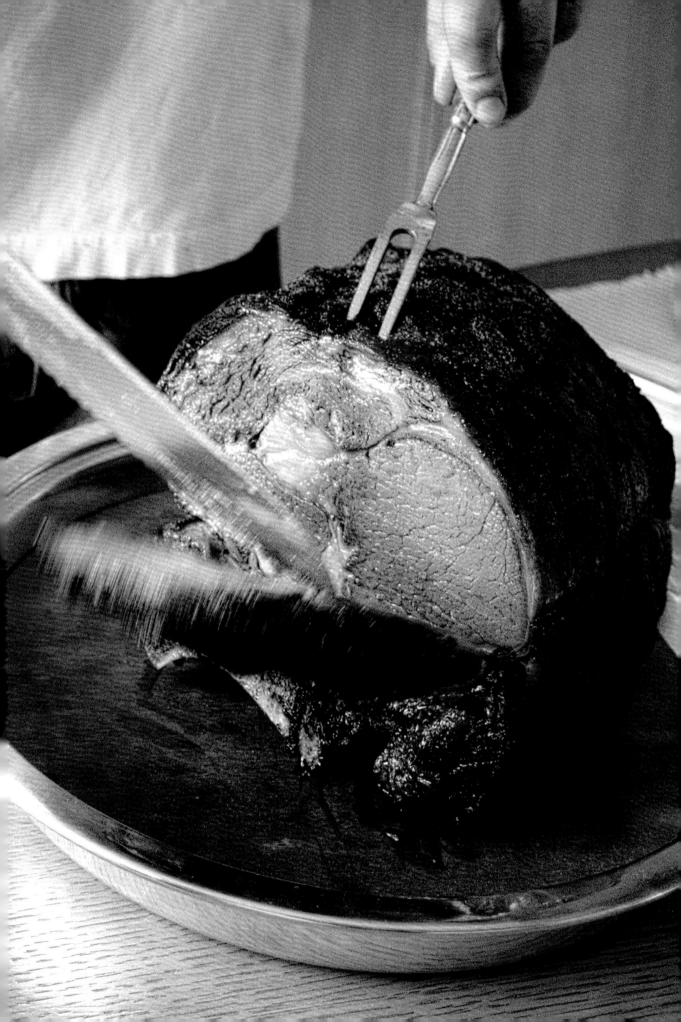

LILIANE'S BOULETTES & PETITS POIS

A: Boulettes et petits pois is one of those easy meals that Moroccans love to cook at home. In mine, we ate them exclusively with yellow mustard, just as we accompanied every meal exclusively with Diet Coke. Now, I've shared a lot of family recipes in this book, but know that you're not making any of them properly unless you're serving them with liters and liters of the fizzy stuff. If we ran out, we'd all wait for my dad to drive to the store and replenish our stock; otherwise, our meal just wouldn't be as enjoyable, not to mention we'd all be pretty pissed. To this day, my younger brother still brings a bottle of it when he comes to my house for dinner.

SERVES 4

1 small clove + 2 smashed cloves garlic

¼ cup (40 g) grated yellow onion

2 lb (900 g) 80/20 ground beef

2 tablespoons Aleppo pepper

1½ teaspoons whole cumin, toasted and ground

1 pinch smoked paprika

1 teaspoon salt

½ teaspoon cracked black pepper

½ teaspoon granulated sugar (optional)

1 pinch baking soda

1½ tablespoons ketchup

3 tablespoons club soda

2 eggs

Tallow or Schmaltz (pg. 169), for frying

1 medium Spanish onion, thinly sliced

1 small pinch ground turmeric

2 (10 oz/284 ml) cans peas, strained[1]

1 cup (240 ml) Chicken Soup Stock (see Matzo Ball Soup, pg. 135) or water

Yellow mustard, for serving

Grate the small clove of garlic into a large bowl along with the onion. Strain out most of the liquid. Add the beef and lightly mix by hand.

In a separate bowl, thoroughly mix together the Aleppo, cumin, paprika, salt, cracked black pepper, sugar, baking soda, ketchup, club soda, and eggs. Add to the bowl with the beef and mix just enough to incorporate so that the meatballs don't become tough.

Using the same method for forming Matzo Balls described in the Matzo Ball Soup recipe (pg. 135), roll the mixture into 1-inch balls. Transfer to a sheet tray as you go, then place in the fridge until firm.

Heat a thin layer of tallow in a large, deep skillet set over medium-high heat. Cooking in batches as needed, brown the meatballs until nicely darkened on all sides and cooked to medium, 6 to 8 minutes. Remove from the pan and set aside.

Lower the heat to medium-low. In the same pan, sauté the sliced onion and the smashed garlic until soft. Add the turmeric and cook for 5 to 10 minutes. Raise the heat to medium-high, stir in the peas, then add the Chicken Soup Stock. Bring to a steady boil, then lower the heat and simmer until the stock is velvety.

Add the meatballs and cook for a few minutes just to warm them through and coat them with the sauce.

Serve with yellow mustard. Eat leftovers the next day in a hot pita sandwich or with a slice of Liliane's Omelet Espagnole (see pg. 223).

---

1 You can use defrosted frozen peas if desired, but we prefer the added sugar of the canned ones.

HONEY OAT BREAD

A: Vermont comes up often in this book, in part because we got married in Stowe at Raegan's family country house. Well, technically we got married in a synagogue in Montreal, but that's only because my mother insisted on an orthodox rabbi (our Vermont rabbi wasn't even kosher—*gasp*). We held our cocktail party at Green Mountain Inn, home to The Whip, where we'd always eat about a loaf of honey oatmeal bread before dinner. As a wedding present, the inn gifted us their original recipe, which we're regifting to you. Our favorite boulangerie in Montreal, Miette, now makes it for Arthurs in their own way, although to taste that version you'll have to visit owner Thea Bryson in person.

MAKES 1 STANDARD LOAF

1 cup + 2 tablespoons + 2 teaspoons (280 ml) water

2 teaspoons active dry yeast

½ cup (45 g) quick-cooking oats + more for topping

1 tablespoon + 2 teaspoons butter, melted and cooled slightly

1½ teaspoons salt

¼ cup (84 g) honey

2½ cups (350 g) flour

1 egg white, for brushing

Heat 2 tablespoons plus 2 teaspoons of the water until very warm. Stir in the yeast and let sit for 5 to 10 minutes, until bubbling.

In a large bowl, stir together the remaining 1 cup (240 ml) water and the oats, butter, salt, and honey. Add the bloomed yeast and mix until incorporated.

Add the flour and knead by hand until a smooth dough forms that is no longer sticky to the touch. You can also do this in a stand mixer fitted with the dough hook attachment.

Oil a large bowl and place the dough inside. Cover with a damp kitchen towel and leave to rise in a warm spot until doubled in size, about 1 hour (rise times will vary on temperature, altitude, etc.).

Once the dough has risen, gently punch it down. Knead for about 5 to 10 minutes, until it slowly springs back when you poke it with a finger.

Roll out the dough into a ½-inch-thick rectangle. Fold the bottom end to the middle, then fold the top end over that, like a letter. Cover with a bowl or damp kitchen towel and let rest for 10 minutes.

Roll out the dough again to the same thickness. Roll it up tightly like a log, again grabbing from the short side, and pinch the seams together. Place the dough, seam side down, into a greased standard loaf pan. Cover and let rise for another 30 to 45 minutes, until it reaches three-quarters of the way up the sides of the pan.

Meanwhile, preheat the oven to 325°F.

Brush the top of the dough with egg white. Sprinkle with a small handful of oats. Bake for about 35 minutes, until dark golden brown—basically, until it looks like a loaf of bread.

Leave the loaf in the pan until it's somewhat cool enough to handle, then turn it out and transfer to a wire rack to finish cooling.

DESSERT

A: # Every time I go out for dinner,

before ordering anything else, I ask to reserve one of each dessert. Raegan always made fun of me until she saw the value in it. Is there anything more disappointing than reaching the end of a meal, good or bad, and being told that the dessert you want is now sold out?

As the final course, dessert is the most important part of any meal. It is the last thing that will linger in your mind and mouth as you leave the restaurant, so it had better be great.

A great dessert, in my opinion, does not taste like the result of hours and hours of work. It may very well be, but your brain shouldn't run in circles chasing down an elusive taste or technique or texture, at least not on the first bite. The first bite should trigger nothing but enjoyment. For a second, your brain should shut off, as you become so involved in what's going on in your mouth that you forget about the muffled world around you. I call it The Pause—the brief, *Ratatouille* food critic moment of silence in which you are eater first, human second. You get that dopamine slam of "Oh fuck, that's delicious" that you used to experience as a kid biting into a plastic-wrapped dép cake or your mom's sugared donuts or whatever tastes you think you've forgotten. I watch for it whenever one of my plates goes out to a table. If there is a sudden lull in conversation as they chew (and they don't proceed to spit into their napkin with disgust), I know I've done it.

To spark that reaction, I'll often develop recipes by recalling foods I've loved, then attempting to reproduce the feeling they gave me while improving upon their flavor (like the West Boston Cream Pie, pg. 273). My goal is never to reinvent anything, but rather to convert preexisting ways of cooking into new ones. And if I don't think I can improve upon the old ways, I won't even try.

I keep saying "I," but almost none of this chapter would have been possible without the help of my staff, particularly pastry chef Nadia Pisaturo. She has put hours into perfecting these recipes, testing and retesting them to help carry out my many, many overbearing requests with total patience and organization.

Before you get started, there's one very important thing to note. We have purposefully listed metric before imperial units for this chapter alone. Why? When we were testing, we found that using imperial measurements (cups, tablespoons, etc.) resulted in a different final product every time. Baking is a work of love, yes, but also of precision. We strongly, strongly recommend that you measure in grams with a scale. Scales are cheap and efficient and will help you become a better baker. Now, if you don't have a little drug-dealer precision scale for things like baking powder, obviously use teaspoons, but everything else is better off in grams.

BIG FAT SUGAR COOKIES WITH CREAM CHEESE FROSTING & SPRINKLES

A: This cookie is a sweet, little, sprinkle-coated piece of hell.

I, like many Jews, have fond memories of begging my mom for a sprinkle cookie when we'd go to the kosher bakery for challah. As with many things from our pasts, however, the sprinkle cookie is best appreciated within the confines of the mind. When I eat that same cookie today, I find it very . . . meh. I'm not saying that the classic, crumbly sprinkle cookie shouldn't live happily ever after at every traditional Jewish bakery. I'm saying that I didn't want it to live at Arthurs.

Using my usual approach to desserts, I set out to create a different sort of sprinkle cookie that captures the nostalgic feel of the original, but through a flavor and appearance better suited to our restaurant style. With our former sous chef, Daina, we developed a thick sugar cookie topped with an almost equally thick layer of cream cheese frosting and dunked in rainbow sprinkles, creating a far cry from its kosher predecessor.

They turned out to be a pain in the ass to produce. With no Daina (who had moved on for reasons unrelated to the cookie), no pastry chef, a tiny stand mixer, a relentless turnover of staff to train and retrain, minimal storage space, and every other hurdle of running a small, independent restaurant, making consistently good cookies proved impossible. Over the years, we've gone back and forth between trying different recipes in-house and outsourcing to local bakeries, with varying success rates. One week they're lopsided; the next they're overbaked; the next they're perfect. As I type this, our prep team is testing three more versions right outside my office door. The truth is that by the time you make this cookie, I'll have already changed it a dozen times.

Good news is, unlike in a restaurant, baking these cookies at home is pure freedom. You can tinge them any color, go crazy with sprinkle varieties, coat them with nuts, swirl jam into the frosting, and more. Sometimes they'll turn out kind of strange, especially if your kids are involved, but that's the fun in it. And if what you do doesn't amuse you, then why do it at all?

MAKES 24 COOKIES

Big Fat Sugar Cookies

670 g (4¾ cups + ½ table-spoon) flour

4 g (1 teaspoon) baking powder

2 g (½ teaspoon) salt

1 g (¼ teaspoon) baking soda

226 g (1 cup) butter, at room temperature

250 g (1¼ cups) granulated sugar

MAKE THE BIG FAT SUGAR COOKIES

In a bowl, whisk together the flour, baking powder, salt, and baking soda.

In a stand mixer fitted with the paddle attachment, beat the butter and both sugars on low for 1 minute. Increase the speed to medium and beat for another 4 minutes. Scrape down the bowl with a large spatula. With the mixer running on medium,

continued . . .

247   DESSERT

156 g (1¼ cups) powdered sugar

168 g (¾ cup) neutral oil

2 eggs, at room temperature

Cream Cheese Icing

113 g (½ cup) butter, at room temperature

227 g (1 cup) cream cheese (preferably Philadelphia), at room temperature

1 g (¼ teaspoon) pure vanilla extract

1 g (¼ teaspoon) salt

594 g (4¾ cups) powdered sugar

250 g (1¼ cups) sprinkles, for dipping

stream in the oil and beat for another 5 minutes. Reduce to low and add the eggs. Mix until the eggs are fully incorporated, about 30 seconds.

Scrape down the bowl. Add the flour mixture in two additions, beating on low for 15 seconds each time. Scrape down the bowl and turn the dough out onto a clean work surface. Knead by hand until completely smooth and firm.

Return the dough to the bowl. Cover and refrigerate for 1 hour. This is essential to allow the flour time to absorb some of the fat.

While the dough is chilling, preheat the oven to 375°F.

Use a large cookie scoop to scoop the chilled dough onto parchment-lined sheet trays, leaving 2½ inches between each one (each scoop should be 65 g/2.3 oz). Flatten the tops slightly with the palm of your hand. Chill for at least 20 minutes or up to overnight. At this point, the dough can also be frozen for up to 3 months.

Bake for 9 to 12 minutes, rotating the trays halfway through. The cookies are done when the edges are golden and the entire surface is covered in small cracks.

Transfer to a wire rack to cool completely before frosting.

MAKE THE CREAM CHEESE ICING

In a stand mixer fitted with the paddle attachment, beat the butter, cream cheese, vanilla, and salt for 2 minutes on medium until pale. Scrape down the bowl and beat for another minute. Reduce the speed to low and gradually add the powdered sugar, scraping down the bowl periodically until all the sugar has been incorporated and the frosting is fluffy and homogeneous.

ASSEMBLE

Transfer the frosting to a piping bag with the tip cut off. Generously pipe the cookies, leaving only a thin ring of cookie visible.

Pour the sprinkles into a wide, shallow dish. Press the surface of each cookie into the sprinkles to flatten and even out the frosting. Lift and repeat, this time more gently, to get full sprinkle coverage. Store in an airtight container at room temperature for up to 2 days, for best freshness.

DELI SPRINKLE COOKIES

Unlike our Big Fat Sugar Cookies (pg. 247), these sprinkle cookies still bear some resemblance to the traditional deli version. They're incredibly easy to put together, and the sprinkle-dunking step makes them the perfect dessert to do with your kids. Their final shape should be slightly domed, almost like a golf ball. If your cookies flatten out, though, don't stress too much. We went through at least a dozen versions to get them to hold their shape (this is, in fact, not at all the original recipe we used at Arthurs). You shouldn't run into too much trouble, though, as we've added chopped almonds to improve the structure. In the end, we're pretty pleased with how this new cookie has come out, much less temperamental and a bit more adult in flavor and texture.

MAKES 24 COOKIES

226 g (1 cup) butter, at room temperature

83 g (⅔ cup) powdered sugar

245 g (1¾ cups) flour

3 g (¾ teaspoon) salt

110 g (¾ cup) toasted almonds, finely chopped

200 g (1 cup) sprinkles

In a stand mixer fitted with the paddle attachment, cream together the butter and sugar on medium until light and fluffy. Turn the mixer to low and add the flour and salt. Mix until just combined, then add the almonds and mix in.

Shape the dough into balls the size of Ping-Pong balls (about 30 g/1 oz each).

Pour the sprinkles into a shallow dish. Roll the balls in the sprinkles, and gently reshape if necessary. Transfer to a sheet tray, and freeze until solid, at least 1 hour and up to overnight. If opting for the longer freeze, transfer to an airtight container once hard to save space and protect them from the freezer air.

When ready to bake, preheat the oven to 375°F.

Arrange the cookies on a room-temperature, parchment-lined sheet tray, leaving 2 inches between them. Bake for 12 to 14 minutes, rotating halfway through. The bottoms should be golden.

Let cool in the pan, then transfer to an airtight container, where they'll keep at room temperature for 3 to 5 days.

BROWN SUGAR WALNUT RUGELACH

R: I have no cutesy tale of nostalgia to sing about this sweet. It's a fun word to say, though—"rugelach!" The main point is the dough; some like it flakier, but we've done ours more like a soft cookie. And you're likely sick of hearing it by now, but I think the ones at Snowdon Deli are supreme.

MAKES 24 RUGELACH

Rugelach Dough

226 g (1 cup) butter, at room temperature

226 g (1 cup) cream cheese (preferably Philadelphia), at room temperature

50 g (¼ cup) granulated sugar

4 g (1 teaspoon) salt

45 g (3 tablespoons) 14% sour cream, at room temperature

4 g (1 teaspoon) pure vanilla extract

280 g (2 cups) flour

Brown Sugar Filling

55 g (packed ¼ cup) dark brown sugar

36 g (3 tablespoons) granulated sugar

6 g (1 tablespoon) cinnamon

Assembly

Rugelach Dough

75 g (⅓ cup) melted butter or 300 g (1 cup) peach jam, for brushing

Brown Sugar Filling

75 g (¾ cup) finely chopped walnuts (optional)

60 g (¼ cup) heavy cream, for brushing

36 g (3 tablespoons) turbinado sugar, for sprinkling

Powdered sugar, for sprinkling (optional)

MAKE THE RUGELACH DOUGH

In a stand mixer fitted with the paddle attachment, cream the butter, cream cheese, sugar, and salt on medium until homogeneous, about 1 minute. Add the sour cream and vanilla and mix until thoroughly combined. Turn the speed to low, then add the flour and mix until a dough forms.

Turn the dough out onto a clean work surface and divide into four pieces. Shape each portion into rough squares. Wrap in plastic wrap and chill for at least 2 hours or overnight.

MAKE THE BROWN SUGAR FILLING

In a small bowl, combine all ingredients.

ASSEMBLE

When ready to bake, preheat the oven to 375°F.

Roll out one piece of chilled dough to an approximate 4½×18-inch rectangle. Brush one-quarter of the melted butter over the entire surface, then sprinkle one-quarter of the Brown Sugar Filling on top. Pat down slightly, then sprinkle with the walnuts. Cut the dough into six strips of about 3×4½ inches. Roll each strip into a spiral, starting from the short side. Repeat with the remaining three pieces of dough.

Place the rugelach, seam side down, onto a parchment-lined sheet tray, spacing them 3 inches apart. Brush with the cream, then sprinkle with the turbinado sugar. Bake for 15 to 25 minutes, until deep golden. Sprinkle with powdered sugar, if desired.

BLACK & WHITE MADELEINES

A: I've always taken issue with black and white cookies. If I wanted a cake, I'd get a cake, not a cookie. It feels deceitful. The madeleine, on the other hand, doesn't pretend to be something it's not. It's a tiny cake, through and through. Of course, my wife loves the black and white cookie, so I attempted something cute with Nadia by combining our two tastes in a B&W madeleine. They're somehow even better frozen!

R: All right, but one day, when we open a bakery, I will have my black and white cookie.

MAKES 24 MADELEINES

Madeleines

113 g (½ cup) butter

140 g (1 cup) flour

4 g (1 teaspoon) baking powder

2 g (½ teaspoon) salt

2 eggs, at room temperature

150 g (¾ cup) granulated sugar

4 g (1 teaspoon) pure vanilla extract

80 g (⅓ cup + ½ tablespoon) 14% sour cream, at room temperature

Icing

150 g (⅔ cup) butter, at room temperature

313 g (2½ cups) powdered sugar + more as needed

53 g (3½ tablespoons) 14% sour cream, at room temperature

2 g (½ teaspoon) pure vanilla extract

48 g (½ cup) dark cocoa powder

10 g (2 teaspoons) whole milk + more as needed

MAKE THE MADELEINES

Melt the butter in a small saucepan. Set aside to cool slightly. In a large bowl, whisk together the flour, baking powder, and salt.

In a stand mixer fitted with the paddle attachment, whip the eggs and sugar on high for 5 minutes, until they reach ribbon stage (when you lift the paddle, the mixture should fall down in thick "ribbons" and linger on the surface for a few moments before disappearing). Beat in the vanilla. Transfer to a large bowl.

Using a large spatula, fold the flour mixture into the egg mixture, then fold in the sour cream. Gradually stir in the melted butter until fully incorporated. The batter should be smooth.

Leave the batter in the bowl and cover, or transfer to a piping bag fitted with a medium, simple round piping tip. Place in the fridge for a minimum of 4 hours and up to overnight.

Preheat the oven to 425°F.

Grease two madeleine pans with butter. Evenly spoon or pipe 1 tablespoon of the batter into each cavity. Bake for 5 to 7 minutes. The edges should be lightly golden and the signature hump should be evident. Do not overbake!

Carefully remove the Madeleines from the tray with the help of an offset spatula, and transfer to a cooling rack. Allow to cool completely before frosting.

MAKE THE ICING

In a stand mixer fitted with the paddle attachment, cream the butter, powdered sugar, sour cream, and vanilla until fluffy and homogeneous. Transfer one half to a separate bowl.

Add the cocoa powder and milk to the stand mixer bowl. Beat on medium until the frosting comes together. Add another teaspoon of milk, if required, until matte and spreadable.

Using an offset spatula, frost each madeleine, with the chocolate on one side and the vanilla on the other. They'll keep in an airtight container at room temperature for a few days.

SANDWICHES

CHALLAH GRILLED CHEESE $8.00
ADD GRILLED KOSHER SALAMI $3.00
ADD 1 FRIED EGG $2.75
ADD REEF SHOOM $7.75

MC ARTHUR $15.00
CHICKEN SCHNITZEL, ICEBERG SLAW, MAYO, PICKLES,
SERVED ON CHALLAH

THE CAPUTO SPECIAL $16.00
ROAST BEEF, SPICY GIARDINIERA, SWEET PEPPERS, GREEN
CHILI CHEESE, AU JUS, SERVED ON A ROLL

$10.00
SALAMI, BALSAMIC MUSTARD, HOUSE
ON A PRESSED ONION ROLL

BASEMENT BABKA

A: Our dear friend Eliot Silverman is the creator of this babka. He has hands the size of tree trunks and fingers the size of kielbasa. With these mighty hands, he made the best flat babka you've ever tasted.

We first knew Eliot for his bagels, which a friend of ours had highly recommended. When it came time for us to get them, he ended up saying that he didn't have his bagel shop butttt, long story short, he could make us babka from the basement of the Jewish Y. It was a glorious, chaotic business deal, with him running in to Arthurs holding trays of steaming babkas whenever he could. Eventually the demand grew too large and we had to transfer production to Josie, over at Léché in St-Henri, but the recipe is still Eliot's. We've still never tasted a babka like his in our lifetime (although he credits the lamination technique to Mordechai Benjamin, a baker at his bagel place).

The plating of it goes back to a now-extinct diner, Moe's Casse-Croûte du Coin, where I'd often drop by for a Danish. They halved it like a sandwich, slathered it with margarine, then toasted it in a panini press. I was so fond of it that we decided to do a very similar procedure for the babkas at Arthurs. For maximum gooey effect, be absolutely sure not to overbake the babka; it should be a little underdone in the middle!

What's Eliot doing now? Even he doesn't know, but he hints it might soon be running his own bakery of Almond Joy babkas or hosting a jazz/political affairs call-in radio show.

MAKES 3 BABKAS

Babka Dough

1 cube (15 g/½ oz) fresh yeast[1]

665 g (4¾ cups) flour

133 g (⅔ cup) granulated sugar

6 g (1½ teaspoons) salt

121 g (½ cup + 2 teaspoons) margarine, at room temperature[2]

1 egg, at room temperature

267 g (1 cup + 2½ tablespoons) water

MAKE THE BABKA DOUGH

Crumble the yeast into the bowl of a stand mixer fitted with the dough hook attachment. Add all remaining ingredients, and mix on medium-low for 5 to 8 minutes, until soft and elastic and a bit sticky, like a soft brioche.

Divide the dough into three pieces of 400 g (14 oz) each (any leftover can be made into a baby babka).

Place each piece in its own greased bowl and cover. Refrigerate overnight.

---

1 Instant yeast is to fresh yeast what instant coffee is to fresh coffee. Fresh yeast has more stamina, adds more flavor, and creates a more robust rise, so we haven't given you a dry yeast alternative.

2 Margarine keeps the babka kosher if you plan to eat it after consuming meat.

Lamination

342 g (3¼-lb sticks) firm margarine, fridge-cold, divided into 3 portions[3]

Neutral oil, for drizzling

Cocoa Filling

21 g (3⅓ tablespoons) high-quality Dutch process cocoa powder[4]

200 g (1 cup) granulated sugar (preferably Redpath)[5]

Neutral oil or melted coconut fat, for brushing

Cinnamon Filling

9 g (1½ tablespoons) cinnamon[6]

200 g (1 cup) granulated sugar (preferably Redpath)

Neutral oil or melted coconut fat, for brushing

Nutella Filling

145 g (½ cup) Nutella

90 g (½ cup) Cocoa Filling

Neutral oil or melted coconut fat, for brushing

Baking

120 g (½ cup) simple syrup, for brushing (see note 1, pg. 69)

Serving

Clarified butter, melted, for drizzling

Maldon salt, for finishing

LAMINATE THE DOUGH

If you have a special lamination rolling pin, like Eliot does, now's the time to use it. Roll out one piece of dough into about a 12×14-inch rectangle. The goal is to get it as thin as possible without ripping the piece of dough, about ¼ cm thick.

Smash one (114 g/¼ pound) stick of the firm margarine to flatten it, and place it in the middle of the rolled-out piece. Using a dough scraper or offset spatula, spread it into a rough square.

Fold the two longest sides to meet in the middle, then fold up the short ends to meet in the middle. Turn the piece 90 degrees.

Roll out the piece of dough as thinly as possible. Fold up the short ends to meet in the middle again. Turn the piece of dough 90 degrees.

Roll out the piece of dough to just about double the length. Fold the bottom end to the middle, then fold the top end over that, like a letter. It should be about the shape of a square. Transfer to a parchment-lined sheet tray.

Repeat with the remaining two pieces of dough. Cover them and place in the fridge overnight.

The next day, roll out one piece of dough as thinly as possible into a rectangle, with the long side facing you. It should be about 8×12 inches. Drizzle about 2 tablespoons of neutral oil over the dough. Spread it evenly over the surface, leaving a 1½-inch border all around. Repeat with the remaining two pieces of dough.

MAKE THE FILLINGS

For the Cocoa Filling, mix together the cocoa powder and sugar in a small bowl. Evenly cover one piece of dough with 3 generous tablespoons of the cocoa mix (keep the remainder to use with the Nutella Filling).

continued . . .

---

3 If you can't find firm margarine, you can use regular margarine firm from the freezer.

4 It is very important to choose a high-quality cocoa, as it is the dominant flavor of the babka.

5 Redpath isn't necessary, but we prefer it for the fillings because we find it caramelizes better than other leading brands.

6 Use the cheapest cinnamon you can find, as it will have a weaker flavor and allow you to use more of the cinnamon sugar, resulting in better caramelization without an overpowering flavor.

For the Cinnamon Filling, mix together the cinnamon and sugar in a small bowl. Taste and adjust the cinnamon if necessary; it shouldn't be too overpowering. Evenly cover the second piece of dough with enough of the cinnamon mix so that you can't see the oil seeping through anymore.

For the Nutella Filling, gently warm the Nutella in a saucepan so that it's easier to spread. Cover the third piece of dough with a thin, even layer of it, then sprinkle the cocoa mixture in a thin layer over top (you may have some left over).

For all fillings, Jackson Pollock a bit more oil over everything for caramelization.

ASSEMBLE & BAKE THE BABKAS

Starting from one long end, tightly roll one piece of dough into a log of about 12 inches. Using a bread knife, cut it in half lengthwise so that you now have two long strands. Twist together the strands, simultaneously twisting the individual strands (which will add textural variation once baked), then very loosely pinch the ends together. Place into a 5½×12-inch pan or a shallow loaf pan as close to those dimensions as possible. Repeat with the two remaining pieces of dough, placing each twisted babka into its own pan.

Cover and let rise in a warm place until doubled in size, about 1 hour. While they proof, preheat the oven to 350°F.

Bake for 20 to 25 minutes, until the outside of each babka is nicely darkened and the loaf is somewhat firm to the touch. (If you touch it and it concaves a bit, put it back in the oven.) Err on the side of slightly underdone, which is always better than an overdone, dry, crappy babka. As soon as they're out of the oven, brush the tops with 2 to 3 tablespoons simple syrup.

To serve, slice the babka in four and place it on a large sheet of parchment paper. Fold over the top of the paper so that the top and bottom of the babka are covered by it. Place it in a panini press and toast for a couple minutes, until gooey and a little smooshed. Alternatively, do this in a pan and press the babka with something heavy.

Drizzle with a bit of melted clarified butter and finish with a sprinkling of Maldon.

The babkas will keep in an airtight container for 3 to 4 days at room temperature. After that, you can reheat them in an oven and they'll be nearly as good as new.

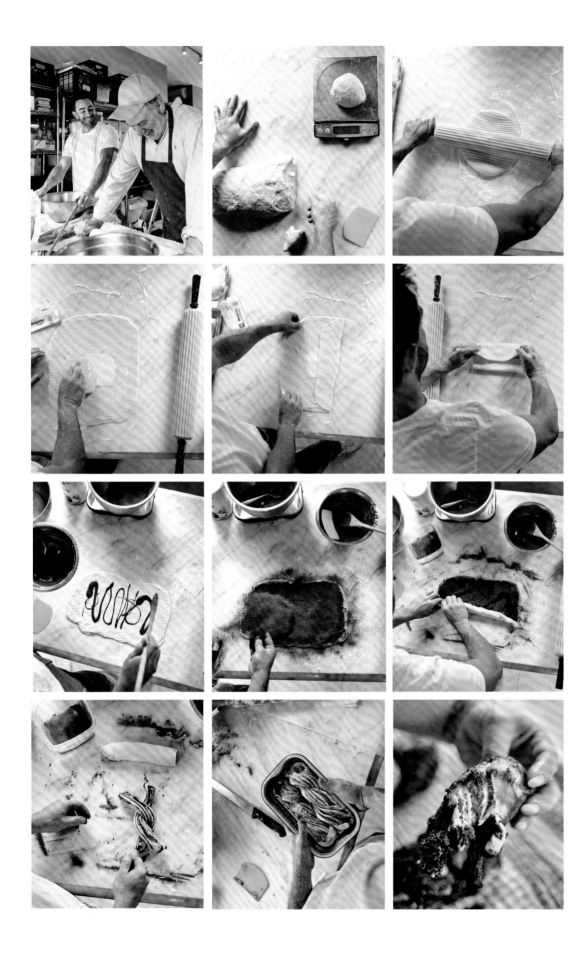

RICE PUDDING

R: Rice pudding isn't technically "Jewish," but Jews seem to have a thing for it. This recipe is our best guess as to how the rice pudding at L'Express is constructed, a craveworthy, creamy, comforting dessert. For such a humble dish, it feels so elegant with dark caramel and crunchy nuts to cut the sweetness.

SERVES 6 TO 8

Bitter Caramel[1]

250 g (1¼ cups) granulated sugar

255 g (1 cup + 1 tablespoon) heavy cream

1 pinch Maldon salt

Butter Walnuts

14 g (1 tablespoon) butter

250 g (2 cups) walnuts

55 g (packed ¼ cup) light brown sugar

60 g (¼ cup) water

4 g (1 teaspoon) pure vanilla extract

2 g (½ teaspoon) Maldon salt

Rice Pudding

1090 g (4½ cups) whole milk

150 g (¾ cup) granulated sugar

1 large cinnamon stick or 2 g (1 teaspoon) ground cinnamon

198 g (1 cup) arborio or carnaroli rice

Scant 340 g (1½ cups) water

4 g (1 teaspoon) pure vanilla extract

240 g (1 cup) heavy cream, cold

5 g (2 teaspoons) powdered sugar

Maldon salt, for finishing

---

1 Instead of Bitter Caramel, you can use cajeta casera (goat's milk dulce de leche) with a bit of salt.

MAKE THE BITTER CARAMEL

In a medium saucepan set over medium heat, add a small amount of the sugar in one even layer. Once melted, add the remaining sugar. As it melts, stir minimally with a heatproof spatula until it turns light amber in color. Remove from the heat. Whisking continuously, add the cream in three additions, taking care not to burn yourself with the steam. Return the pan to low heat and whisk until homogeneous. Add the Maldon and cool completely before storing in the fridge. It will keep in an airtight container there for up to 3 weeks.

MAKE THE BUTTER WALNUTS

Preheat the oven to 375°F.

In a small skillet, melt the butter. Add the walnuts and lightly toast them, then stir in the brown sugar. Add the water and stir to make a syrup, then add the vanilla. Continue to cook until the walnuts are nicely coated, the sugar is melted, and the water has mostly evaporated.

Transfer to a parchment-lined sheet tray and bake for 3 to 5 minutes. Remove from the oven and immediately sprinkle on the Maldon. Let cool completely before breaking apart or chopping. Store in an airtight container in a cool, dry place for up to 1 month.

MAKE THE RICE PUDDING

In a medium saucepan, combine the milk, sugar, cinnamon, rice, and water. Bring to a steady simmer. Cook until the rice is tender, stirring often, about 35 minutes. Remove from the heat. Remove the cinnamon stick, if using, and stir in the vanilla. Let cool to room temperature.

By hand or with a stand mixer, whip the heavy cream to soft peaks. Add the powdered sugar and continue whipping to stiff peaks. Gently fold into the Rice Pudding until just incorporated. Transfer to individual ramekins or a large serving dish.

Serve with Bitter Caramel, Butter Walnuts, and a sprinkling of Maldon. The Rice Pudding can be made up to 1 day in advance and stored in the fridge in an airtight container.

CINCO DE MAYO PIE

A: At some point in my years of pie development with Nadia, it dawned on me that most cakes are potentially better off as pies. They have more structural integrity, which allows for more free play with different layers and textures. Tres leches cake, for instance, is perfectly delicious as is. When changed into a pie, however, we're able to add a crust for crunch, a side milk sauce that won't make the base too sweet or soggy, and a stable vanilla custard for further creaminess. It is possible to add these things to a cake, but there is always the fear of too much weight or height or bulk. Or maybe my small, non-pastry chef mind is just too lazy to find a solution.

In any case, this pie is not supposed to be "better" than classic tres leches cake, just somewhat different. You may disagree with the concept, but why not try it first? It's a good baking project for when you're looking for a challenge.

MAKES 1 (10×12-INCH) PIE

Drizzling Sauce

1 (300 ml/10 oz) can condensed milk

60 g (¼ cup) whole milk

14 g (1 tablespoon) butter

8 g (2 teaspoons) pure vanilla extract

Sweet Sour Cream

300 g (1⅓ cups) 14% sour cream

42 g (⅓ cup) powdered sugar

1 g (¼ teaspoon) pure vanilla extract

Tres Leches Cake

113 g (½ cup) butter, at room temperature

200 g (1 cup) granulated sugar

5 eggs, at room temperature

4 g (1 teaspoon) pure vanilla extract

210 g (1½ cups) flour

4 g (1 teaspoon) baking powder

4 g (1 teaspoon) salt

1 (396 ml/14 oz) can condensed milk

1 (340 ml/12 oz) can evaporated milk

500 g (2 cups + 1 tablespoon + 1 teaspoon) whole milk, at room temperature

MAKE THE DRIZZLING SAUCE

Place all ingredients in a saucepan and stir over low heat until the butter has melted. Store in the fridge until ready to use, where it will keep in an airtight container for up to 1 month.

MAKE THE SWEET SOUR CREAM

In a bowl, whisk together all ingredients until smooth. Store in the fridge until ready to use, where it will keep in an airtight container for up to 1 week.

MAKE THE TRES LECHES CAKE

Preheat the oven to 375°F. Grease and line a half sheet tray with parchment paper.

In a stand mixer fitted with the paddle attachment, cream the butter and sugar until pale and fluffy. Add the eggs one at a time, and mix until homogeneous. Add the vanilla and beat to combine. Whisk together the flour, baking powder, and salt in a bowl. With the mixer on low, mix in the flour mixture until just combined.

Pour the batter into the prepared sheet tray and smooth with an offset spatula. Bake for 6 to 9 minutes, until the cake is beginning to pull away from the sides of the pan and a tooth-pick comes out almost clean.

While the cake is baking, whisk together the condensed, evaporated, and whole milks in a bowl. This will be the soaking liquid.

continued . . .

Vanilla Crunchies

129 g (½ cup + 1 tablespoon) butter

2 (300 ml/10 oz) cans condensed milk[1]

187 g (1⅓ cups) flour

125 g (½ cup + 2 tablespoons) granulated sugar

2 g (½ teaspoon) salt

Assembly

3 recipes Vanilla Custard (pg. 295)

2½ recipes Sugar Cookie Bagel Crust (pg. 294, baked in a 10×12-inch baking dish and cooled)[2]

Vanilla Crunchies

Maldon salt

Sweet Sour Cream

Tres Leches Cake

2 recipes Chantilly Cream (pg. 295)

Mexican cinnamon, for sprinkling

Drizzling Sauce, for serving

While the cake is still hot out of the oven, brush it with some of the soaking liquid to nicely moisten it. Lay a piece of parchment paper over the cake and flip into another pan so that the bottom of the cake is now the top. Brush on more soaking liquid until the cake is fully moistened but not soggy (you may not use all of it). Cool completely before continuing with assembly. Leave the oven on for the Vanilla Crunchies.

MAKE THE VANILLA CRUNCHIES

Melt the butter in a small saucepan. Set aside to cool slightly.

Remove the label from the condensed milk cans. Fill a large pot with enough water to submerge the cans by 1 to 2 inches. Bring to a boil, then lower to a simmer. Simmer for 5 to 6 hours for a dark, thick dulce de leche that won't soak through during assembly.[3]

In a large bowl, mix together the flour, sugar, and salt. (If making for the Poached Peach Ricotta french toast, pg. 69, add 1 g/½ teaspoon of cinnamon.) Add the melted butter and stir until everything is moistened. Transfer to a parchment-lined sheet tray and break apart into smaller clusters. Bake for 15 to 20 minutes total, stirring the crunchies and rotating the pan halfway through. Allow to cool completely. Leave the oven on for assembly.

When ready to assemble, cut the Vanilla Crunchies into even smaller pieces. Stir 400 g (3 cups) of them into the dulce de leche. Store leftovers in an airtight container at room temperature for up to 3 weeks.

---

1 If you can, use cajeta casera (goat's milk dulce de leche) instead of cow's milk dulce de leche; it has an inexplicable depth of flavor and thickness that just makes everything better.

2 Pay attention! Only the Bagel Crust ingredients from the Sugar Cookie Bagel Crust recipe need to be multiplied by 2½. For the Sugar Cookie Crumbs and Bagel Crumbs, make as instructed in the recipe (they already make enough for 2½ crusts as is).

3 If using store-bought dulce de leche, empty the contents of the can into a saucepan and boil for 10 minutes to darken and thicken it.

ASSEMBLE

Pour the chilled Vanilla Custard into the Sugar Cookie Bagel Crust, and smooth with an offset spatula. Bake for 20 to 25 minutes, until the edges are set and the center jiggles slightly. Don't worry if the top is darker in some spots, but be careful not to overbake. Allow to cool completely at room temperature, then refrigerate until cold before assembling the rest of the pie.

Once cooled, spread on the dulce de leche–coated Vanilla Crunchies, using as little pressure as possible so as to not pierce the custard. Top with a light sprinkling of Maldon. Spread the Sweet Sour Cream over top.

Trim the Tres Leches Cake to fit the shape of your pie tin. Place it on top of the Sweet Sour Cream. Spread the Chantilly Cream on top of the Tres Leches Cake (if you want a prettier pie, transfer the Chantilly to a piping bag and pipe it onto the cake as you see fit). Use a mini fine-mesh strainer to sprinkle on a bit of Mexican cinnamon.

Refrigerate for at least 4 hours, preferably overnight, before serving. Cut the pie and drizzle the Drizzling Sauce onto each piece. It will keep in the fridge for up to 5 days.

BEST FUDGING CHOCOLATE PIE

A: I'm no pastry chef, but I can say with certainty that this is the perfect chocolate pie. Nadia and I built it for indulgence. It is constructed of chocolate in every form imaginable—crunchy cookie crust, airy chocolate mousse, gooey fudge sauce, cooling chocolate pudding, and fluffy chocolate cake. While it is a lot of work, many of the components can be made days in advance and used in various other ways. If you spread out the workload, the only thing you have to do on celebration night is assemble and enjoy.

MAKES 1 (10-INCH) PIE

Chocolate Cookie Crumbs

170 g (¾ cup) butter, at room temperature

188 g (1½ cups) powdered sugar

1 egg, at room temperature

4 g (1 teaspoon) pure vanilla extract

175 g (1¼ cups) flour

87 g (¾ cup + 1 tablespoon) Dutch process cocoa powder (preferably Cacao Barry Extra Brute)

2 g (½ teaspoon) salt

Chocolate Cookie Crust

98 g (¼ cup + 3 tablespoons) butter

245 g (2¼ cups) Chocolate Cookie Crumbs

50 g (¼ cup) granulated sugar

4 g (1 teaspoon) salt

Gelatin Mass

70 g (¼ cup + 2 teaspoons) very cold water

14 g (1½ tablespoons) gelatin powder

MAKE THE CHOCOLATE COOKIE CRUMBS

Preheat the oven to 375°F.

In a stand mixer fitted with the paddle attachment, cream the butter and powdered sugar on low until combined, then increase the speed to medium and mix until light and fluffy. Add the egg and vanilla and mix until well incorporated, scraping down the sides of the bowl as needed. With the mixer running on low speed, add the remaining ingredients and mix just until a dough forms.

Turn the dough out onto a floured work surface and roll it out to a ⅛-inch thickness. Transfer to a parchment-lined sheet tray and bake for 5 to 8 minutes, rotating halfway through. The top will be matte and the edges crisp.

Let cool completely, then blitz in a food processor to make fine crumbs. They will keep in an airtight container for up to 2 weeks.

MAKE THE CHOCOLATE COOKIE CRUST

Preheat the oven to 375°F.

Melt the butter in a small saucepan. Set aside to cool slightly.

In a medium bowl, mix together the Chocolate Cookie Crumbs, sugar, and salt. Stir in the melted butter until moistened.

Transfer to a 10-inch pie tin. Using a measuring cup and your hand, shape the pie crust, evenly spreading it on the bottom and up the sides of the tin, applying even pressure to ensure it is compact and sturdy. Bake for 5 to 9 minutes. If it shrinks, reshape while still warm and pliable. Let cool completely before using. It can be made up to 4 days in advance and stored, covered, at room temperature.

continued . . .

Chocolate Mousse

110 g (⅓ cup + 2 tablespoons) whole milk

18 g (1½ tablespoons) granulated sugar

10 g (2 teaspoons) Gelatin Mass

143 g (¾ cup + 1½ tablespoons) chopped 58% chocolate

210 g (¾ cup + 2 tablespoons) heavy cream

Toffee Sauce

120 g (½ cup) heavy cream

56 g (¼ cup) butter

55 g (packed ¼ cup) dark brown sugar

38 g (2 tablespoons) golden corn syrup

1 g (¼ teaspoon) salt

20 g (1 tablespoon) date syrup[1]

4 g (1 teaspoon) pure vanilla extract

Chocolate "Oreo" Crumbs

113 g (½ cup) butter, at room temperature

100 g (½ cup) granulated sugar

1 egg, at room temperature

140 g (1 cup) flour

81 g (¾ cup) Dutch process cocoa powder (preferably Cacao Barry Extra Brute)

4 g (1 teaspoon) salt

1 g (¼ teaspoon) baking soda

4 g (1 tablespoon) instant coffee crystals

3 g (¾ teaspoon) Maldon salt

Chocolate Fudge Sauce

128 g (⅓ cup + 1 tablespoon) pure maple syrup

---

1 If you're unable to find date syrup, you can replace it with an equal amount of corn syrup plus at least 50 g (¼ cup) dark brown sugar.

MAKE THE GELATIN MASS

Place the very cold water in a small bowl and sprinkle the gelatin on top. Let sit for about 10 minutes, until firmed up, then stir.

MAKE THE CHOCOLATE MOUSSE

In a small saucepan set over medium heat, warm the milk and sugar until scalding, but not yet boiling. Add the Gelatin Mass.

Place the chocolate in a large bowl, then pour the hot milk mixture over top. Stir until fully melted and combined, to make a ganache. Let cool slightly.

Whip the cream to medium peaks. Fold one-third of the whipped cream into the ganache to lighten the mixture. Gently fold in the rest until no streaks remain. Cover and refrigerate until fully set, at least 8 hours. It will keep there for a few days.

MAKE THE TOFFEE SAUCE

In a small saucepan set over medium heat, reduce the cream by one-third. Once reduced, add the butter, brown sugar, corn syrup, and salt. Bring to a boil, then lower the heat and simmer for 3 minutes. Remove from the heat. Whisk in the date syrup and vanilla. It can be stored in an airtight container in the fridge for up to 1 week.

MAKE THE CHOCOLATE "OREO" CRUMBS

Preheat the oven to 375°F.

In a stand mixer fitted with the paddle attachment, cream the butter and sugar on medium until light and fluffy. Add the egg and mix until well incorporated, scraping down the bowl as needed. On low speed, add the remaining ingredients and mix just until a dough forms.

Turn the dough out onto a floured work surface and roll it out to a ⅛-inch thickness. Transfer to a parchment-lined sheet tray and bake for 5 to 8 minutes, rotating halfway through. The top will be matte and the edges crisp. Let cool, then weigh out 215 g (2½ cups) and pulse in a food processor a few times to break it up. (You will have leftovers, which will keep in an airtight container at room temperature for about 1 week.)

Add the coffee crystals and Maldon and pulse a bit more until it reaches coarse crumbs.

MAKE THE CHOCOLATE FUDGE SAUCE

In a medium saucepan, combine all ingredients, minus the chopped chocolate, and simmer for 3 to 5 minutes over medium

120 g (½ cup) heavy cream

24 g (packed 2 tablespoons) dark brown sugar

22 g (1½ tablespoons) butter

12 g (2 tablespoons) cocoa powder

2 g (½ teaspoon) pure vanilla extract

1 g (¼ teaspoon) salt

128 g (⅔ cup + 1½ tablespoons) 58% chopped chocolate

Chocolate Pudding

79 g (⅓ cup + 1 tablespoon) sugar

18 g (3 tablespoons) cocoa powder

15 g (1½ tablespoons) cornstarch

1 g (¼ teaspoon) salt

320 g (1⅓ cups) whole milk

14 g (1 tablespoon) butter

10 g (2 teaspoons) Gelatin Mass

1 g (¼ teaspoon) pure vanilla extract

"McD's" Caramel

100 g (½ cup) granulated sugar

19 g (1 tablespoon) golden corn syrup

98 g (⅓ cup + 1 tablespoon) evaporated milk

1 g (¼ teaspoon) salt

28 g (2 tablespoons) butter, cubed

2 g (½ teaspoon) pure vanilla extract

Date Puree, for cake (optional)

100 g (⅔ cup) pitted dates

Chocolate Cake

75 g (¼ cup + 2 tablespoons) granulated sugar

123 g (¾ cup + 2 tablespoons) flour

42 g (¼ cup + 3 tablespoons) cocoa powder

heat. Remove from the heat, then whisk in the chocolate a little at a time until homogeneous. Let cool slightly before transferring to an airtight container. It can be made 4 days in advance and stored in the fridge. Let it come to room temperature before assembling the cake.

MAKE THE CHOCOLATE PUDDING

In a small saucepan, whisk together the sugar, cocoa powder, cornstarch, and salt, then whisk in the milk. Bring to a boil over medium heat and continue whisking for 1 minute longer, until thickened. Remove from the heat and stir in the butter, Gelatin Mass, and vanilla. Strain into a bowl and store in the fridge with a layer of plastic wrap touching the surface to prevent a skin from forming. It can be made 4 days in advance and stored in the fridge. Use from cold, and stir before using.

MAKE THE "MCD'S" CARAMEL

In a medium, deep saucepan[2] set over medium heat, melt the sugar and corn syrup without touching the mixture at all. Once it starts to darken in color, use a heatproof spatula to gently move the sugar around in the pan so that it doesn't burn, but not so much that sugar crystals form on the side of the pot or spatula.[3] Once it reaches a medium caramel color, remove from the heat.

While whisking, add the evaporated milk in two additions, taking care not to burn yourself, as the mixture will steam. Return to low heat and continue whisking until homogeneous, scraping down the sides of the pot as needed. Add the salt.

Remove from the heat, then add the butter, piece by piece, while whisking. Add the vanilla. Allow the caramel to cool completely before assembling the pie. It can be made 4 days in advance and stored in the fridge. Let it come to room temperature before using.

MAKE THE DATE PUREE, FOR CAKE (OPTIONAL)

Remove any tough bit on the dates (usually near where the stem was), and place them in a small saucepan. Add enough water to just barely cover them. Bring to a boil, then cover and

continued . . .

[2] Ideally, your pot or pan is wide enough to hold the sugar in a fairly thin, even layer. If the sugar is too deep, the bottom layer is more likely to burn.

[3] If you overstir or stir too early and the sugar lumps, lower the heat and continue stirring until it comes back together. Any remaining lumps can be strained out.

3 g (¾ teaspoon) baking powder

3 g (¾ teaspoon) baking soda

2 g (½ teaspoon) salt

25 g (1½ tablespoons) Date Puree (optional)

1 egg, at room temperature

120 g (½ cup) whole milk, at room temperature

60 g (¼ cup) neutral oil

125 g (½ cup + 1 teaspoon) hot water

4 g (1 teaspoon) pure vanilla extract

30 g (3 tablespoons) chopped 58% chocolate (optional)[4]

120 g (½ cup) Toffee Sauce

Assembly

Chocolate Cookie Crust

Chocolate Fudge Sauce

Maldon salt

Chocolate Pudding

Chocolate Cake

Chocolate Mousse

"McD's" Caramel

Chocolate Oreo Crumbs, for topping

---

4 This adds extra chocolate to the cake and is optional. You can use any percentage you want as long as it is less than 85%, or it won't melt well.

5 We prefer disposable pie tins because they seem to result in a more even bake. They are also easier to maneuver and cut into and can be reused a few times.

take the pan off the heat. Let sit until softened, about 5 minutes. Strain the dates, reserving their cooking liquid.

Puree the dates with an immersion blender (or mash with a fork or blitz in a food processor). Adjust the consistency with their cooking liquid as needed, until it resembles applesauce in texture. It will keep for up to 2 weeks in the fridge.

MAKE THE CHOCOLATE CAKE

Preheat the oven to 375°F. Grease and dust a 10-inch disposable pie tin[5] with cocoa powder.

In a medium bowl, whisk together the sugar and other dry ingredients. Mix in the Date Puree, egg, milk, and oil. Stream in the hot water while whisking, scraping down the bowl as needed. Add the vanilla.

Fill the pie tin halfway full with the batter (about 400 g/14 oz). Top with the chopped chocolate, if using, and bake for 8 to 12 minutes, until a toothpick inserted in the center of the cake comes out slightly wet. Don't overbake! Remove from the oven and let cool for 5 minutes.

If you made the Toffee Sauce in advance, warm it slightly.

Invert the cake onto a half sheet of parchment paper, and place back into the pie tin, so that the bottom of the cake is now the top. Poke a few holes into the cake and pour over the warmed Toffee Sauce, taking care to enrobe the whole cake and sides. Allow to cool completely before assembling the pie. This can be done 1 day in advance and kept, covered in plastic wrap, at room temperature.

ASSEMBLE (FINALLY!)

Place the Chocolate Cookie Crust onto a sheet tray to catch any fallout.

Pour the Chocolate Fudge Sauce into the crust until it reaches halfway up the sides. Sprinkle a bit of Maldon on top. Spread on enough of the chocolate pudding so that it reaches the top of the crust. Next, gently place the Chocolate Cake, domed top side still facing down, on top of the Chocolate Pudding. Spread the Chocolate Mousse all over the cake so that the entire top and sides are fully covered. Drizzle the "McD's" Caramel in a spiral motion on top of the mousse, concentrating it in the center, as it will naturally spread outward. Cover the surface with the chocolate crumbs in an even coating. The assembled pie will keep in the fridge for up to 5 days.

WEST BOSTON CREAM PIE

A: This cake-pie hybrid is a perfect example of how nostalgia-based our desserts are. I feel like every kid had a favorite prepackaged snack cake they would spend their allowance on at the dép, usually either a Jos Louis or May West. I was team May West, so long as I ate it out of sight of my mom, who had banned her fat kids from eating more junk food. (For any non-Canadians who don't know, a May West cake is a little, round white cake filled with cream and covered in chocolate, kind of like a Hostess.)

I also love a Boston cream donut, which—comprising sponge cake, pastry cream, and chocolate glaze—is not so distant from my childhood cake. This recipe is my attempt to cross the two. The different stages take some time, so you should tackle it on a weekend when you have extra time on hand. We've made some adjustments, using a crust made of Montreal bagels and pretzel salt, a chiffon cake, and a chocolate donut glaze. There you have it, the West Boston Cream Pie. The only comment my wife has about it is "This pie is goddamn delicious."

MAKES 1 (10-INCH) PIE

Vanilla Chiffon Cake

2 eggs, yolks + whites separated, at room temperature

37 g (2½ tablespoons) neutral oil

2 g (½ teaspoon) pure vanilla extract

60 g (¼ cup) cold water

79 g (½ cup + 1 tablespoon) flour

4 g (1 teaspoon) baking powder

1 g (¼ teaspoon) salt

66 g (⅓ cup) + 36 g (3 tablespoons) granulated sugar

Chocolate Glaze

83 g (⅔ cup) powdered sugar

37 g (2½ tablespoons) whole milk

15 g (2½ tablespoons) cocoa powder

2 g (½ teaspoon) pure vanilla extract

MAKE THE VANILLA CHIFFON CAKE

Preheat the oven to 375°F. Grease and flour a 10-inch disposable pie tin.

In a medium bowl, whisk together the egg yolks, oil, vanilla, and cold water.

Into a large bowl, sift the flour, baking powder, salt, and 66 g (⅓ cup) sugar. Add the liquid mixture to the dry mixture and whisk until smooth.

In a stand mixer fitted with the whisk attachment, whisk the egg whites on medium-high until frothy. Turn the mixer to low and gradually add the remaining 36 g (3 tablespoons) of sugar. Increase the speed to high and whip until stiff peaks form.

Gently whisk one-third of the whites into the cake batter to lighten it up. Using a large spatula, gently fold in the rest of the whites until no streaks remain. Pour into the prepared tin and spread evenly with a small offset spatula.

Bake for 12 to 15 minutes, until a sharp knife or toothpick inserted in the center comes out nearly clean. As soon as it's out of the oven, run a knife or small offset spatula around the edge of the pan, then turn it out onto a cooling rack. (If the cake remains in the pan as it cools, it will shrink and become dense.) Allow to cool completely before assembling the pie.

continued . . .

Assembly

Vanilla Custard (pg. 295)

Sugar Cookie Bagel Crust
(pg. 294), baked and
cooled

Vanilla Chiffon Cake

Chantilly Cream (pg. 295)

Chocolate Glaze

MAKE THE CHOCOLATE GLAZE

In a bowl, whisk together all ingredients, and set aside until ready to assemble. It will keep in an airtight container at room temperature for 2 to 3 days.

ASSEMBLE

Preheat the oven to 375°F.

Pour the chilled Vanilla Custard into the Sugar Cookie Bagel Crust, and smooth with an offset spatula. Bake for 20 to 25 minutes, until the edges are set and the center jiggles slightly. Don't worry if the top is darker in some spots, but be careful not to overbake. Allow to cool completely at room temperature, then refrigerate until cold before assembling the rest of the pie.

Once cooled, smooth a ¼-inch layer of Chantilly over top. Invert the chiffon cake so that the domed top is now the bottom, and gently place it on top of the Chantilly. Spread more Chantilly onto the cake to thinly cover the top and sides. Pour the Chocolate Glaze over the entire pie. To neaten things up, you could transfer the remaining Chantilly to a piping bag and pipe a border on the top of the pie. The assembled pie will keep in the fridge for up to 5 days.

MAMI'S CHEESECAKE

R: I fucking love cheesecake. I especially love rich, dense, New York cheesecake with a coulis on top. This recipe is a subtle ode to the famous one from Junior's in NYC, which replaces the classic graham cracker crust with a light sponge cake. Because Alex always ate a marble sponge as a kid, that's what we went with. Additionally, the cheesecake he grew up with was always a bit burnt and bitter, so we did the same to ours, making it reminiscent of the Basque variety. He and his brothers would sneak a slice in the middle of the night, until nothing was left for his mother the next day. He never confessed to the serial crime, until now.

MAKES 1 (10-INCH) CHEESECAKE

Marble Sponge Base

43 g (3 tablespoons) butter

70 g (½ cup) cake flour

4 g (1 teaspoon) baking powder

2 g (½ teaspoon) salt

3 eggs, yolks + whites separated, at room temperature

67 g (⅓ cup) + 20 g (1½ tablespoons) granulated sugar

8 g (2 teaspoons) pure vanilla extract

Pinch (⅛ teaspoon) cream of tartar

6 g (1 tablespoon) cocoa powder

Simple Syrup Soak

50 g (¼ cup) granulated sugar

60 g (¼ cup) water

Cheesecake

750 g (3⅓ cups or 3 blocks) cream cheese (preferably Philadelphia), at room temperature

230 g (1 cup) mascarpone, at room temperature

300 g (1½ cups) granulated sugar

3 eggs + 5 egg yolks

3 g (¾ teaspoon) salt

240 g (1 cup + 1 tablespoon) 14% sour cream, at room temperature

MAKE THE MARBLE SPONGE BASE

Preheat the oven to 375°F. Grease and line the base and sides of a 10-inch springform pan with parchment paper.

Melt the butter in a small saucepan. Set aside to cool slightly. Sift the cake flour, baking powder, and salt into a large bowl.

In a stand mixer fitted with the whisk attachment, whisk the egg yolks on high for 2 minutes, until pale and increased in volume. With the mixer running on low, gradually add 67 g (⅓ cup) of the sugar. Add the vanilla. Continue whisking on high until ribbon stage is achieved, about 4 minutes (when you lift the whisk, the mixture should fall down in thick "ribbons" and linger on the surface for a few moments before disappearing).

Using a large spatula, fold the flour mixture into the egg yolk mixture until no streaks remain. Stir in the melted butter until fully incorporated. Transfer the mixture to a new bowl.

Thoroughly clean the stand mixer bowl and whisk attachment. (Any residual fat will interfere with the next step.) In the cleaned bowl, whip the egg whites and cream of tartar on high until soft peaks form. With the mixer running on low, add the remaining 20 g (1½ tablespoons) sugar. Continue whipping until stiff peaks form, being careful not to overwhip.

Using a large spatula, fold a portion of the whites into the batter to lighten it. Gently fold in the rest until no streaks remain.

Transfer 75 g (about ⅓ cup) of the batter to a small mixing bowl and whisk in the cocoa powder. Pour the remaining vanilla batter into the springform pan and spread evenly. Spoon the chocolate batter on top sporadically. Using a toothpick or the tip of a knife, swirl the batters together to create a marble pattern.

continued . . .

120 g (½ cup) heavy cream, at room temperature

8 g (2 teaspoons) pure vanilla extract

47 g (⅓ cup) flour

Raspberry Coulis

375 g (3 cups) fresh or frozen raspberries

100 g (½ cup) granulated sugar

13 g (4 teaspoons) cornstarch

20 g (1⅓ tablespoons) water

4 g (1 teaspoon) freshly squeezed lemon juice

4 g (1 teaspoon) pure vanilla extract

For Serving

Whipped Cream (see Hot Cocoa, pg. 312)

Bake for 8 to 10 minutes, until a toothpick inserted in the center comes out nearly clean with a few moist crumbs. Don't overbake!

MAKE THE SIMPLE SYRUP SOAK

While the cake is baking, make the simple syrup. In a small saucepan, bring the sugar and water to a boil. Once the sugar has dissolved, remove from the heat.

Once the cake is out of the oven, poke a few holes on its surface with a toothpick or paring knife. Brush the simple syrup evenly on top. Set aside on a cooling rack and allow to cool completely.

MAKE THE CHEESECAKE

Raise the oven temperature to 400°F.

In a 14-cup (3 L) capacity food processor (work in two batches if using a smaller size), blitz the cream cheese, mascarpone, sugar, eggs, egg yolks,[1] and salt until very smooth, scraping down the sides as needed. Add the sour cream, heavy cream, and vanilla and blitz until homogeneous. Add the flour and pulse three times. Let the batter rest at room temperature for 20 minutes.

Pour the batter into the pan on top of the sponge base. Bake for 45 to 60 minutes, until the top is dark brown and the center is slightly jiggly. Cool completely at room temperature, then refrigerate. The cheesecake can be made up to 3 days in advance and kept covered in the fridge.

MAKE THE RASPBERRY COULIS

In a medium saucepan, combine the raspberries, sugar, cornstarch, and water. Cook over medium heat, stirring constantly, until it boils, thickens, and is no longer cloudy. Remove from the heat, then stir in the lemon juice and vanilla. Let cool before using.

SERVE

Spread the whipped cream over the cheesecake and smooth with an offset spatula. Serve with a spoonful of Raspberry Coulis on top of each slice.

---

[1] To ensure you get no weird clumpy egg bits in the cake, whisk the eggs through a fine-mesh strainer before adding them.

CRISSE DE COFFEE CAKE

R: Alex and I both grew up eating the same My Grandma's of New England coffee cake, although I had always thought mine was made fresh at a bakery in Stowe. I loved it so much that I brought Alex there to try it. He told me that it was incredible but tasted exactly like the one his mom bought from Costco. We asked the staff, and sure enough, he was right. I was a little crushed by the news, but we've since come up with this, our own homemade version of our favorite, non-homemade coffee cake. Alex being Alex, he had to try out 50 different versions of the recipe before circling back to the original. He kept trying to turn it into a poundcake, which is what his family always ate with coffee. But after days and days of baking, none of his elaborate cakes ended up being actually better than the first, especially not the one that he dropped all over our kitchen floor. Crisse de coffee cake!!! Some things are best left alone.

MAKES 1 (9-INCH) CAKE

Streusel Filling

100 g (packed ½ cup) dark brown sugar

65 g (⅓ cup + 2 tablespoons) flour

43 g (3 tablespoons) salted butter, cold, cubed

9 g (1½ tablespoons) cinnamon

Streusel Topping

115 g (packed ½ cup + 1 tablespoon) dark brown sugar

140 g (1 cup) flour

85 g (¼ cup + 2 tablespoons) salted butter, cold, cubed

9 g (1½ tablespoons) cinnamon

Glaze (optional)

125 g (1 cup) powdered sugar

60 g (¼ cup) whole milk

MAKE THE STREUSEL FILLING

Place all ingredients in a medium bowl. Use your hands to mash everything together until the butter is in pea-sized pieces.

MAKE THE STREUSEL TOPPING

Place all ingredients in a medium bowl. Use your hands to mash everything together until the butter is in pea-sized pieces. It will be slightly drier than the Streusel Filling.

MAKE THE GLAZE (OPTIONAL)

In a bowl, whisk together the sugar and milk.

MAKE THE CAKE

Preheat the oven to 350°F. Grease and line a 9-inch square pan with parchment paper.[1]

Sift the cake flour, sugar, baking powder, and salt into the bowl of a stand mixer fitted with the paddle attachment. Start the mixer on low, and pour in the coconut oil. Gradually increase the speed to high, then continue beating for 2 minutes until velvety. Add 1 egg, then the buttermilk. Beat to combine. Add the remaining egg, then the milk. Beat to combine, then add the vanilla.

continued . . .

---

1 We baked this cake in a bundt pan for the photo shoot because it looks prettier, but it's more annoying to make that way. It takes a lot longer to bake, and if you have any scratches on your bundt pan, the cake won't come out cleanly. If you want to use a bundt pan, multiply the recipe based on your pan size, lower the oven temperature, and increase the bake time.

Cake

420 g (3 cups) cake flour

275 g (1¼ cups + 2 table-
spoons) granulated sugar

12 g (1 tablespoon) baking
powder

6 g (1½ teaspoons) salt

112 g (½ cup) coconut oil or
butter, melted and cooled
slightly[2]

2 eggs, at room temperature

120 g (½ cup) buttermilk

120 g (½ cup) whole milk

4 g (1 teaspoon) pure vanilla
extract

Streusel Filling

Streusel Topping

Turbinado or granulated sugar,
for sprinkling

Glaze (optional)

Fill the prepared pan with two-thirds of the batter. Sprinkle over the Streusel Filling in an uneven manner, then use a knife to make one swirl across the top. You want the filling to be thicker in some spots so that the end texture is more interesting. Pour the remaining batter over top and spread it evenly with an off-set spatula. Sprinkle on the Streusel Topping evenly, followed by a bit of turbinado or granulated sugar.

Bake for 20 to 30 minutes, until an inserted toothpick comes out with a few moist crumbs. (If it comes out clean, you've overbaked it.) Let cool for 10 minutes on a wire rack, then remove from the pan. Drizzle on the Glaze as desired; for a breakfast-time cake, you can omit it entirely. This cake is better the next day. It will keep for at least 3 days, covered, at room temperature (after that point, heat it up before eating).

---

2 We like coconut oil because it keeps the cake moister longer, but you can use butter if you prefer.

HOT COCOA BROWNIE

This is the brownie made for our Hot Cocoa (pg. 312). It's very moist on its own, but to experience it in all its full, spoonable glory, we really encourage you to use it as instructed in the drink recipe.

MAKES 1 (8-INCH SQUARE) BROWNIE

60 g (¼ cup) chopped 58% chocolate

2 g (½ teaspoon) cornstarch

120 g (½ cup) buttermilk

1 egg, at room temperature

3 g (¾ teaspoon) pure vanilla extract

55 g (¼ cup + 1½ teaspoons) Crisco shortening, at room temperature

212 g (1 cup + 1 tablespoon) granulated sugar

140 g (1 cup) flour

38 g (⅓ cup + 1 tablespoon) cocoa powder

6 g (1½ teaspoons) salt

3 g (¾ teaspoon) baking soda

2 g (½ teaspoon) baking powder

120 g (½ cup) freshly brewed coffee, hot

Toffee Sauce (see Best Fudging Chocolate Pie, pg. 270), for topping (optional)

Preheat the oven to 375°F. Grease and line an 8-inch square pan with parchment paper.

In a small bowl, dust the chocolate with the cornstarch, then toss together. This will ensure it doesn't sink to the bottom of the brownie.

In a medium bowl, whisk together the buttermilk, egg, and vanilla.

In a stand mixer fitted with the paddle attachment, combine the shortening, sugar, flour, cocoa, salt, baking soda, and baking powder. Mix on medium until the mixture resembles wet sand.

Add the wet mixture and mix until fully combined. Lower the speed and stream in the hot coffee, then mix until incorporated. Stir in half of the chopped chocolate. The batter should have the consistency of fudge sauce.

Pour the batter into the prepared pan. Scatter the remaining chopped chocolate on top. Bake for 20 minutes. Remove the pan from the oven and tap it on the counter four times. Place back in the oven for another 10 minutes, then remove and tap twice. The tapping will help increase the brownie's density, which is what we want.

While it's still hot, poke holes in the brownie and spread on a thin layer of Toffee Sauce, if using. Let cool on a wire rack. This tastes even better from the fridge the next day. It will keep there, covered, for up to 1 week.

PASSOVER MATZO BRITTLE

A: Every good Jewish mom (except Raegan's) makes a version of this treat during Passover, which is a grueling holiday in terms of food restrictions, especially for kids. On this holiday, we commemorate our ancestors who freed themselves from Egypt by eating their unleavened food, matzo. To make it more tolerable, we load it with toffee and chocolate. Generally speaking, people tend to not care what it looks like. But seeing as it's a holiday and all, why not make it cute? We're not implying that ours is any less junky, and we don't want it to be. It just looks a lot prettier and makes a potentially nice gift. Be creative with it; matzo is actually a decent base for desserts, if you buy the right kind (Streit's) and treat it a bit like a graham cracker. You could add date puree, peanut butter, nice dark chocolate, nuts, sea salt, etc., etc. The idea is, matzo brittle doesn't need to be the same every single year.

MAKES 5 SHEETS MATZO BRITTLE

Matzo Brittle Base

5 full sheets matzo

190 g (¾ cup + 1½ tablespoons) butter

186 g (packed ¾ cup + 2 tablespoons) dark brown sugar

1 g (¼ teaspoon) Maldon salt

Strawberries & Cream Topping
(optional)

450 g (2½ cups + 1 tablespoon) chopped white chocolate

2 drops pink gel food coloring (optional)

10 g (½ cup) freeze-dried strawberries

Disco Blackberry Topping
(optional)

450 g (2½ cups + 1 tablespoon) chopped white chocolate

2 drops violet gel food coloring (optional)

2 drops yellow gel food coloring (optional)

Edible gold dust (optional)

3 g (1½ teaspoons) ground freeze-dried blackberries

MAKE THE MATZO BRITTLE BASE

Preheat the oven to 375°F.

Arrange the matzo on parchment-lined sheet trays.[1]

In a medium saucepan, melt the butter and brown sugar over medium heat. Cook for 2 minutes, whisking constantly, until the mixture boils and bubbles. Carefully pour it over the matzo and spread evenly with an offset spatula. Bake for 4 to 6 minutes, watching carefully so as not to burn the caramel. When the caramel has browned, bubbled, and absorbed into the matzo slightly, remove from the oven. While it's still hot, respread the caramel to the corners of the matzo, if necessary. Sprinkle with the Maldon. Once cool, transfer the matzo to a wire rack set over a sheet tray before adding the topping.

STRAWBERRIES & CREAM TOPPING (OPTIONAL)

Melt the white chocolate in the microwave in 10-second intervals, stirring between each one until completely melted, watching carefully to not burn it. Place about 2 tablespoons of the melted chocolate into a small bowl, and stir in the food coloring. Alternating between the plain white chocolate and pink, spoon the chocolates over the matzo. Swirl them together with a toothpick to create a marble effect. While the chocolate is still wet, sprinkle with the freeze-dried strawberries.

continued . . .

---

1 If your matzo is stale, place it in the oven for 2 to 3 minutes at 350°F to crisp it back up before proceeding with the recipe.

Chocolate Maldon Topping
(optional)

450 g (2½ cups + 1 table-
    spoon) chopped 58%
    chocolate

4 g (1 teaspoon) Maldon salt

DISCO BLACKBERRY TOPPING (OPTIONAL)

Melt the white chocolate in the microwave in 10-second intervals, stirring between each one until completely melted,
watching carefully to not burn it. Place about 1 tablespoon of
the melted chocolate into each of two small bowls. Stir the violet
food coloring into one of the bowls, and the yellow into the
other. Stir the gold dust into the bowl with the yellow coloring.
Alternating between the two colors, spoon the chocolates over
the matzo. Swirl them together with a toothpick to create a
marble effect. While the chocolate is still wet, sprinkle with the
freeze-dried blackberries.

CHOCOLATE MALDON TOPPING (OPTIONAL)

Melt the chocolate in the microwave in 10-second intervals,
stirring between each one until completely melted, watching
carefully to not burn it. Spoon over the matzo, and spread with
a small offset spatula, then sprinkle with the Maldon.

SERVING

After topping, allow the matzo to set completely before cutting
and serving. Store in an airtight container at room temperature
for up to 1 week.

CHEESE BLINTZES

R: I've loved baked blintzes since I was a kid, when my parents would bring home a box of them from Snowdon Deli. My dad would warm them up in the microwave and top them with a quick mix of sour cream, vanilla, and sugar. It was so delicious.

A: You know, we could say a blintz is sort of like a hot Jewish cannoli wrapped in a crêpe.

R: What a disgusting way to describe it.

A: Well, that's what it is.

R: Definitely not.

MAKES 10 TO 12 BLINTZES

Cheese Filling

300 g (1⅓ cups) high-quality ricotta

250 g (1 cup + 2 tablespoons) full-fat cottage cheese

120 g (½ cup + 1½ teaspoons) cream cheese (preferably Philadelphia)

1 egg

55 g (⅓ cup + 2 tablespoons) powdered sugar

Lemon zest (optional)

Crêpes

4 eggs, at room temperature

200 g (½ cup + ⅓ cup) whole milk, at room temperature

175 g (1¼ cups) flour

16 g (4 teaspoons) granulated sugar

2 g (½ teaspoon) salt

45 g (3 tablespoons) 14% sour cream

56 g (¼ cup) butter, melted and cooled slightly

14 g (1 tablespoon) neutral oil or melted coconut oil

Clarified butter, for frying

MAKE THE CHEESE FILLING

Place the ricotta in a cheesecloth-lined fine-mesh strainer set over a bowl. Let sit overnight in the fridge. In a separate bowl, use the same method to strain the cottage cheese. This step is common in restaurants, used to intensify flavor and attain a velvety texture by removing excess water.

The next day, blend the strained cottage cheese in a blender until smooth. Transfer it to a large bowl, along with the strained ricotta, cream cheese, egg, powdered sugar, and a bit of lemon zest. Stir to combine.

MAKE THE CRÊPES

In a medium bowl, whisk together the eggs and milk until fully smooth.

In a large bowl, mix together the flour, sugar, and salt.

Transfer one-third of the liquid mixture to a small bowl, and stir in the sour cream little by little until there are no lumps. Add the butter and oil and mix until incorporated. Transfer back into the original liquid mixture and whisk to combine.

Pour half of the liquid mixture into the dry mixture. Using a large spatula, mix until no lumps remain. Add the rest and stir well to fully combine. Let rest for 20 minutes before using.

continued . . .

For Serving

Jam

Fresh fruit

Sour cream mixed with granulated sugar

Meringue, crumbled (optional)

COOK THE CRÊPES

Set an 8-inch nonstick skillet over medium-low, and lightly brush it with clarified butter.

Tilt the pan toward you, then ladle about ⅓ cup of batter into the pan. Rotate the pan to evenly spread the batter in a circle. Cook just until the side facing up is cooked through (it will turn matte). Repeat the process for each crêpe, brushing the pan with clarified butter between each one.

FILL THE CRÊPES

Lay one crêpe on a plate, browned side facing up. Place about ⅓ cup of Cheese Filling at the lower-middle part of the crêpe, leaving a bit of space around the edges. (As you go you'll figure out what the best amount of filling is and where to place it.) Fold in the short ends and roll it, burrito style, making sure the closing seam faces down and is somewhat centered. If you don't get a perfect roll, it's not a huge deal, but it will help seal the blintz when you fry it.

FRY THE BLINTZES

Add some more clarified butter to the nonstick skillet and set over medium heat. Place the blintzes, seam side down, in the pan. Fry until golden, then flip and repeat. Work in batches to avoid crowding.

Serve immediately with jam, fresh fruit, sweetened sour cream, and crumbled meringue. If serving at a later time, reheat in a 300°F oven for a few minutes, or gently resear in a pan.

SFENJ

A: Sfenj is a Moroccan donut I've been fed on high holidays by my mom and grandma since I was a baby. Mimouna, celebrated the day after Passover, is basically Maghrebi Jews' Halloween. We'd go door to door, stopping in to converse with neighbors and pick at their spread of pastries, sfenj being one of them. God willing I'll make it for my kids one day—now that I'm basically the only Moroccan person with a written recipe, I really have no excuse.

The dough is super sticky and as wet as a pizza's, resulting in an airiness 10 times that of a donut. When you cut into it, you find big, focaccia-level holes (in Arabic, *sfenj* literally means "sponge"). Classically, it is never glazed, only drizzled with honey or dipped in sugar, meaning you could eat a dozen before realizing you shouldn't have.

I make it in the old method, toasting the dough in a pan before shallow-frying it, which improves the crust, browning, and structure. You can form any shape you want, leaving out the hole if you want to fill them. For a savory fried bread, add a bit more salt and leave out any sugary coatings.

MAKES 12 DONUTS

500 g (3½ cups + 1 table-spoon) flour[1]

12 g (1 tablespoon) salt

8 g (4½ teaspoons) active dry yeast

5 g (2 teaspoons) powdered sugar

480 g (2 cups) water

Extra-virgin olive oil, for greasing

Neutral oil, for frying

Granulated sugar or honey, for finishing

In a large bowl, stir together the flour, salt, yeast, and sugar.

Warm the water to about 110°F, until very warm to the touch.

Create a well in the center of the dry ingredients, then stir in the water in two additions, using your hands to mix together thoroughly after each addition. For 5 to 10 minutes (the longer the better), knead the dough in the bowl. It will still be extremely wet and difficult to handle, like playing with slime. Scrape any dough that ends up on your fingers back into the bowl.

Transfer the dough into a tall, rectangular dish oiled with olive oil. Cover and let sit in a warm spot until doubled in size, 30 minutes to 1 hour.[2]

Oil your hands, and punch down the dough. Pick it up and smack it onto the counter, repeating this throwing motion for 5 to 10 minutes. Place it back in the dish and cover. Let rise until doubled again. (If desired, you can do this second rise overnight in the fridge for a more fermented flavor.)

continued . . .

---

1 For a "bouncier" interior texture, replace 100 g (about ¾ cup) flour with 100 g (about ⅔ cup) fine semolina flour.

2 At this point, you could proceed directly to making the balls and frying, but they will be significantly lacking in crispiness.

Once doubled, lightly oil your hands again. Rip off 12 golf-ball-sized pieces from the dough and place them on a lightly oiled tray. It is normal for the dough to still be very loose, wet, and sticky.

Fill a cast-iron skillet or heavy-bottomed pan with no more than 1 inch of oil. (Less than half the dough ball should be submerged when you place it in the oil.)

Oil your hands again. Grab each dough ball and push your fingers into the center of it to make a hole, then stretch it into a donut shape. Lay the dough in the oil, working three to four at a time. Fry the first side until lightly golden. As it fries, baste the exposed side with the hot oil. It should puff up as little bubbles of air form inside. Being careful not to break these bubbles, gently flip the donut and fry the other side for 1 to 2 minutes.

Transfer to a paper towel–lined plate and sprinkle with a tiny bit of salt. While they're still warm, toss them in sugar or drizzle them with honey. If using a glaze of any sort (such as Maple Glaze; see Chicken Butter Biscuit Sandwich, pg. 75), let them cool fully beforehand. These are best eaten the day of. If you plan to eat them more than a few hours later, heat them in an oven until crispy, then transfer them to a paper towel–lined plate and proceed with the coating.

SUGAR COOKIE BAGEL CRUST

If making this crust to use in the Cinco de Mayo Pie (pg. 265), make the Sugar Cookie Crumbs and Bagel Crumbs according to their quantities below, but use 2½ times the ingredients for the Bagel Crust. This means: 283 g (1¼ cups) butter, 250 g (1¾ cups + 2 tablespoons) Sugar Cookie Crumbs, 250 g (1¾ cups + 2 tablespoons) Bagel Crumbs (recipe below), 125 g (½ cup + 2 tablespoons) granulated sugar, 23 g (2½ tablespoons) sesame seeds, and 8 g (1¾ teaspoons) pretzel salt. As indicated in Cinco de Mayo, be sure to use a 10x12-inch baking dish.

MAKES 1 (10-INCH) PIE CRUST

Sugar Cookie Crumbs

280 g (2 cups) flour

2 g (½ teaspoon) baking powder

2 g (½ teaspoon) salt

113 g (½ cup) butter, at room temperature

212 g (1 cup + 1 tablespoon) granulated sugar

1 egg, at room temperature

6 g (1½ teaspoons) pure vanilla extract

Bagel Crumbs

4 Montreal-style sesame bagels

Bagel Crust

113 g (½ cup) butter

100 g (¾ cup) Sugar Cookie Crumbs

100 g (¾ cup) Bagel Crumbs

50 g (¼ cup) granulated sugar

9 g (1 tablespoon) sesame seeds

3 g (¾ teaspoon) pretzel salt[1]

---

1 We like pretzel salt in the crust because it doesn't melt, so the saltiness hits more intensely in some spots than in others. It makes for a more interesting eating experience, like the salt is teasing you.

MAKE THE SUGAR COOKIE CRUMBS

Preheat the oven to 375°F.

In a large bowl, whisk together the flour, baking powder, and salt.

In a stand mixer fitted with the paddle attachment, cream the butter and sugar until pale and fluffy. With the mixer running, add the egg and vanilla. Scrape down the bowl and continue to mix together until homogeneous. On low speed, gradually add the flour mixture. Mix together just until a dough forms.

Turn the dough out onto a clean work surface and divide it in half. Roll out each half to ¹⁄₁₀ inch thick. Carefully transfer each half onto two parchment-lined sheet trays. Bake for 5 to 10 minutes, until the edges are golden and the "cookie" is matte. Let cool completely. Leave the oven on for the Bagel Crumbs.

Break up the cookies with your hands, then transfer to a food processor. Pulse until it reaches the texture of cookie crumbs. Store leftovers in an airtight container for up to 3 weeks.

MAKE THE BAGEL CRUMBS

While the cookie crust is cooling, make the Bagel Crumbs. Slice the bagels horizontally ¼ inch thick and spread them on a sheet tray. Bake for 4 to 7 minutes, flipping them halfway through. The bagel chips should be dry and crisp, but not too browned. Let cool completely, then break up with your hands. Leave the oven on for the Bagel Crust.

Pulse the bagel chips in the food processor until they're the texture of crumbs. Store in an airtight container for up to 3 weeks.

MAKE THE BAGEL CRUST

Melt the butter in a small saucepan. Set aside to cool slightly.

In a large bowl, stir together all remaining ingredients. Then, stir in the melted butter until everything is moistened. Transfer the mixture to a 10-inch pie tin (or a 10x12-inch pie tin for the Cinco de Mayo Pie). Using the bottom of a measuring cup, bring it up the sides of the pie tin and evenly flatten the bottom. Bake for 5 minutes (or 12 to 18 minutes for the Cinco de Mayo Pie), or until golden.

If necessary, reshape the crust while it's still warm and pliable. Let cool completely before using.

CHANTILLY CREAM

MAKES ABOUT 4 CUPS

480 g (2 cups) heavy cream, cold

63 g (½ cup) powdered sugar

3 g (1½ teaspoons) dried milk powder (optional, for stability)

2 g (½ teaspoon) pure vanilla extract

In a stand mixer fitted with the whisk attachment, whip the cream to soft peaks. Lower the speed and add the powdered sugar and milk powder. Increase the speed to medium and beat for 10 seconds. Add the vanilla and continue whipping on high speed until JUST SHY OF stiff peaks, about 30 seconds longer. Do not overwhip, or you'll lose the velvety quality we want. This is best used the same day.

VANILLA CUSTARD

MAKES ABOUT 2 CUPS

255 g (1 cup + 1 tablespoon) whole milk

80 g (⅓ cup) heavy cream

12 g (1 tablespoon) + 50 g (¼ cup) granulated sugar

½ vanilla pod, cut lengthwise and seeds scraped, or 6 g (1½ teaspoons) pure vanilla extract

1 egg + 1 egg yolk

20 g (2 tablespoons) cornstarch

1 g (¼ teaspoon) salt

60 g (¼ cup + 1 teaspoon) mascarpone, at room temperature

In a medium saucepan, bring the milk, cream, 12 g (1 tablespoon) sugar, and vanilla pod and seeds to a simmer.

Meanwhile, in a small bowl, whisk together the remaining 50 g (¼ cup) sugar, and the egg and egg yolk, cornstarch, and salt until pale. Once the milk mixture is simmering, slowly stream a small amount of it into the egg mixture, whisking constantly to temper the eggs.

Transfer the mixture into the same saucepan. Cook over medium-low heat, whisking often, until it begins to thicken and bubbles appear. Switch to a spatula (to avoid incorporating air) and stir vigorously for an additional 30 seconds, moving the pot off the heat as necessary to avoid overcooking the custard. Strain through a fine-mesh sieve into a large bowl.

Using a hand blender, blend the mascarpone into the hot custard.[1] Cover with plastic wrap so that it touches the surface of the custard. Let cool completely in the fridge, at least 4 hours or overnight. It will keep in the fridge for about 1 week.

---

1 If using a whisk, gradually whisk the custard into the mascarpone to prevent clumping (not vice versa).

DRINKS

R: Despite being a nosh "bar," we're not exactly known for our drinks. People come to Arthurs for the food, but considering that we're a brunch restaurant, some late afternoon debauchery is bound to occur from time to time. Our cocktail style therefore errs on the side of classic. Save for our one regular who'll come in at 9 a.m. on a Tuesday to chase his whiskey with pancakes and a pint of Krombacher, easy drinking is the end game before 4 p.m. If there is one thing you can assuredly recreate in this book, it's these familiar friends: spritz, bellini, sangria, margarita, et al.

One classic you will never find at Arthurs is the screwdriver, which I've been turned off by ever since my dad started sneaking them to me at bar mitzvahs. Inevitably, I'd end up leaving the party wretchedly sick. May you have better luck with these boozy recipes.

ARTHURS CAESAR

R: This is our most celebrated and elaborate cocktail, made with house Caesar mix and garnished with a baby version of The Classic (pg. 46). I hopped on the Caesar bandwagon when my girlfriends in Vancouver roped me into their obsession for it, which seemed logical enough to me—it's alcohol that comes with a snack. Given that ours is garnished with a mini bagel, smoked salmon, tomatoes, and cream cheese, you can even pretend it's a well-rounded meal.

SERVES 1

Arthurs Caesar Mix

2½ cups (600 ml) Clamato

Juice of ½ lemon

1 tablespoon canned pickled horseradish

1 tablespoon Worcestershire

¾ teaspoon pickle juice

½ teaspoon Tabasco

Mini Classic

1 mini Classic (pg. 46)

Caesar

2 lemon wedges, for rimming + garnish

Celery salt, for rimming

1 oz (30 ml) vodka

½ to ¾ cup (120 to 180 ml) Arthurs Caesar Mix

¼ pickle, for garnish

Green olive, for garnish

½ radish, for garnish

Mini Classic, for garnish

MAKE THE ARTHURS CAESAR MIX

Combine all ingredients in a large container and whisk together thoroughly. For a spicier drink, add more horseradish and Tabasco. Store it in the fridge for up to 2 weeks, and remix before using.

MAKE THE MINI CLASSIC

Follow the instructions for the Classic on pg. 46, substituting a mini bagel and downsizing all ingredients accordingly.

MAKE THE CAESAR

Rim a chilled highball glass with the lemon wedge and celery salt. Fill the glass with ice, pour in the vodka, and top it with your desired amount of Caesar mix. Garnish with a skewer of pickle, lemon wedge, green olive, and radish, and a Mini Classic.

MIMOSA

R: The mimosa is a brunch gal's favorite way to get wrecked on a Saturday afternoon. We don't do bottomless at Arthurs for this reason—people who drink more stay longer. It's not that we want to rush off our customers just so we can flip the table and make money; it's that we want to make sure the people who are waiting in line have to wait "only" two hours, not five. We know you don't need a recipe for this, but we're giving you one anyway because, you know, brunch is what we do.

SERVES 1

Bubbles of choice

High-quality orange juice

Orange wheel, for garnish

You know the drill: Fill a coupe glass halfway with the bubbles, then add a splash of orange juice. Garnish with the orange wheel, and drink drink drink.

BLACKBERRY BASIL SMASH

This simple gin drink, destined for slow sipping outdoors, was brought to the menu by our former longtime server, Olivia Butler. She bid us farewell to embark on an inspiring, year-long journey around the earth, but this drink has stayed put. The subtle bittersweetness of blackberries, paired with the herbal notes of the basil and the slight acidity of the lemon, makes them the ideal *petit fruit* for this cocktail. Really smash the basil to extract all its essence and make the drink worthy of its name.

SERVES 1

Blackberry Syrup

2 cups (480 ml) water

1 (6 oz/170 g) package blackberries

1¼ cups (250 g) granulated sugar

Juice of ½ lemon

Berry Basil Smash

3 to 4 leaves fresh basil + more for garnish

1 oz (30 ml) Blackberry Syrup

1 oz (30 ml) freshly squeezed lemon juice

2 oz (60 ml) gin

Blackberries, for garnish

Lemon wheel, for garnish

MAKE THE BLACKBERRY SYRUP

In a medium saucepan, bring the water to a boil. Once boiling, add the blackberries, sugar, and lemon juice. Stir to dissolve the sugar, then lower the heat and simmer for about 30 minutes, stirring occasionally. Once the blackberries have softened, mash them with the back of a wooden spoon to break them up. Let cool before using. Store in an airtight container in the fridge for up to 3 months.

MAKE THE BERRY BASIL SMASH

Fill a shaker with ice. Place the basil in the palm of your hand and give it a good, solid whack with your other hand to release its aromas. Add it to the shaker with the Blackberry Syrup, lemon juice, and gin. Shake it up, then strain into a highball glass and top with ice. Garnish with basil leaves, blackberries, and a lemon wheel.

BELLINI

R: The key to a good bellini is a high-quality bellini mix. It's true that you could make your own from fresh peaches, but if you're making a batch of this cocktail, chances are it's hot out and you're in the mood to just chill the fuck out. We order ours from Cipriani, which I discovered at their SoHo location during my bellini-chugging bachelorette weekend (not sponsored—we wish). We recommend you also opt for something on the "craft" side rather than buy a giant jug of the sickeningly sweet stuff from the grocery store.

SERVES 1

¼ oz (7 ml) freshly squeezed lemon juice + more for rimming

Granulated sugar, for rimming

¼ oz (7 ml) peach schnapps

2 oz (60 ml) nonalcoholic bellini mix (like Cipriani)

4 oz (120 ml) prosecco

Strawberry slice, for garnish

Peach slice, for garnish

Rim half of a highball glass with a bit of lemon and sugar. Pour in the schnapps, lemon juice, and bellini mix, and stir. Fill the glass halfway with ice. Top it off with the prosecco.

Garnish with a strawberry and peach slice, if it's the season.

FROSÉ

Like all good frozen alcoholic drinks, this frosé goes down like a dép slushy in mid-July. In other words, she sneaks up on you, so you might want to schedule sunbathing in the park as your only plan for the afternoon. Our recipe calls for white peach puree, but we imagine you could make this with any stone fruits on special at the market. Just be sure that if working from fresh, you peel, chop, and freeze the fruit before blending it.

MAKES ABOUT 6 TO 7 CUPS, ENOUGH FOR A SMALL CROWD

2 cups (480 ml) water

2 cups (480 ml) simple syrup (see note 1, pg. 69)

1¼ cups (300 ml) peach schnapps

1 cup (250 g) store-bought frozen white peach puree

2 (6 oz/180 ml) bottles non-alcoholic bellini mix (like Cipriani)

½ cup (120 ml) freshly squeezed lemon juice

Strawberries, sliced, for garnish

Add all ingredients, minus the strawberry slices, to a blender and blend until smooth, adding more water as needed. Pour the slush into chilled wine glasses and garnish with sliced strawberries.

APEROL SPRITZ

R: Forget the fucking wine pairing—I'm the girl who goes to the Italian restaurant and pairs Aperol spritz with everything. Have I ever been to Italy? No. Do I need to put another Aperol spritz recipe into the world? No. Do I want to? Yes.

SERVES 1

2 oz (60 ml) Aperol

3 oz (90 ml) prosecco

Club soda, to taste

Orange slice, for garnish

Olive, for garnish

Pour the Aperol into a wine glass and fill it halfway with ice. Add the prosecco and top with as much club soda as desired. Garnish with an orange slice and a skewered olive.

GRAPEFRUIT SPRITZ

R: This may seem like a basic drink, but it pairs super well with a brunch spread, and we can't imagine anyone complaining if you hand them a cold glass of it on a lazy Sunday morning—it's super refreshing, tastes great, and looks cute. As in the Bellini and Frosé (pg. 304), be sure to select a bellini mix of quality. For the orange and grapefruit juices, we actually recommend you use a cold-pressed, bottled variety, unless your citrus fruits are extra sweet. Otherwise, you may need to add more simple syrup to up the sugar level.

SERVES 1

1½ oz (45 ml) vodka or gin

2 oz (60 ml) cold-pressed grapefruit juice

1 oz (30 ml) cold-pressed orange juice

1 oz (30 ml) freshly squeezed lemon juice

1 oz (30 ml) nonalcoholic bellini mix (like Cipriani)

½ oz (15 ml) simple syrup (see note 1, pg. 69)

Club soda, to taste

Orange wheel, for garnish

Grapefruit wheel, for garnish

Add the vodka, citrus juices, bellini mix, and simple syrup to a highball glass. Fill the glass with ice until nearly full, then stir it up. Top with club soda to taste. Garnish with orange and grapefruit wheels.

ICED TEA (CLASSIC & PEACH)

R: Here's another pair of stupid-easy recipes for you. If you wanna be a good host, you should always keep a jug of at least one of these in your fridge. Sweeten them with maple syrup, top them with orange juice, or use them as a base for a summer cocktail.

MAKES 14½ CUPS

Classic Iced Tea

6 bags orange pekoe tea

½ lemon, sliced into wheels

14½ cups (3.5 L) hot water

Peach Iced Tea

7 bags peach tea

1 bag orange pekoe tea

14½ cups (3.5 L) hot water

Place all ingredients of your variation of choice into a very large container. Let cool, then place in the fridge overnight. Store in the fridge for up to 1 week and enjoy over ice.

MAPLE BOURBON LEMONADE ICED TEA

This is a drink to make you feel like a happy grandma sitting in her rocking chair on her wraparound porch staring dreamily out onto acres of unspoiled land. Or just a happy person on their front stoop early in the warm evening.

SERVES 1

2 oz (60 ml) Classic Iced Tea (pg. 308)

1½ oz (45 ml) bourbon

1 oz (30 ml) freshly squeezed lemon juice

½ oz (15 ml) pure maple syrup

Lemon wheel, for garnish

Fill a highball glass halfway with ice. Add all ingredients to a shaker with some ice, and shake well. Pour into the glass and garnish with a lemon wheel.

SHAKEN ICED COFFEE

R: Viviane Pedersen is a ray of sunshine who was with us in the front of house for years. If you live around St-Henri, there's a high chance you've seen her around. She is an expert in styling thrifted clothes, organizing community pop-ups, covering food in dill, picking snacks from the trash can, giving squeezy happy hugs, and creating yummy drinks (including at Bonheur d'Occasion on Notre-Dame, where she runs the café side). We entrusted her with tending our bar and sneaking her coworkers concoctions during rough services; this drink is one of many that got them through the day. Cheers to Vivi!

SERVES 1

3 oz (90 ml) freshly brewed coffee, cooled

1 oz (30 ml) Baileys (optional)

½ oz (15 ml) Tia Maria (optional)

½ oz (15 ml) pure maple syrup

¼ teaspoon pure vanilla extract

1 dash cinnamon

Milk of choice, to taste

Fill a shaker with ice. Add all ingredients minus the milk, and SHAKE SHAKE SHAKE until your arms burn, for maximum frothiness. (If you want, add the milk to the shaker as well for extra volume.) Strain into a tall glass and finish with the milk and as much ice as you like.

HOT COCOA

A: This is the ideal slurping hot cocoa. Its consistency falls between that of its American and French sisters, thanks to a blend of cocoa powder, chocolate pastilles, whole milk, and condensed milk. The real treat lies at the bottom of the mug, where the brownie has been absorbing the hot chocolate all the while, turning itself into a gooey consistency akin to an Oreo soaked in milk. Unfortunately, what often happened when we served it this way was that a lot of mugs arrived at the dish pit with the brownie left at the bottom, mistaken for clumped chocolate left over from the drink. We switched it to a garnish so people would know to eat it, but this defeated the whole purpose. Point being, a lot of cool concepts get washed down the drain (literally) in a restaurant, but at home, anything is possible.

SERVES 2 TO 4 (DEPENDING ON THE SIZE OF YOUR MUGS)

Whipped Cream

2 cups (480 ml) heavy cream, very cold

1 teaspoon powdered sugar

2 teaspoons pure vanilla extract

Hot Chocolate

4 cups (960 ml) whole milk

⅓ cup (60 g) granulated sugar

½ cup (85 g) chopped 58% chocolate pastilles

½ cup (42 g) Dutch process cocoa powder

¼ cup (60 ml) condensed milk (preferably Eagle Brand)

½ teaspoon salt

2 to 4 squares Hot Cocoa Brownie (pg. 282)

Whipped Cream, for garnish

Sprinkles, for garnish

MAKE THE WHIPPED CREAM

In the bowl of a stand mixer fitted with the whisk attachment, or by hand, whip the heavy cream with the powdered sugar and vanilla until soft peaks form.

MAKE THE HOT CHOCOLATE

In a medium saucepan, combine the milk, sugar, chocolate pastilles, cocoa powder, and condensed milk. Whisk together over medium-low heat until the chocolate has melted. Lower the heat and keep stirring until everything is well combined, then add the salt.

Grab your favorite glasses or mugs and place one square of Hot Cocoa Brownie at the bottom of each. Fill three-quarters of the way with Hot Chocolate. Top with a swirl of Whipped Cream and some sprinkles.

Thank You

Thank you from Raegan and Alex:

We couldn't have done any of this without the following people. When they say it takes a village, they're not lying.

First and foremost, we want to thank our parents for all their love and support:

Alex's parents, Liliane and Solomon Cohen. We can always count on you to tell us when the french fries are not up to standard or the eggs are cold. Thank you for inspiring so much of the food we make today that so many people have grown to love. You have helped us make our dreams a reality. On vous aime.

Raegan's mother, Marilyn Steinberg, for her encouragement and unquestioning belief in us. For being Arthurs' number one fan and unpaying customer, and for continuing to come to us to order bones for your dogs and carrots for your horses. Had you not taken a leap of faith for us, Arthurs would never exist. Love you so much!

To those beside us as we opened our doors. We couldn't have done it without you:

Heather Avrith, our restaurant landlord, who took a chance on two kids with a very disorganized dream.

Dr. Swift, one of our oldest customers, for all your sharp advice and ongoing kindness.

Fred Morin and Diane Solomon, two amazing figures in Raegan's cheffing career.

To every single staff member, whether or not your name is here. Thank you endlessly for the time and labor you've offered to this restaurant. If not for you, the world wouldn't have Arthurs at all.

To Evelyne Eng: Yes, you are currently writing your own thank-you. You are amazing, and we could not have written this book without you. You have been so patient and organized and have created something so beautiful from the chaos of our lives. We are so grateful you decided to work on this *lengthy* project with us and wish you only the best in your future career.

To the opening team: Jackie Biberkraut; Austin Burke, chef; Marlee Felberbaum; Alejandro Martinez; Chris Kek; Melanie Vanderpool; Daina Antikacioglu; Sean Heitner; MJ Hodhod; Oswald Rowe, MVP!!; Bentely; Anne Marie Tidman; Kelsey Thomas; and Jon Reed.

To everyone who came after and helped us build our business into what it is today: Luka LeCavalier, chef; Charlotte Mofford; Lindsay Weller; Lauren Scholefield; Clara Mesguen; Alessandra Ruffolo; Viviane Pedersen; Olivia Butler; India Simmons; Renata Ottati; Sofia Griffin (also for taking care of our babies so we could work); Sheryl Kaufman, our former bookkeeper; Albert Greenspoon, our trusted lawyer; and Robbie Weitzman, our financial adviser.

To everyone working with us during the period of writing of this book. We love you all and we are so grateful for you every day: Kirk Prillo; Serena Bugler; Alice Chemel, chef; Jeremy Goldberg; Noemie Lessard; Talia Sinagra; Alexandra Galy; Carlos Flores Perez; Mason Kreissl.

To our trusty suppliers: The boys at Boucherie de Tours; Phillip Viens at Aliments Viens; Josie Weitzenbauer at Léché Desserts; Thea Bryson at Miette Boulangerie; The whole family at Marois et Frères; Birri Farms; Adar Supermarket; Fairmount Bagel; Almazara; Snowdon Bakery; Miel Dubreuil; Les Aliments Bien-être et Bon Goût; Zack Eberts at Épicerie Mange-Tout; Mello Foods; and Lenny Lighter.

To our neighbors for feeding and caffein-ating us through long days: Campanelli; Cordova; Rustique; Dalla Rose; Tran Cantine; Bernice; and Tuck Shop.

To our loyal customers and supporters from day one: Henri Neufeld; Peter Gélinas and Elysia Bryan-Baynes; Chris Mackenzie; Arié Benchetrit; Corey Shapiro; and Elad Cohen.

To all who worked on this book: Evelyne Eng, co-author; Karolina Victoria Jez, pho-tography extraordinaire; Lindsay Paterson, Appetite by Random House editor; Nadia Pisaturo, pastry guru; Caroline Haurie, sup-plier of the most beautiful pottery; Vanessa Laberge, illustrator; Kelly Hill, designer; and Kendra McKnight, recipe tester.

From Raegan to Alex:

Thank you to my husband, my partner in crime. Although you drive me insane some-times, I could not, nor would I want to, do this with anyone else. I'm always in awe of your creativity and patience; watching you grow as a chef and partner has been the most rewarding experience. Love you so much. I can't wait for the next chapter of life!

From Alex to Raegan:

Any married couple you talk to will tell you that the hardest thing you can do—after mar-rying—is working with the person you married. You've asked me before about how our lives would be had we not stuck together. It's not something I've ever wondered; when you know you're exactly where you need to be, you can't even envision another possibil-ity. That is all thanks to you, to your intense drive and passion for this life we have, to your support and partnership, and to how you always push me to be better. Even though, you know, I wish sometimes you would lay off a bit.

Thank you from Evelyne:

Raegan and Alex, obviously, for giving an uncertain 21-year-old her first writing job and entrusting her to help tell your stories. You are hilarious, honest, good-hearted people. I am forever indebted to you both.

Kirk Prillo, for answering endless recipe questions and tolerating me as I rummaged around the prep kitchen while you worked.

Clara Mesguen, for having the answer to nearly anything I needed to know about Arthurs and for being my office buddy.

Serena Bugler, for always sticking around after work-sies to get ice cream with me (and thank you to Nick at Dalla Rose for supplying the goods).

Every coworker, from beginning to end, who helped me in the making of this book or who hustled alongside me through the ups and downs of service. I fricking love you guys. You have made Arthurs a home for me.

Mom and Dad, for letting me be your roommate while I finished this book, and for supporting me as I ventured onto a creative job path.

Index

RAEGAN STEINBERG is a self-proclaimed "retired" cook in charge of business development at Arthurs Nosh Bar HQ Inc. Co. and married to her partner in work and life. Her love of food started at a very young age; she believes it was a genetic disorder passed down by her father, Arthur. She started her career at Mandy's Gourmet Salads and has worked at famed restaurants such as the Blue Water Cafe and Joe Beef. This laid the foundation for her career as a professional butter pasta maker, or as her kids call her, "the best cooker." She hopes to build a global Arthurs empire, with a location in every major city, taking pancake batter and sprinkle cookies international. She dreams of retiring in Vermont and opening a small business there with her husband, summering in Italy, and eating her way around the world with her family.

ALEXANDER COHEN is the co-owner and executive chef of Arthurs. Before becoming a self-taught cook, he was the popcorn boy at the late, great Blockbuster, then a professional gamer. One day, he hopes to open Nothing but Butts, a restaurant that only serves the butt-ends of foods. His most embarrassing kitchen moment was melting 36 liters of deep-fryer oil through a garbage bin and staying four hours late to clean the entire floor. As for hobbies, he has none, but is working on it as per his therapist's recommendation. Raegan and Alex live in Montreal with their children, Freya and Abel, who are their entire world. They also shared their home with Pumak, their beloved Alusky dog, who was as much a part of Arthurs as anyone else.

EVELYNE ENG (@ev_eng) is a writer and novice pastry cook from San Diego, California. After obtaining her bachelor's in English literature from McGill, she started working on this book, simultaneously doing expo and whatever FOH position needed filling at Arthurs. In 2023, she moved to Rome, where she completed pastry school and narrowly survived a stage in one of the top restaurants in Italy. She now lives and bakes in Montreal, waiting around for news from any other desperate chefs in need of a hand with cookbook writing.